IMAGES
of America

DALLAS COUNTY

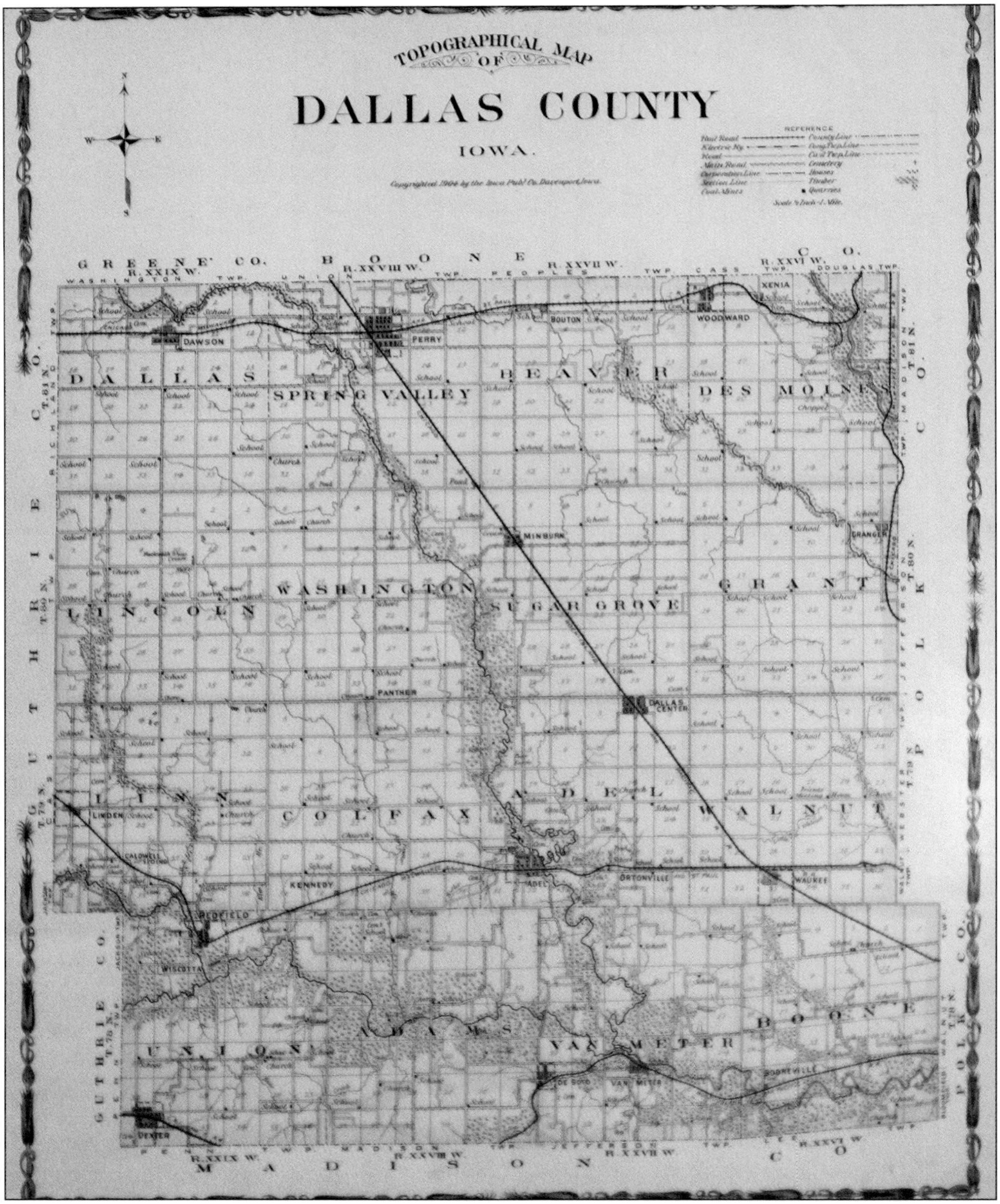

Historic Dallas County at a Glance. Located just west of Iowa's capital city of Des Moines, Dallas County was organized in 1847, shortly after Iowa statehood in 1846. Not since the period of early settlement has Dallas County experienced such significant growth as it has during its current population increase. With 80,133 people (a 2015 Census Bureau estimate), Dallas County is the 10th-most populous of Iowa's 99 counties. (Courtesy of Dallas County Conservation.)

On the Cover: Van Meter Matrons Club. These dynamic ladies of the Van Meter Matrons Club socialized while improving their knowledge of Iowa heritage and current events. When the club celebrated its 50th anniversary in 1959–1960, historian Hazel Lauterbach said the club "helped me be a better homemaker, citizen, and community member and has taught me the true meaning of teamwork." (Courtesy of Van Meter Public Library.)

IMAGES
of America

DALLAS COUNTY

Darcy Dougherty Maulsby

ARCADIA
PUBLISHING

ISBN 978-1-4671-2630-4

Published by Arcadia Publishing
Charleston, South Carolina

Printed in the United States of America

Library of Congress Control Number: 2016960889

For all general information, please contact Arcadia Publishing:
Telephone 843-853-2070
Fax 843-853-0044
E-mail sales@arcadiapublishing.com
For customer service and orders:
Toll-Free 1-888-313-2665

Visit us on the Internet at www.arcadiapublishing.com

This book is dedicated to all those in Dallas County and beyond who love Iowa history, protect this precious legacy, and look to the future while honoring the past.

Contents

Acknowledgments

The history of Dallas County reflected here is a rich legacy indeed, and it is worth preserving.

I am forever grateful to my friends at the Dexter Museum, including Doris Feller, Rod Stanley, and Joy Neal Kidney, for sharing their vast knowledge of all things Dexter, including the Dexfield Park shoot-out and President Truman's visit to the 1948 plowing match—pivotal events that inspired me to write this book.

There is no way I could have completed this book without Pete Malmberg, museum curator at Forest Park Museum in Perry. Pete has spent years delving into Dallas County history and is a tremendous resource.

Thank you, Delbert Countryman, for letting me research for hours in the Redfield Museum, and Jan Price, for extending this same courtesy at the Adel Historical Museum. Thanks, also, go to Julie Bailey of Redfield, who gave me priceless, first-person insights about Bob Feller. Thank you, Dorothy Knight, director of the Van Meter Public Library, for letting me dig through the archives, where I found the perfect cover image for this book.

I am inspired by the people of Perry, including Brian Eiteman with the Iowa Fire Museum, Jay Hartz with the Hotel Pattee, and the Perry Historic Preservation Commission (including Jeanette Peel-Peddicord and Larry Vodenik).

I cannot forget Lyn Wilkinson, who has been the driving force to preserve the iconic Lake Robbins Ballroom. Thanks, also, are extended to Paul and Carolyn Snyder, along with Deanette Snyder of Minburn, for sharing the history of Washington Township School and the fabulous Singing Wheels.

I truly enjoyed hearing Don Beneventi tell stories of Granger in years gone by. Life is changing fast in eastern Dallas County, including Waukee, so I appreciate everyone who is keeping local history alive, including Terry Snyder and Sue Ellen Kennedy with the Waukee Area Historical Society and Kristine Larson with the Waukee Public Library. Thank you, also, to the Woodward Public Library, Granger Public Library, and Roy R. Estle Memorial Library in Dallas Center for all your assistance.

While I have done my best to record this history accurately, I am sure there are still gaps to fill. The research continues. Through it all, thanks go to the Arcadia Publishing team, including my title manager, Caroline Anderson, for helping bring this history to life and preserving this tremendous legacy.

Introduction

Discovering the remarkable history of Dallas County presents a real-life adventure, complete with drama, action, horror, romance, comedy, mystery, and more. It also weaves in unforgettable stories that transformed Iowan and American history.

Located in central Iowa just west of Des Moines, Dallas County was organized in 1847, not long after Iowa became a state on December 28, 1846. The county was named after George M. Dallas, who served as vice president of the United States when James K. Polk was president.

The county was first opened for settlement on April 30, 1843. A year earlier, the land had been purchased from the Sac and Fox Indians. The region's gently rolling hills and miles of prairie with rivers and abundant streams seemed like the ideal place to homestead. When the first settlers began moving into the area in the 1840s, the nearest trading post was at Fort Des Moines.

At Dallas County's first census in 1850, the county had approximately 854 residents. Dallas County soon became a hub of western migration, from pioneers seeking fertile Iowa farmland to travelers with "gold fever" seeking their fortunes in the California Gold Rush from the late 1840s to early 1850s. Adel became the first relay station on the stagecoach line between Des Moines and the "Wild West." By the 1850s, branches of the Underground Railroad also ran through southern Dallas County, helping fugitive slaves escape east across Iowa.

The expansion of the railroads was critical to the settlement of Dallas County. Many towns in the county were established when the railroad arrived. As Dallas County grew, it became known as the home of many famous Iowans, including George W. Clarke, governor of Iowa (1913–1917); Nile Kinnick, the University of Iowa football star after whom the stadium in Iowa City is named; and major-league baseball pitchers Bob Feller, the "Heater from Van Meter," and his cousin, Hal Manders.

Dallas County also became a destination for some of the most famous (and infamous) Americans of their era, such as Bonnie and Clyde and other members of the Barrow Gang, including Buck Barrow, who did not survive a shoot-out at Dexfield Park on July 24, 1933.

Fifteen years later, Dallas County helped propel Harry Truman to an unlikely victory in the 1948 presidential campaign following a fiery speech he delivered to 100,000 farmers on a sweltering September day at the National Plowing Match near Dexter.

Much of Dallas County's history reflects the immigrant experience. Many of the first settlers were European immigrants seeking a new start in a new land. Some became farmers, others became merchants, and many became community leaders in the pioneer towns that flourished in Dallas County.

By the late 19th and early 20th centuries, coal mining attracted more immigrants to Dallas County, from Waukee to Woodward. Many of these newcomers hailed from Italy and other parts of Europe. The social and economic challenges plaguing these mining families spurred the development of the Granger Homesteads, which became one of the most successful New Deal programs of the 1930s. The 225-acre Granger Homesteads, built in 1935, included approximately

50 modern houses for low-income mining families, along with approximately four acres for raising crops and livestock for food. Some of these four-, five-, and six-bedroom houses, built for roughly $2,232 on average, can still be seen today.

The 1930s also marked the debut of the famous Lake Robbins Ballroom near Woodward. While ballrooms were once common throughout Iowa, few remain, making Lake Robbins not only a Dallas County icon but also an Iowa treasure.

Other pieces of Dallas County's unique history have vanished with the passage of time. Perhaps the most bizarre story involves the Van Meter Visitor, which terrorized the southern Dallas County town of Van Meter for several nights in the fall of 1903. Witnesses reported seeing an eight-foot-tall winged monster that shone a bright light, emanated a strong odor, and ran on all four feet before extending its wings and disappearing near a coal mine. The case continues to fascinate people more than a century later.

In the early 1920s, Dallas County history took another strange twist when the Ku Klux Klan (KKK) staged huge rallies in the Perry area. Nearly 15,000 people (almost triple the population of Perry) witnessed a KKK parade, complete with robed Klansmen, and a semipublic meeting in Perry on May 31, 1924. The evening rally "attracted the largest crowd which has ever visited the city," reported the local newspaper.

While this occurred in Dallas County's largest city, small towns throughout the county also influenced local history. Now a ghost town, Ortonville (located between Adel and Waukee) was the winter headquarters of the popular Orton Bros. Circus, which toured the Midwest for decades. In 1906, Granger became the winter headquarters for Fred Buchanan's Yankee Robinson Show, a midwestern traveling circus that lasted until the Great Depression.

From 1950 to 1963, Minburn became known for its beloved Singing Wheels roller-skating performances. These three-day summer extravaganzas that showcased up to 150 local skaters required the whole community of 350 people to work together, from planning the choreography to sewing the costumes.

Much has changed since those days. Modern Dallas County is essentially a tale of two counties, as communities like Waukee in the east experience unprecedented suburban growth while much of western Dallas County remains distinctly rural.

The population growth has been so strong in parts of the county that Dallas County has become one of the fastest-growing counties in America. After a century of stagnant population growth between 1890 and 1990, when the county's population hovered between 20,000 and 30,000 residents, the westward growth of the Des Moines metro area began pushing into Dallas County in the 1990s, igniting the county's current growth trend.

Dallas County has more than doubled in population in the last two decades, growing from 29,755 residents in 1990, according to the US Census Bureau, to 66,000 residents by 2010. Dallas County became one of the fastest-growing counties in the nation by 2015–2016, with an estimated population of more than 84,500 in 2016. The county has not experienced such significant growth since the period of early settlement in Iowa, when the county's population of 5,244 residents in 1860 soared to 20,479 by 1890.

Through all these changes, Dallas County remains a region of opportunity with a rich heritage of small-town living, farming, and the immigrant experience. While the world in which Dallas County exists today is vastly different from the one the pioneers created in the 1800s, people's hopes, fears, and dreams have not changed all that much. Enduring values like family and faith continue to link the past and the present in Dallas County.

Come along on this exciting journey into the past through the eyes of those who lived it and discover what makes Dallas County so unforgettable.

One

Adel

Dallas County's First Town

History is inescapable in Adel, from the brick streets to the stunning Dallas County Courthouse. Founded in 1847, the town was originally called Penoach, a Native American name meaning "far away." In 1849, the city's name was changed to Adel in honor of a pretty young lady, according to local lore. The community has remained the county seat despite numerous efforts years ago to move the seat of government to Perry, Dallas Center, or Waukee.

The first courthouse in Adel, a log cabin, was built in 1848. The current courthouse, made of white Bedford stone, was completed in 1902 at a cost of $109,000. In September 1902, when Adel's population was roughly 1,200 residents, 2,000 people attended the dedication of the courthouse, which is listed in the National Register of Historic Places.

Just a few years before this, on March 6, 1895, Adel witnessed one of the most violent events in Dallas County history. The robbery of the Adel State Bank left one man dead and six others wounded.

Located on the west side of the square, the bank was targeted by Orlando "Rowdy" Wilkins and Charles Crawford from Patterson, Iowa. On the morning of March 6, the criminals drove a team and buggy into Adel and entered the bank around 9:00 a.m. Wilkins shot cashier S.M. Leach and a customer. The robbers grabbed a bag and filled it with approximately $267.

The ruckus caught the attention of George Clarke, an attorney whose office was above the bank. When Clarke came down the stairs, Wilkins stuck his shotgun into Clarke's chest and pulled the trigger. The gun clicked but did not fire. Clarke dashed back up the stairs. (Clarke later became the governor of Iowa and was also the grandfather of University of Iowa football star Nile Kinnick.)

Wilkins and Crawford took off at breakneck speed in their buggy but were soon captured. Wilkins was shot and killed, and his body was brought back to Adel. Before being taken to the undertaker, his body was displayed sitting in a chair in front of the bank so the public could view the dead outlaw.

The former bank building still graces downtown Adel. With a population of more than 3,600 residents today, Adel retains its small-town charm, from its town square to its historic buildings. Located just minutes from Des Moines, the community continues to grow and comes together each summer for the annual Sweet Corn Festival.

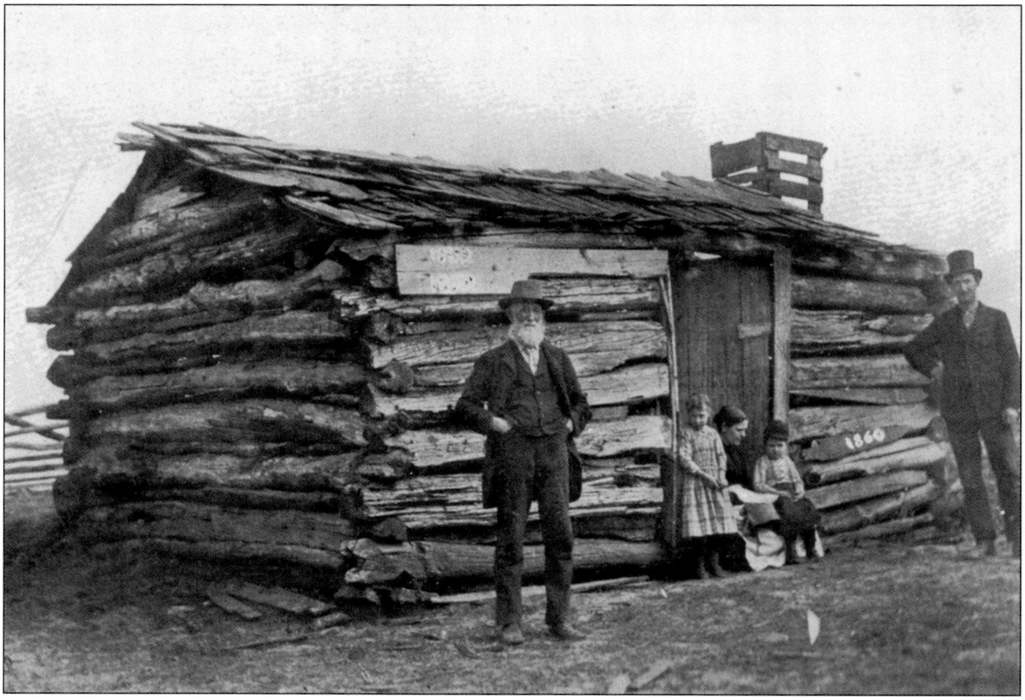

DALLAS COUNTY PIONEERS. A man named Mr. Lindsey built this log cabin southwest of Adel on a claim in Section 4 of Adams Township in southwest Dallas County in 1852. It was later the home of Anderson Van Cleave. The photograph shows members of the Van Cleave family, including Anderson and Thomas Van Cleave. (Courtesy of Dallas County Conservation.)

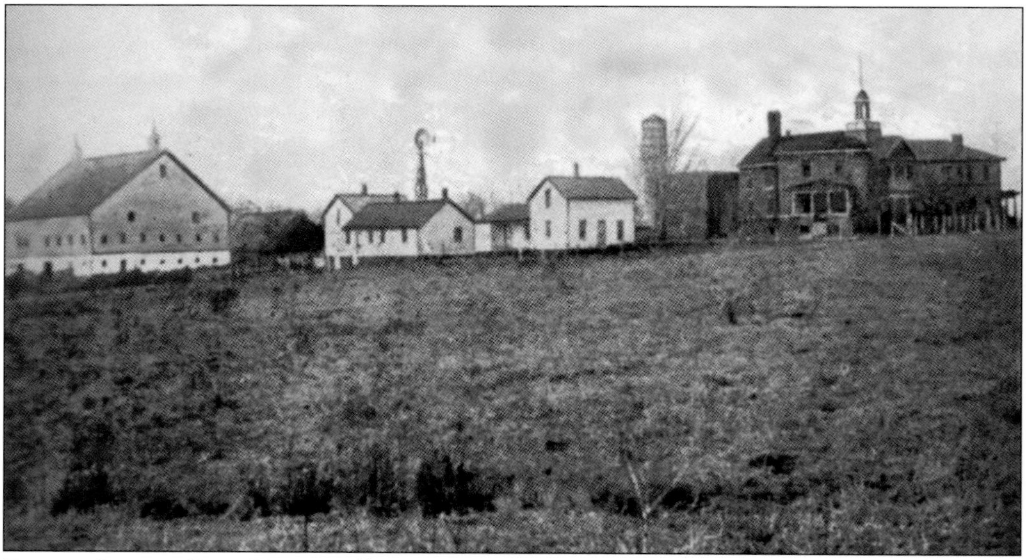

DALLAS COUNTY POOR FARM. Dallas County purchased 160 acres for $4,000 in 1869 to establish a poor farm to care for "paupers, the disabled and the feeble minded." Residents were expected to work to help raise food and cover expenses. The farm, which expanded to more than 500 acres, still includes a spacious barn and a two-story brick building constructed in the 1930s through the Works Project Administration. The farm now houses the Dallas County Human Services campus. (Courtesy of Roy R. Estle Memorial Library, Dallas Center.)

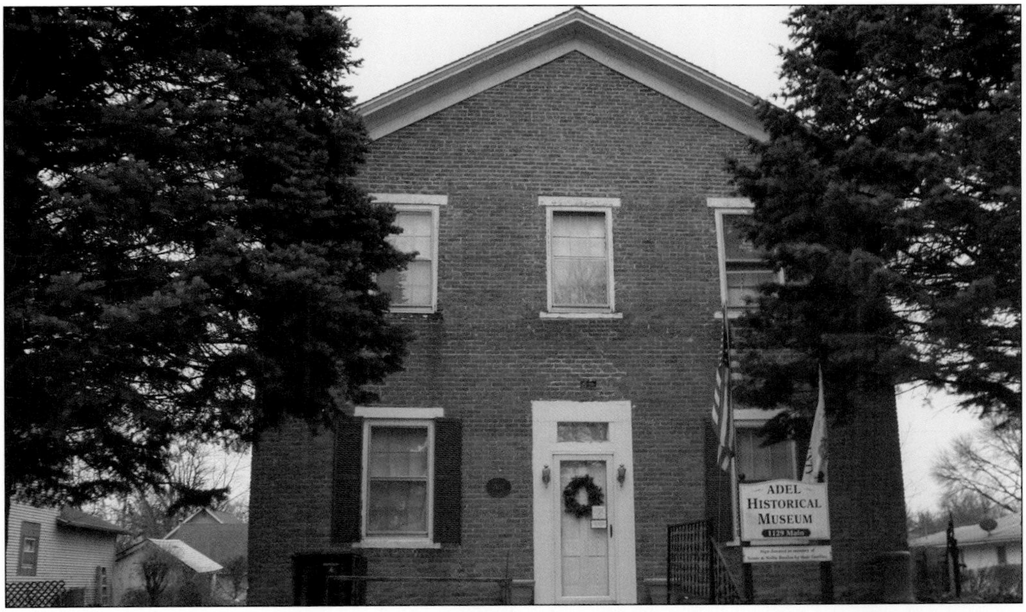

First School in Adel. The first school in Adel opened in 1857 in this two-story brick schoolhouse, which served the community until the 1870s. From 1872 to 1898, the building was home to Adel banker and state lawmaker Leroy Lambert. The property became a boarding and rooming house that the Thornton family ran from 1898 to 1943. It then became a private home until the early 1970s. Located close to the town square, the structure remains one of Adel's oldest buildings and houses the Adel Historical Museum. (Author's collection.)

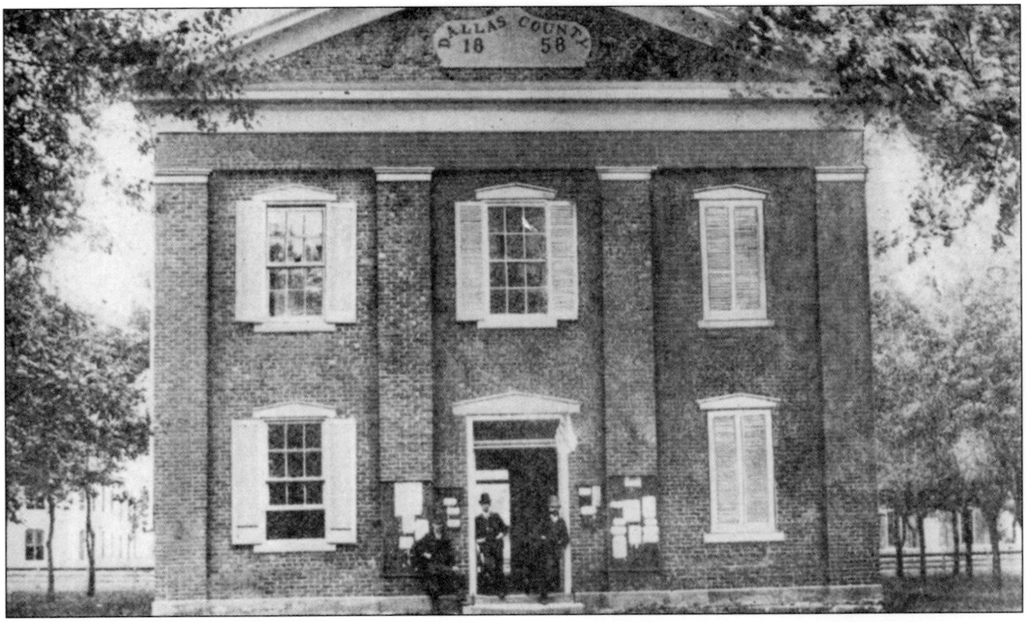

Brick Courthouse. Built in 1858, Dallas County's third courthouse replaced the first one, a double log cabin built in 1848, as well as the second, a one-story frame structure built in 1853. The 1858 courthouse cost $20,000 and was located on the town square. Standing in front of the courthouse are, from left to right, J.M. Roland, W.L. Mitchell, and Ralph E. Joy. (Courtesy of Roy R. Estle Memorial Library, Dallas Center.)

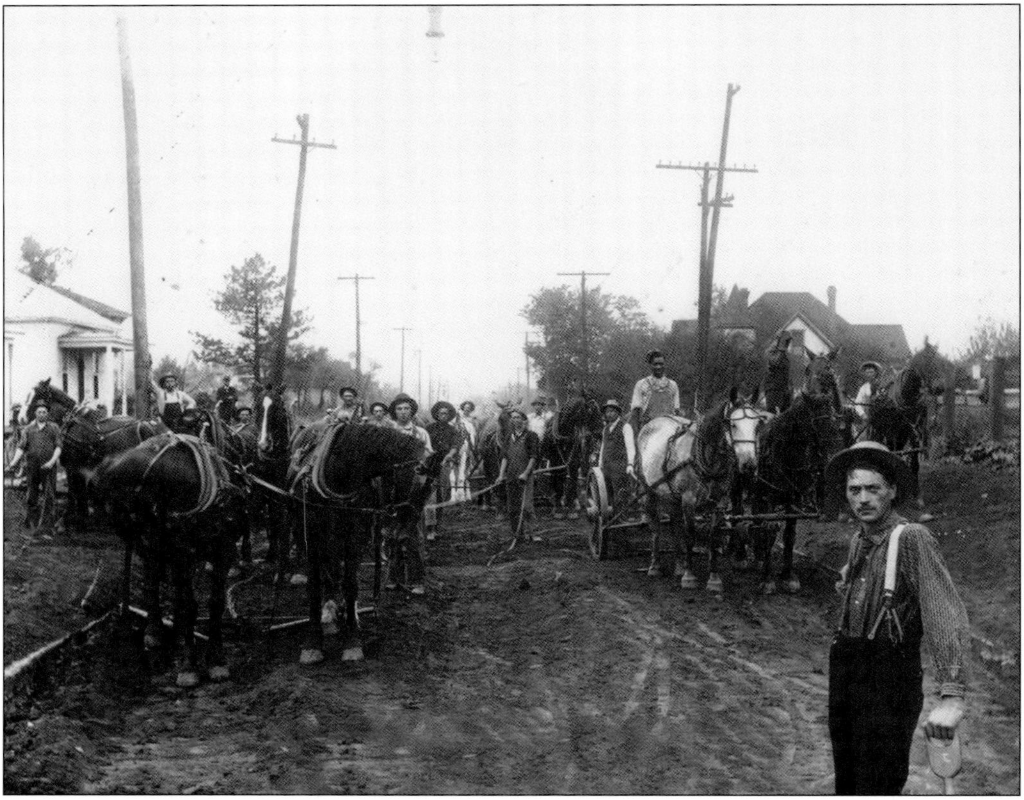

STREETS PAVED WITH HISTORY. Adel features paved and brick streets. This crew paved Adel's side streets sometime after 1897. In the mid-1920s, J.S. McLaughlin and Sons Construction Company received a contract to install more paved streets. City planners favored brick instead of concrete, because Adel had its own brickyard. Also, sand for concrete had to be shipped in from Des Moines, raising the cost to pave the streets. (Courtesy of Adel Historical Museum.)

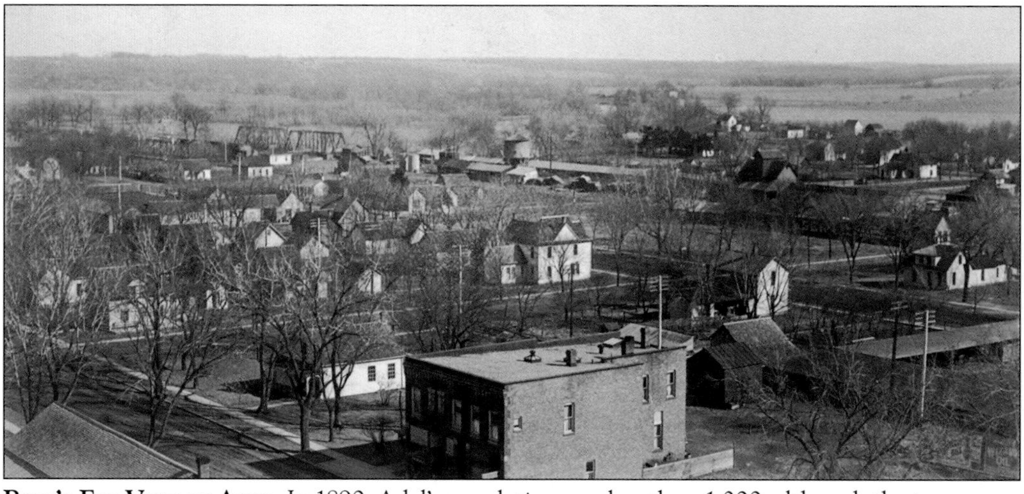

BIRD'S-EYE VIEW OF ADEL. In 1890, Adel's population was less than 1,000, although the town grew to 1,455 residents by 1920. As more homes and businesses were built, barns were also common throughout the town in the 19th century and into the early 20th century, before the age of the automobile. (Courtesy of Van Meter Public Library.)

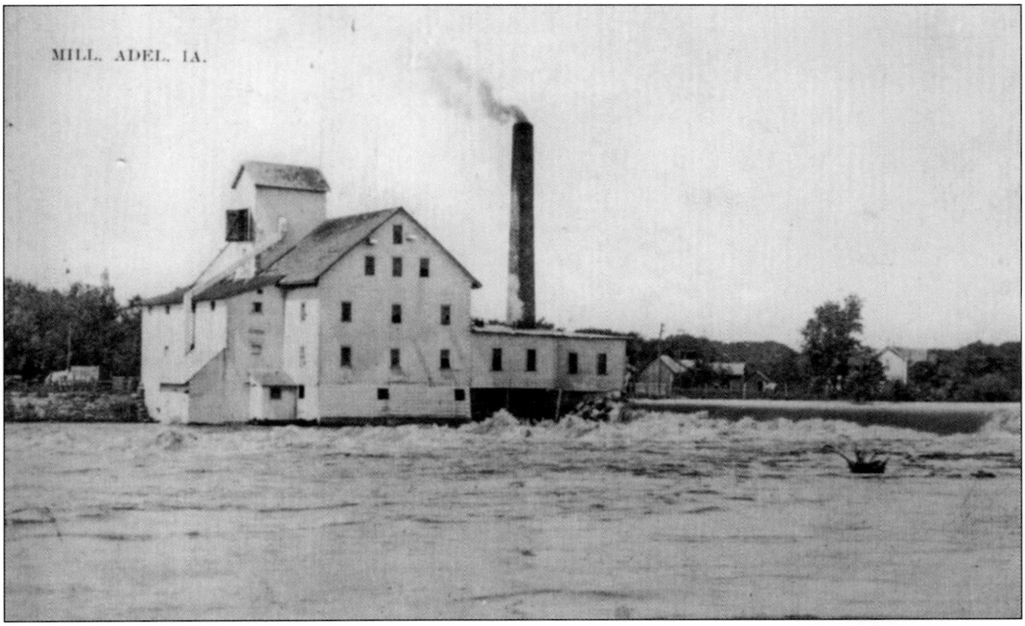

Milling in Dallas County. Thanks to the nearby Raccoon River, milling enterprises of various types thrived in many Dallas County communities, including Adel, in the 19th and early 20th centuries. Pioneers in communities like Redfield started operating sawmills in 1850. Other settlers built mills to produce cracked corn and flour. (Courtesy of Dallas County Conservation.)

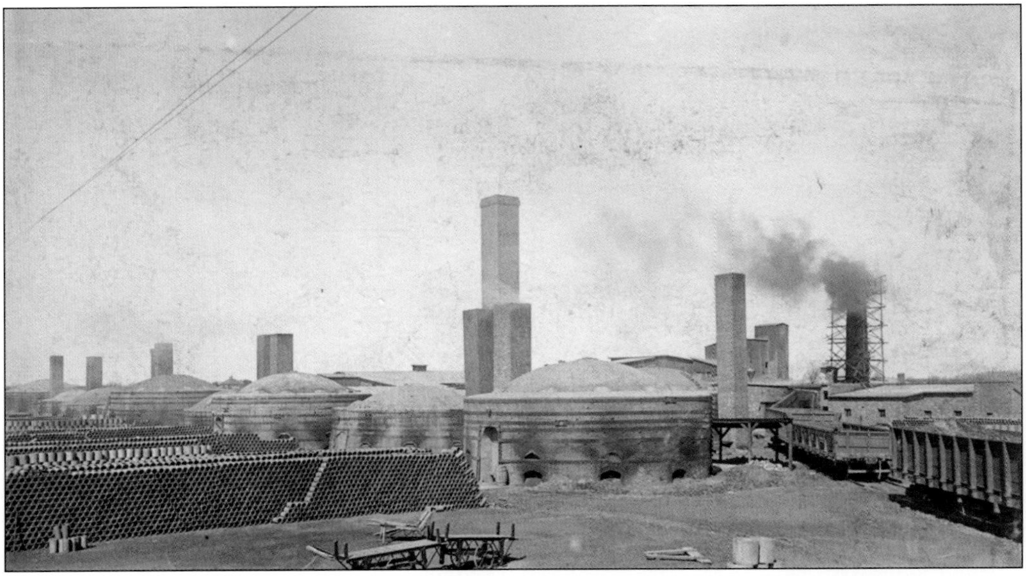

Adel's Tile Factory. Adel has had a brick and tile factory for more than a century. This photograph shows the kilns that produced thousands of tiles that helped drain excess water from farm fields. In 1958, Sioux City Brick & Tile purchased the plant at Adel. Today, United Brick and Tile Company, a division of Sioux City Brick & Tile, remains one of Adel's largest industrial plants. (Courtesy of Redfield Museum.)

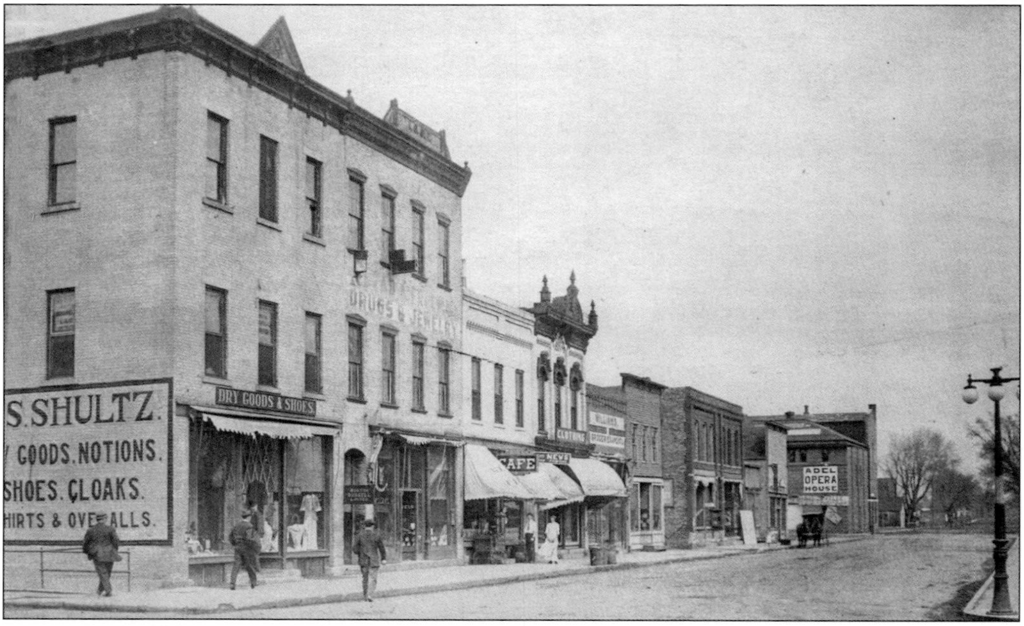

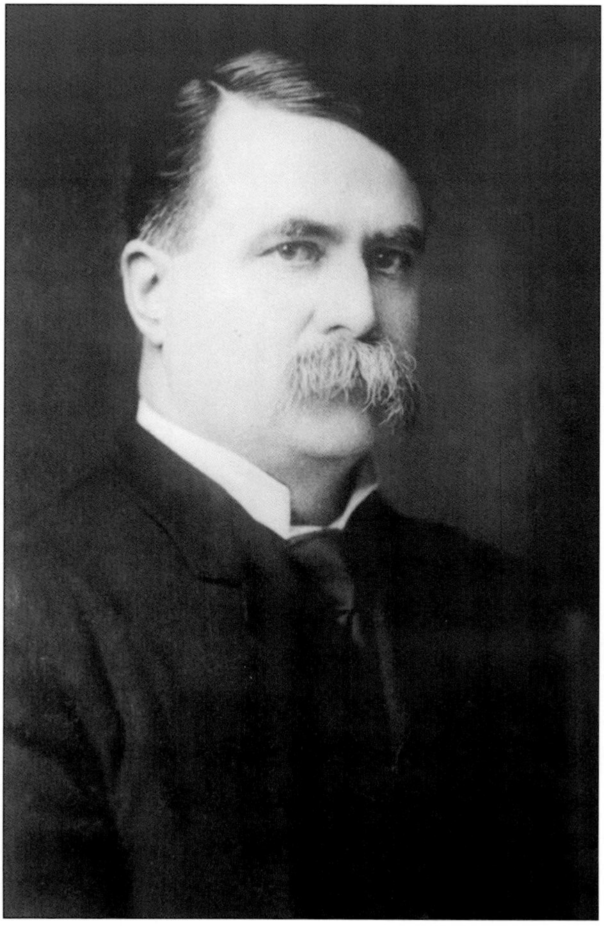

1895 Bank Robbery. This c. 1906 photograph shows the Adel State Bank (third building from the left), which was robbed on March 6, 1895. Orlando "Rowdy" Wilkins and Charles Crawford from Patterson, Iowa, drove a team and buggy into Adel and entered the bank around 9:00 a.m. Wilkins pointed a shotgun at cashier S.M. Leach, shot him in the shoulder and neck, and escaped with approximately $267. Wilkins was shot and killed on a farm near Adel. (Courtesy of Adel Historical Museum.)

George Clarke, Iowa Governor. George Washington Clarke was Iowa's 21st governor and the grandfather of Iowa football legend Nile Kinnick. Clarke settled in Adel by the 1880s, established a law practice, and served as governor of Iowa from 1913 to 1917. During his tenure, the Republican advocated for workmen's compensation and the creation of a state highway commission. Clarke died in 1936 and is buried in Adel. (Courtesy of Adel Historical Museum.)

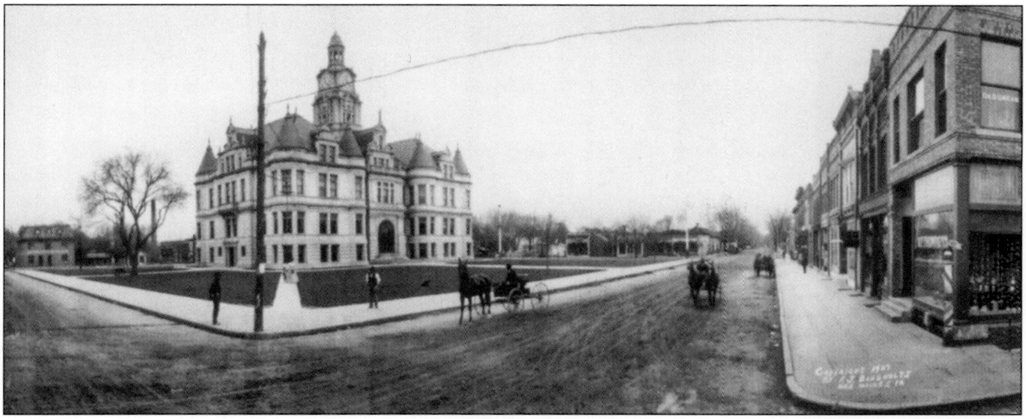

DALLAS COUNTY COURTHOUSE. The stunning Dallas County Courthouse was built in 1902 for more than $109,000 after voters approved a new courthouse in November 1900. George Bird, a partner in the Des Moines architectural firm Proudfoot and Bird, was inspired by the Château d'Azay-le-Rideau—located in the town of the same name in Indre-et-Loire, near Tours, France, southwest of Paris—when he designed this majestic courthouse, which still serves Dallas County and is listed in the National Register of Historic Places. (Courtesy of Library of Congress.)

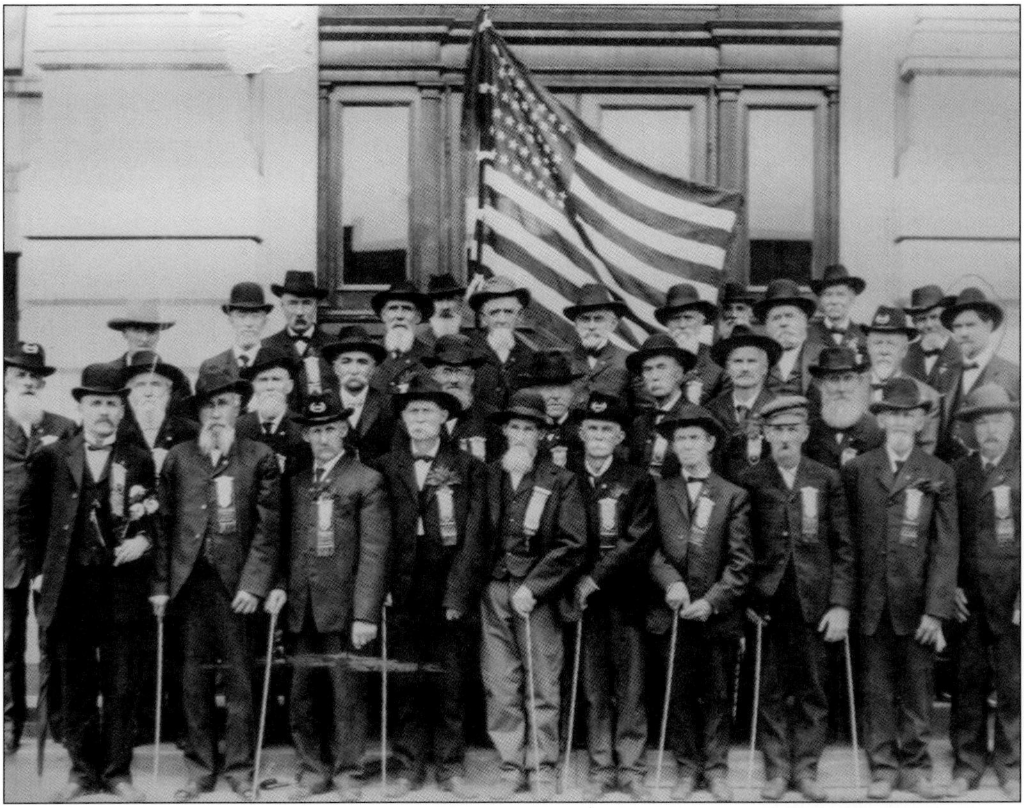

GAR MEMBERS IN 1907. These Civil War veterans, pictured near the Dallas County Courthouse on Memorial Day, 1907, are Grand Army of the Republic (GAR) members from Redfield. The GAR was an aging but active force in Iowa. Of the roughly 76,000 Iowans who fought for the Union, a vast majority were affiliated with the GAR. In 1949, James P. Martin, 101, of Sutherland, was the last Civil War veteran to die in Iowa. (Courtesy of Adel Historical Museum.)

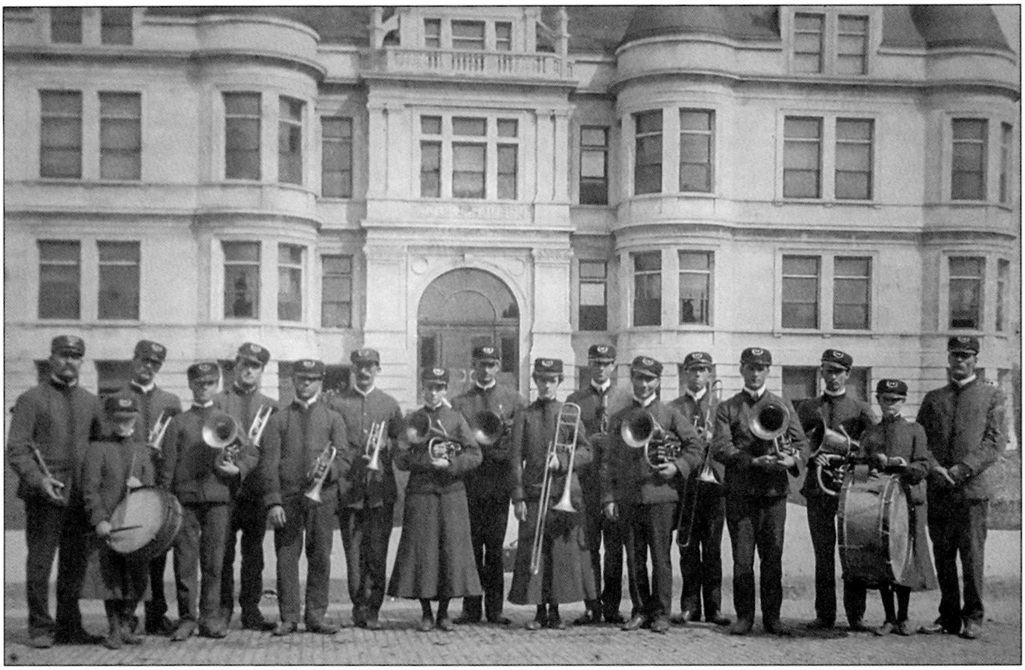

CADWELL BAND. Adel's Cadwell family band performed frequently in Dallas County in the early 20th century and is shown in this undated photograph outside Dallas County's iconic courthouse. By 1910, the band included Althea Cadwell Mann, Bess DeAtley Cadwell, Susie Cadwell Snyder, Lepha Cadwell Barrett, H.N. Cadwell, Edith Cadwell Pearson, Fred Cadwell, George Mann, Alfred Cadwell, Ben Merical, Den Mann, T.A. Husband, Clarence Cadwell, Myron Leonard, Charles Cadwell, and Weaver Merical. (Courtesy of Dallas County Conservation.)

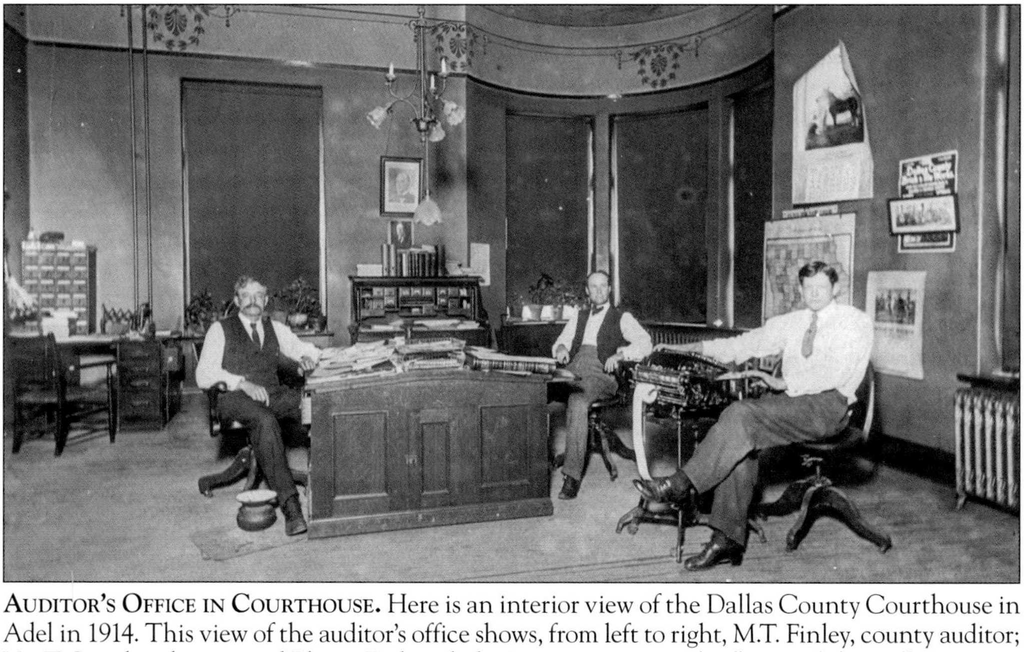

AUDITOR'S OFFICE IN COURTHOUSE. Here is an interior view of the Dallas County Courthouse in Adel in 1914. This view of the auditor's office shows, from left to right, M.T. Finley, county auditor; Vic T. Sweeley, deputy; and Blaine Finley, clerk. A spittoon sits on the floor and the Dallas County Brick & Tile Works poster is on the wall. (Courtesy of Dallas County Conservation.)

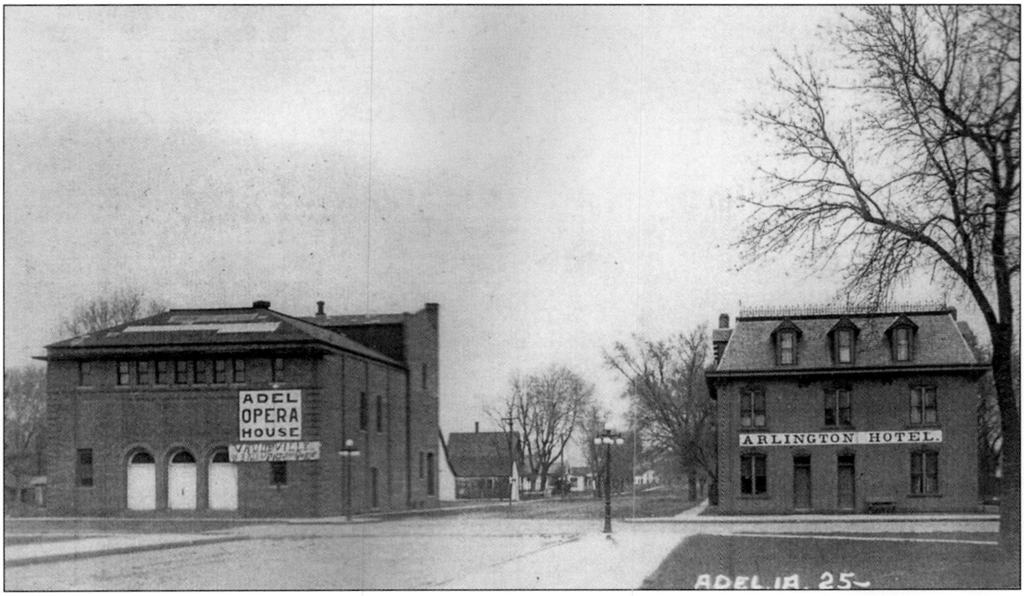

Adel's Opera House and Hotel. Located northwest of the Dallas County Courthouse, Adel's opera house was built in 1890. (A vaudeville sign can be seen in the picture.) It later became the Rialto Theater, where kids paid 10¢ to enjoy Westerns on Saturday afternoons in the 1940s. The theater burned down in 1956. Across the street, the Arlington Hotel served the community from 1888 until it was demolished in 1972. (Courtesy of Adel Historical Museum.)

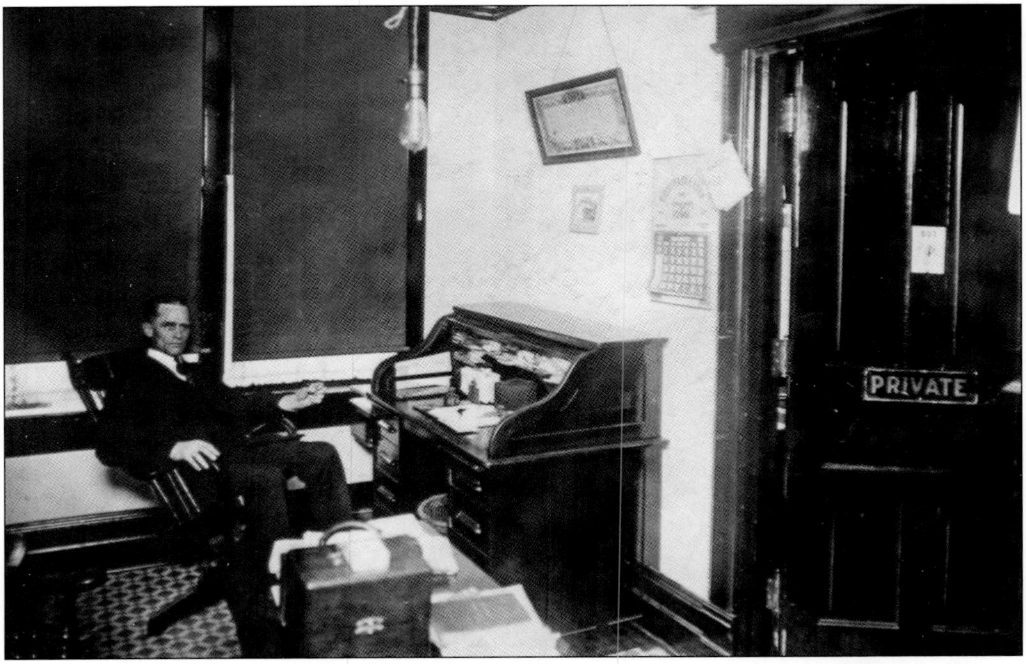

Small-Town Doctor. Dr. Clinton E. Mershon, an Iowa native born in 1870, served the community's medical needs for more than 50 years. Mershon came to Adel in 1900 after graduating from the University of Iowa. In 1907, he was appointed physician for the Des Moines & Central Iowa Railroad, a position he held until the 1950s. During World War I, Mershon (shown here around 1918) provided medical examinations for local military recruits. (Courtesy of Adel Historical Museum.)

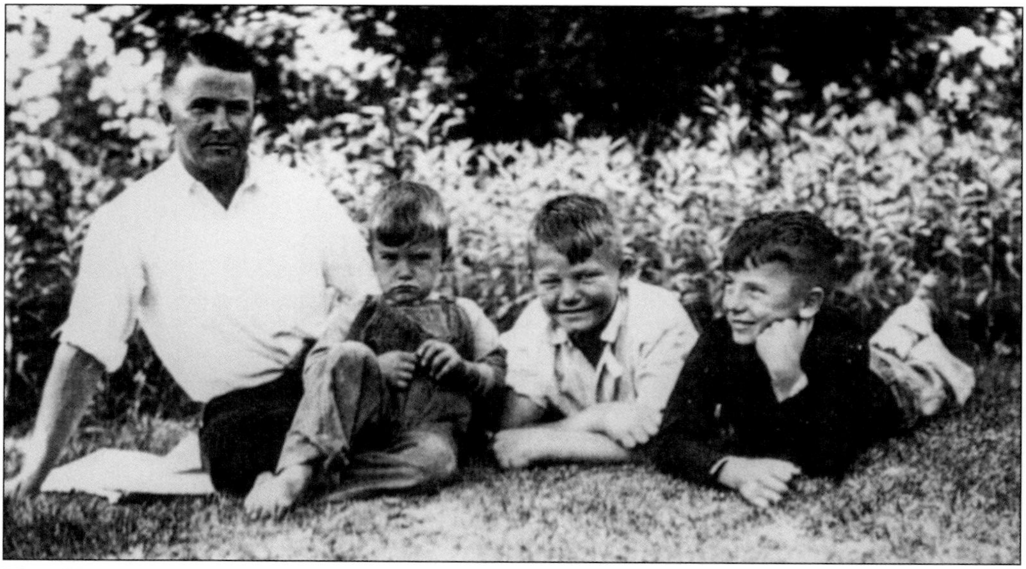

NILE KINNICK, A HOMETOWN HERO. Football star Nile Clarke Kinnick Jr. was born on July 9, 1918, in Adel to Nile Sr. and Frances Clarke Kinnick. He became a standout athlete at Adel High School and played many sports. He was a catcher for future baseball pro Bob Feller during American Legion games in Dallas County. Kinnick (second from right) is shown with his father and younger brothers Ben (right) and George. (Courtesy of Adel Historical Museum.)

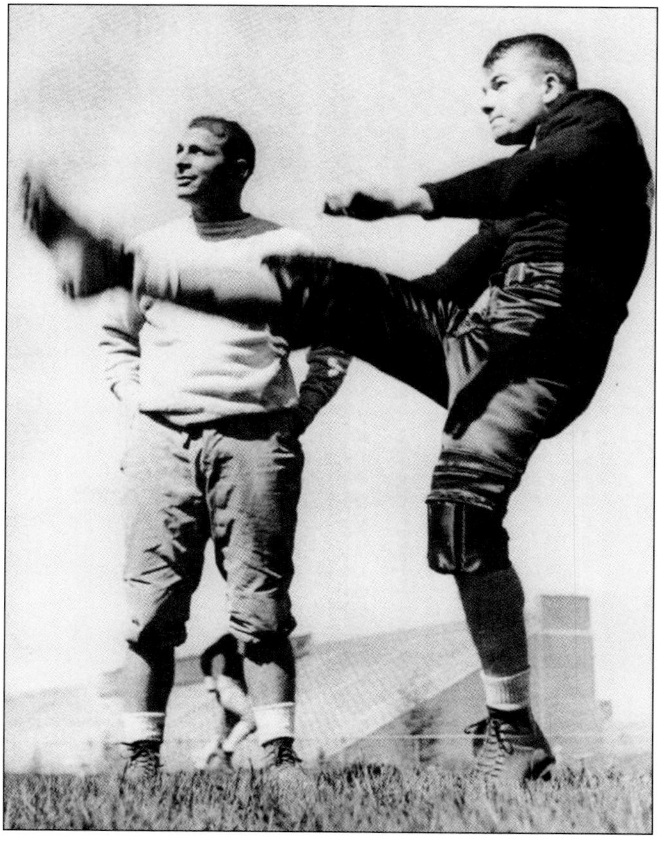

RETURNING TO IOWA. The grandson of Iowa governor George Clarke, Nile Kinnick moved with his family to Omaha, Nebraska, after his junior year at Adel High School. The five-foot-eight, 170-pound Kinnick returned to his home state to attend the University of Iowa. He played halfback on the football team, which struggled in those days. The team went 1-7 in 1937 while Kinnick (a sophomore) earned All–Big Ten honors. (Courtesy of Adel Historical Museum.)

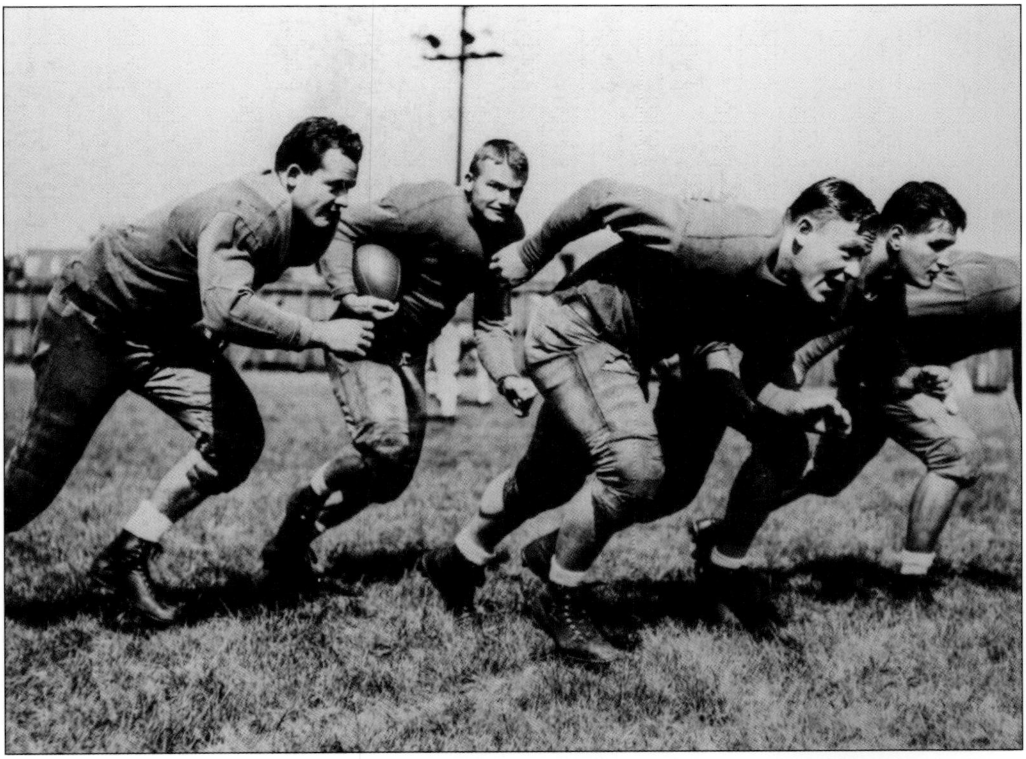

"CORNBELT COMET." Although his running style earned him the nickname "the Cornbelt Comet," Nile Kinnick suffered an ankle injury, possibly a broken ankle, in the 1938 season. Nothing could slow Kinnick too long, however. By passing, running, or kicking, Kinnick was directly involved in 107 of Iowa's 130 points during the 1939 season. He also made eight interceptions and became the backbone of Iowa's legendary "Ironmen" football squad. (Courtesy of Adel Historical Museum.)

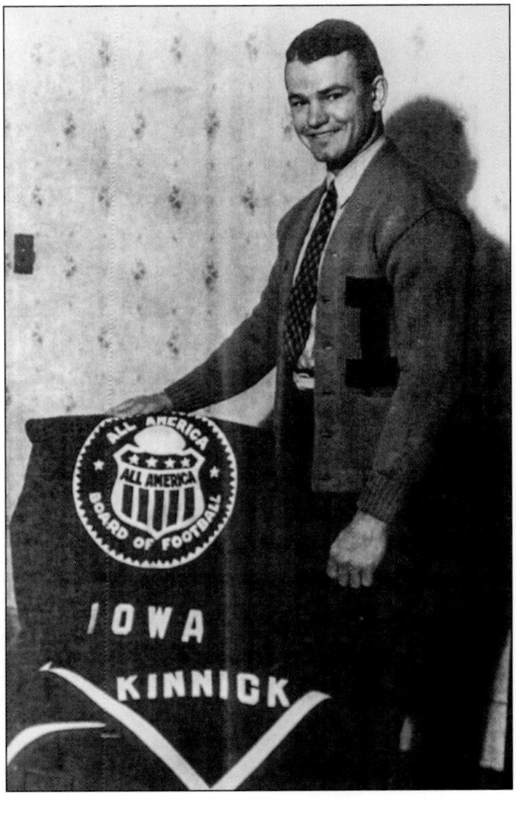

1939 HEISMAN TROPHY WINNER. While the word "hero" is overused in sports, Adel native Nile Kinnick fit the description. While a senior at the University of Iowa, Kinnick won all the major football awards, including the 1939 Heisman Trophy and the Maxwell Award, which is presented to the best college football player in America. Kinnick was also named Athlete of the Year in 1939 by national sportswriters, who selected him over notables like Joe DiMaggio. (Courtesy of Adel Historical Museum.)

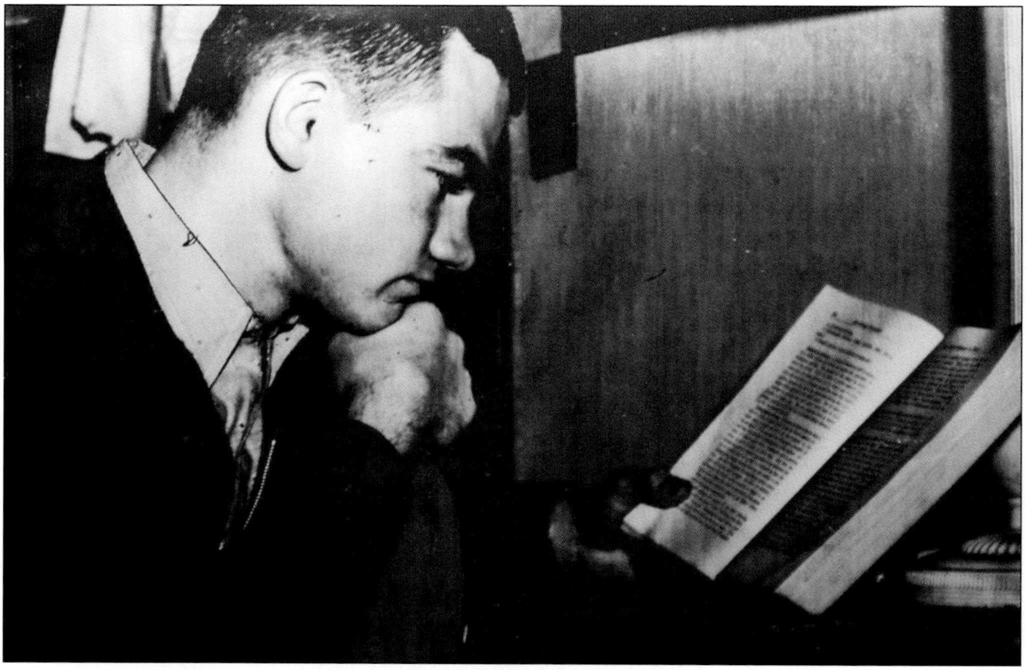

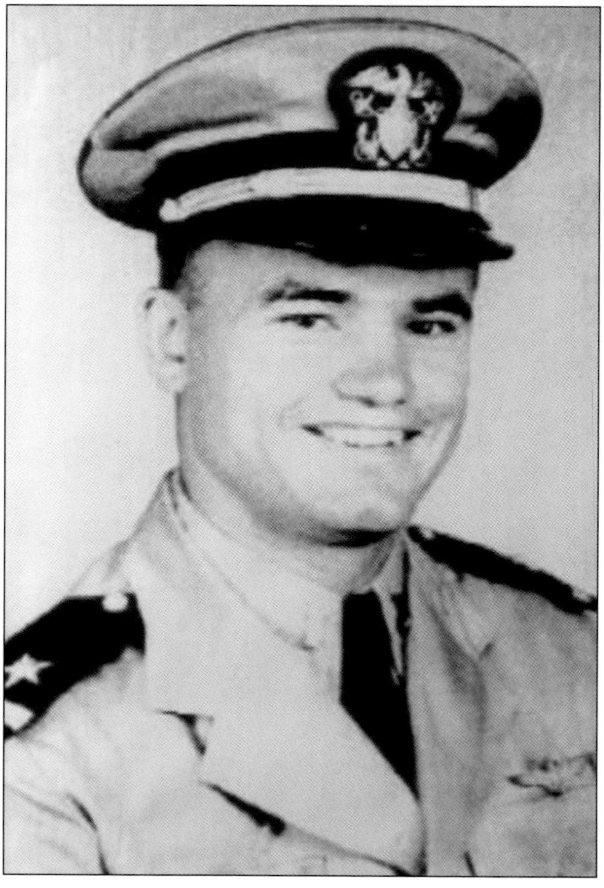

Hitting the Books. Nile Kinnick was much more than a great athlete. A Phi Beta Kappa, Kinnick was elected senior class president for the College of Liberal Arts and earned his bachelor's degree in commerce from the University of Iowa in 1940. Refusing draft offers from the National Football League, Kinnick entered law school. The young Republican also campaigned for Wendell Willkie, the 1940 Republican nominee for president. (Courtesy of Adel Historical Museum.)

Killed in Action. After a year in law school, Nile Kinnick enlisted in the Navy Air Corps Reserve and was called to active duty three days after Pearl Harbor was attacked. Kinnick died on June 2, 1943, after his fighter plane crashed into the Caribbean Sea off the coast of Venezuela during a training flight. His body was never recovered. In 1972, the University of Iowa named its football stadium in Kinnick's honor. (Courtesy of Adel Historical Museum.)

NUMBER, PLEASE. The Iowa Telephone Company provided Adel with telephone service until the company was purchased by Northwestern Bell in 1896. In 1938, magneto-type phones that had to be cranked by hand were converted to battery-type phones. Northwestern Bell converted Adel to a dial telephone system in 1961. This c. 1939 photograph shows telephone operators Cora DeCamp Danielson and Dorothy Stephens Stacy. (Courtesy of Adel Historical Museum.)

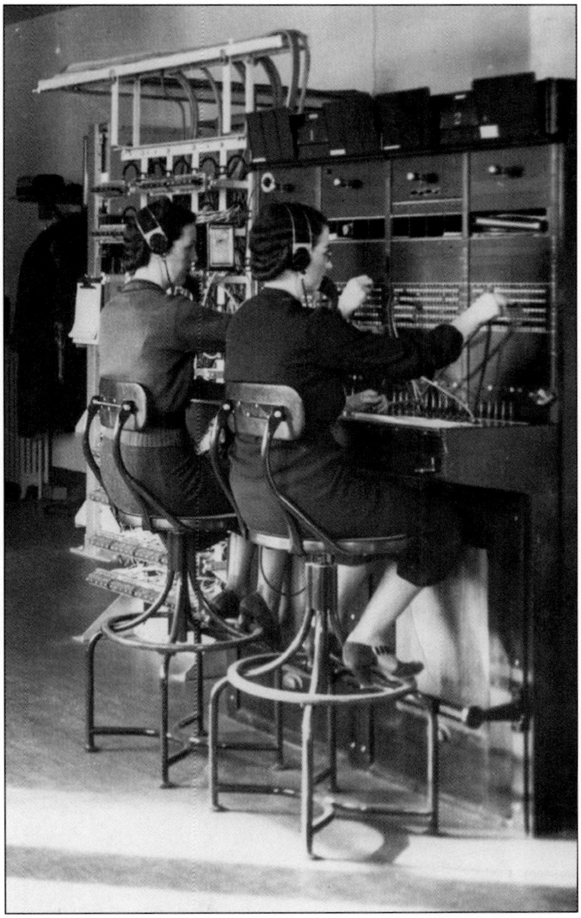

PANTHER STORE. In the days before automobiles, it was often difficult for residents of rural Dallas County to travel to towns like Adel. The Panther Cooperative Association and Panther Store started in 1898 when local farmers bought shares in the business. While Panther is now a ghost town, a marker at the intersection of Highway 44 and County Road P58 west of Adel tells how Panther boasted a store, blacksmith shop, tin shop, post office, and creamery. (Courtesy of Adel Historical Museum.)

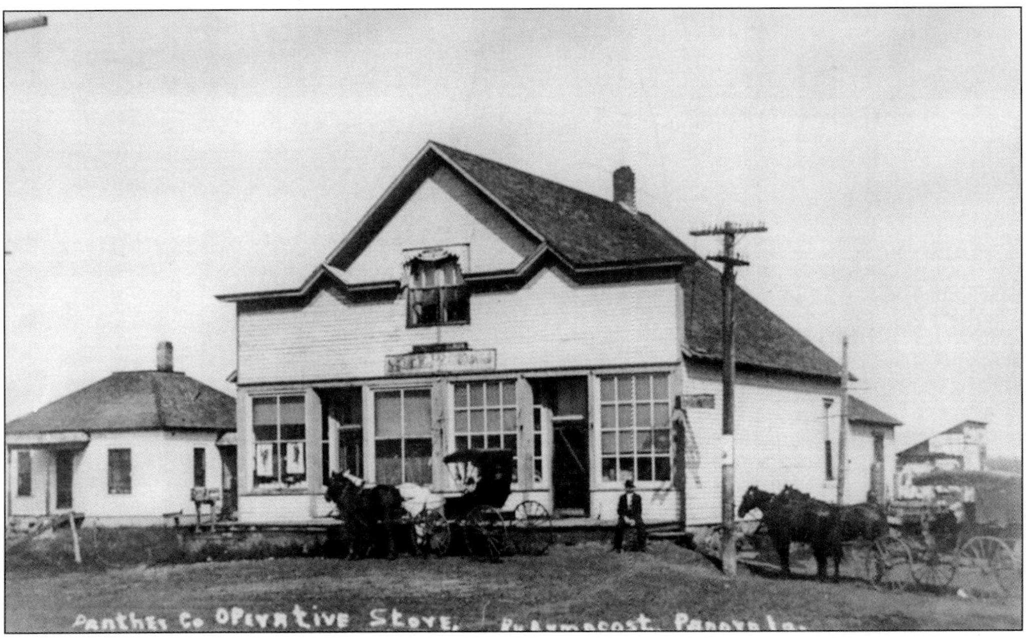

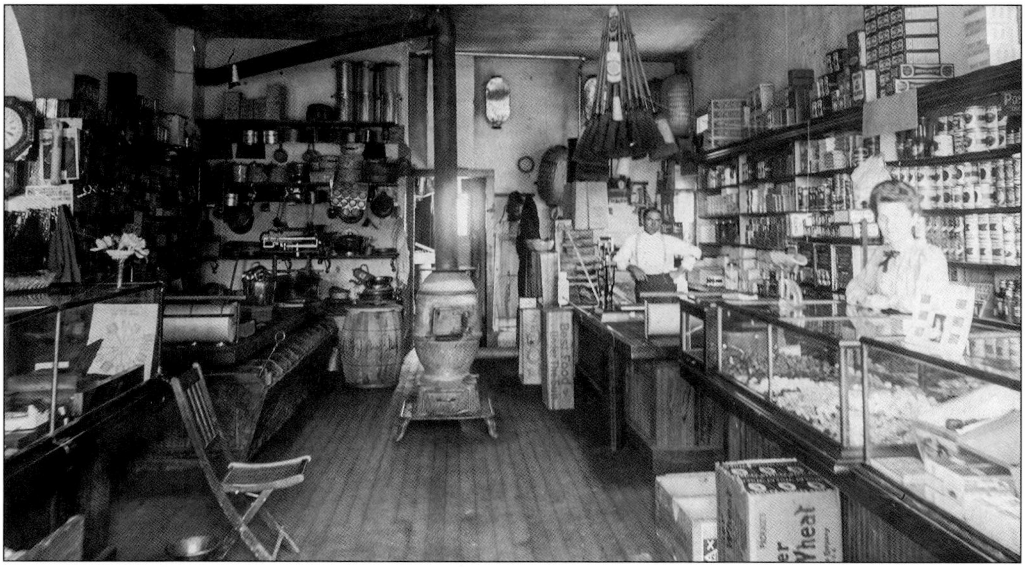

Inside the Panther Store. The Panther Store was usually open from 7:00 a.m. to 10:00 p.m. and sold a little bit of everything, from flour and kerosene to ammunition and men's overalls. This c. 1905–1909 photograph shows Martin and Valeria Bechtel in the store. The business even had an icehouse where ice cut from the Raccoon River was stored and sold. Store managers also bought items to sell, including poultry, cream, butter, and eggs. (Courtesy of Deanette Snyder.)

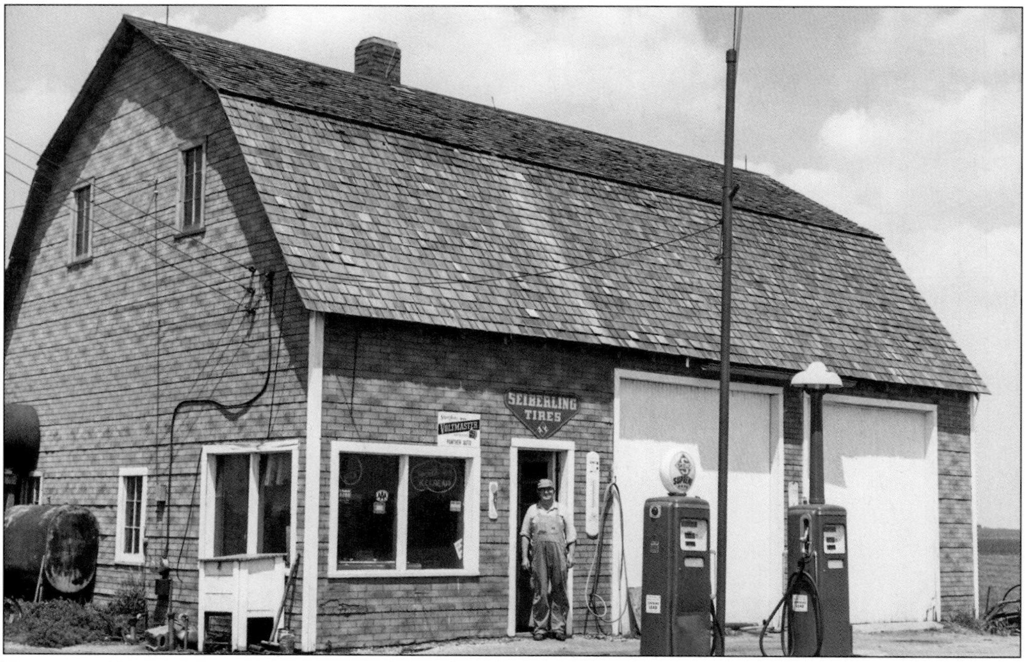

Panther Filling Station. Remaining in business until the early 1970s, the filling station on the east side of County Road P58 was one of the last traces of Panther. It outlasted the Panther Store, which had been a popular gathering spot for folks to swap stories and catch up on local news. Before the store closed around 1958, ball games, wrestling matches, boxing matches, and horse races were held near the store, while quilting bees were held in the attic over the store, located west of County Road P58 and across from the filling station. (Courtesy of Deanette Snyder.)

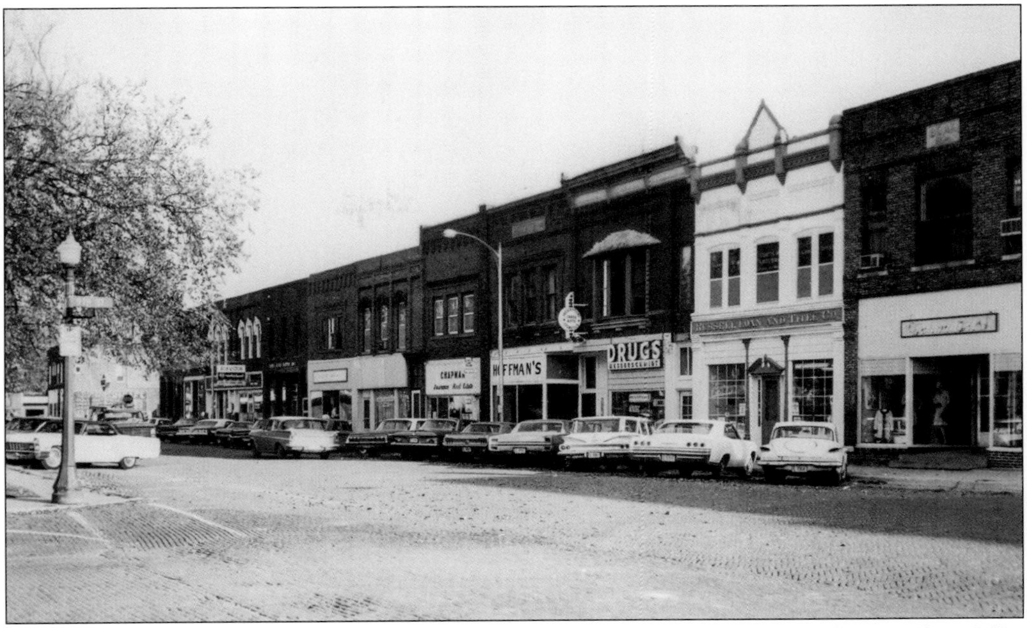

SOUTH SIDE OF THE SQUARE. Adel's downtown business district was a busy place in the 1960s, as seen in this photograph showing the south side of the square, where people could stop by the drugstore and other businesses. (Courtesy of Adel Historical Museum.)

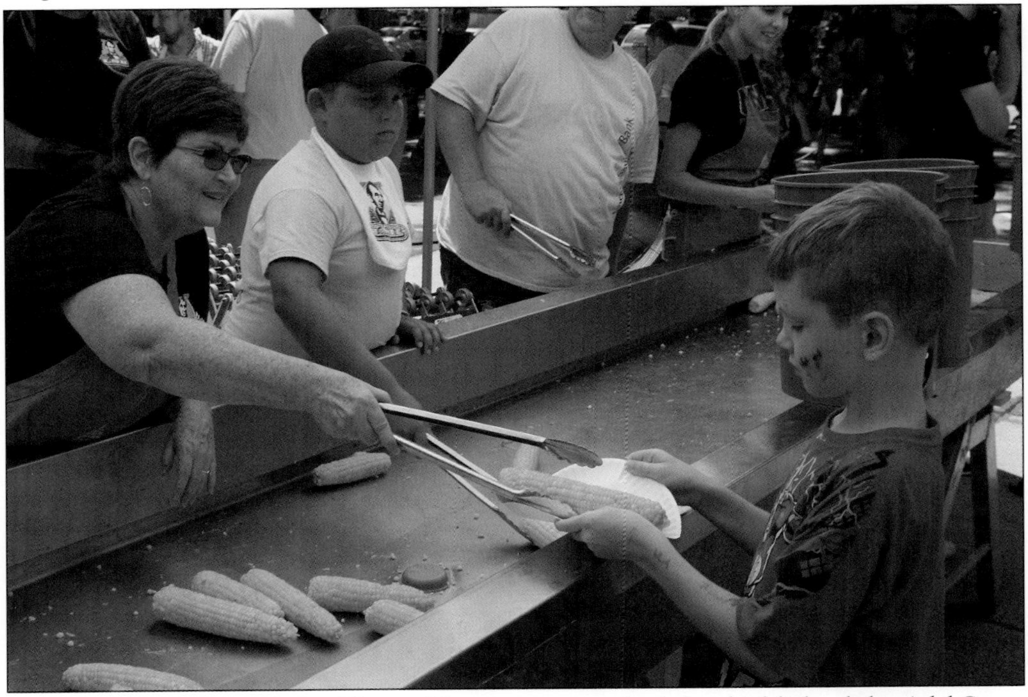

SWEET CORN FESTIVAL. One of Iowans' favorite summer foods has highlighted the Adel Sweet Corn Festival for nearly 40 years. In August 2016, more than seven tons of locally grown sweet corn were husked, cooked, and given away for free. Hundreds of people attended the festival, which also included a parade, car show, food and craft vendors, and 5K run on Adel's scenic brick streets. (Author's collection.)

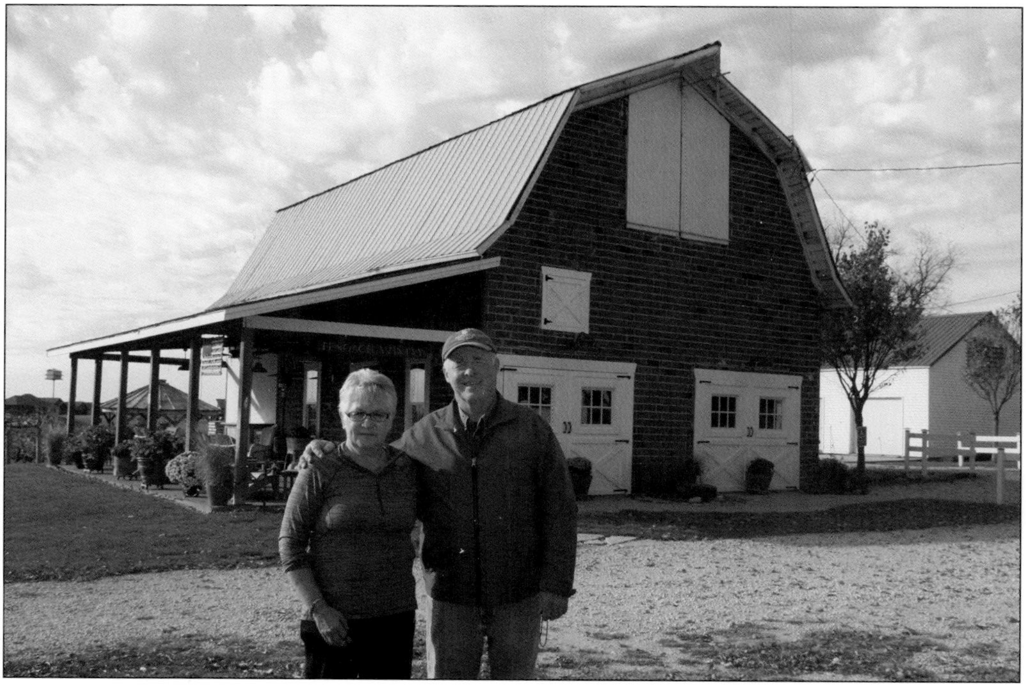

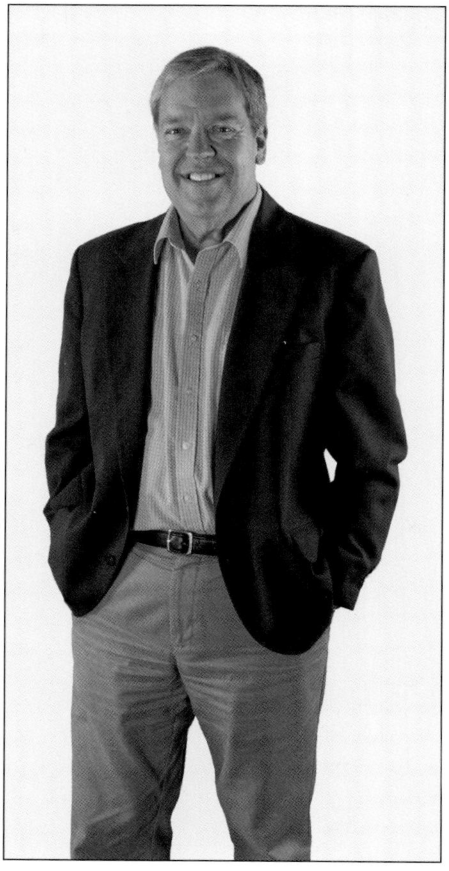

Drink in History at Penoach Winery. Stan and Joanie Olson incorporated a former 1920s-era dairy barn just north of Adel into Penoach Winery. The clay-tile barn, which was built on the H.B. Kinnick farm, was likely constructed with blocks made in Adel. Penoach Winery opened in 2006 and reflects Adel's original name. The winery includes four acres of grapes and produces 18 varieties of wine. (Author's collection.)

Van Harden, Radio Broadcaster. Well-known Iowa radio personality, author, and inventor Van Harden grew up in Adel. Radio has always been a passion for Harden, who got his first radio job in 1971 at KDLS FM in Perry, Iowa. After a stint in Tulsa, Oklahoma, Harden worked at KRNT Radio in Des Moines before joining WHO 1040 Radio in Des Moines in 1986. He cohosts WHO's popular *Van and Bonnie* morning show. (Courtesy of WHO Radio.)

Two

Redfield
A Crossroads of Local History

Founded in 1860, Redfield is one of the oldest towns in Dallas County, and its unique location has connected the community with some of the major migrations of the 19th century, from the California Gold Rush to the Underground Railroad.

The town was originally named New Ireland by the Cavanaugh brothers. Another town, Wiscotta, was laid out by Col. James Redfield about one mile south of New Ireland. Efforts were made to establish both towns, with Wiscotta being the larger community for some time. New Ireland was purchased by Colonel Redfield, and the name was changed to honor him. Colonel Redfield was killed in Georgia during Sherman's March to the Sea in 1864. By the 1890s, Redfield had grown to nearly 400 residents.

Redfield's history reflects the area's natural landscape. The Redfield Dam spans the Middle Raccoon River. Starting in the mid-1800s, sawmills and grain mills harnessed waterpower to provide the essentials of daily life for settlers.

Not far from the dam is Hanging Rock, which features a massive outcrop of sandstone and limestone that has served as a landmark for years. The area just downstream was a ford used by wagon trains heading west during the mid-1800s.

Rich clay deposits contributed to Redfield's long tradition of brick and tile manufacturing. Redfield was once known as the town with two brickyards, although only one remains.

Patriotism is another proud tradition in Redfield, population 835 (based on 2010 US Census data). Not only is Redfield well-known for its American Legion breakfasts, but the town also includes a restored GAR Hall, the only one of its kind in Iowa. Founded in 1866, the GAR promoted comradeship among Union veterans of the Civil War and worked to increase pensions and assist war widows and orphans. In Iowa, hundreds of posts (including the Marshall Post in Redfield) held meetings in small towns and cities across the state. Reaching its largest enrollment in 1890 with nearly half a million members nationwide, the GAR wielded considerable political clout for years.

Redfield's GAR building eventually fell into disrepair, but it was restored around 2008 and now includes a museum. Redfield also boasts a local history museum in a historic building on First Street downtown.

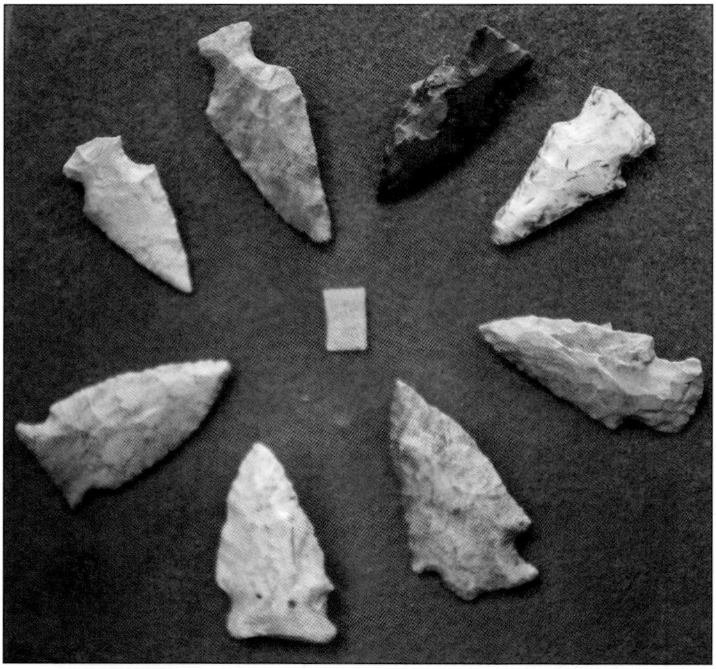

Arrowheads Reflect Native American Heritage. These Iowa artifacts, on display at the Redfield Museum, came from the collection of Redfield native Leo M. Harvey (1912–1972). They reflect Dallas County's Native American heritage as well as Harvey's lifetime of collecting items from the fields and woodlands of central Iowa. "May his deep appreciation for those who came before be passed on to those who follow," reads the museum display. (Author's collection.)

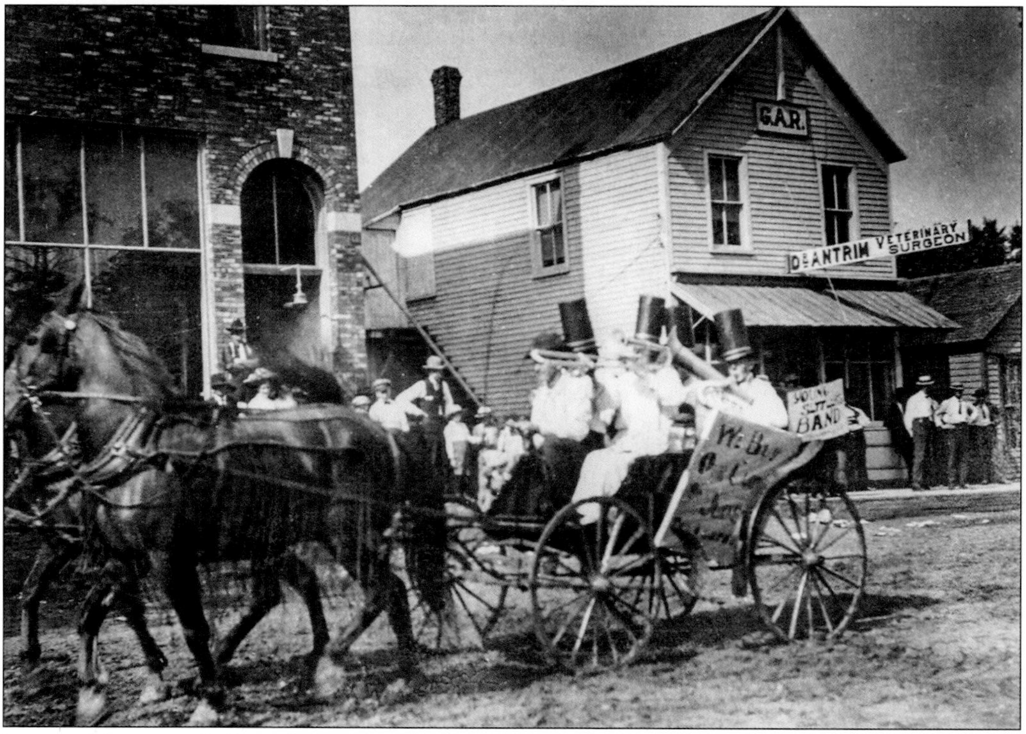

Parade Past the GAR. This Old Settlers Day parade is headed west on Thomas Street past the GAR Building, which was constructed in the 1880s and has been restored as a museum. Comprising Northern Civil War veterans, the GAR wielded considerable political clout nationwide at the time. Note the sign for Dr. John Delman Antrim, veterinary surgeon, whose office was located on the first floor of the GAR Hall. (Courtesy of Redfield Museum.)

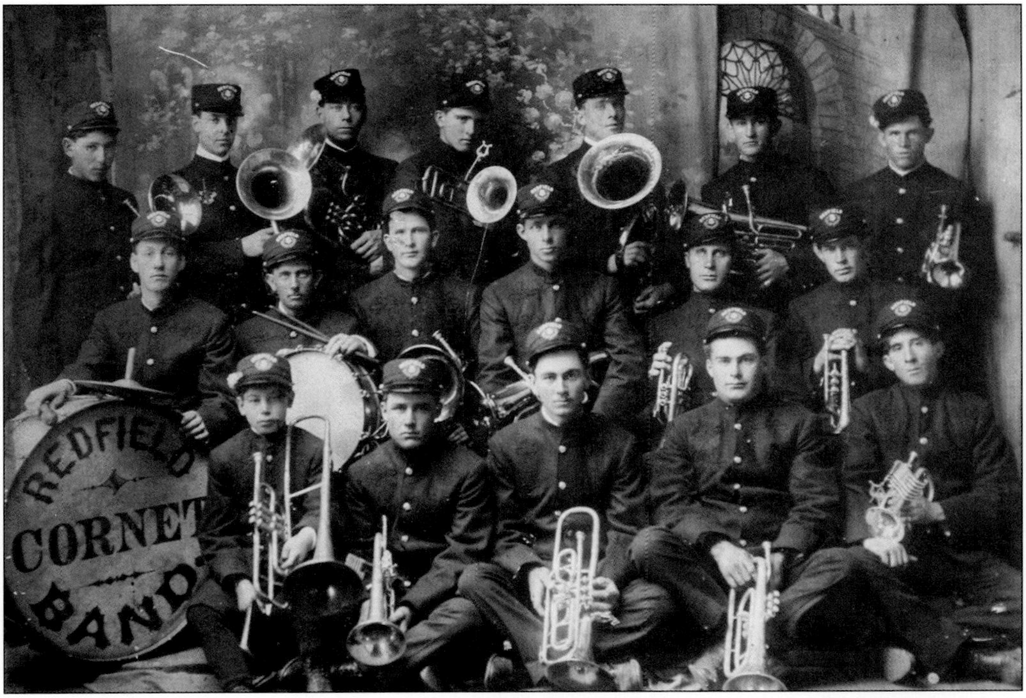

Small-Town Band Glory Days. In the years before radio and television, small-town brass bands were immensely popular. This Redfield Cornet Band includes, from left to right, (first row) Jack Colton, Roy Bates, Perry Hutchins, Albert Pitts, and Don Hodson; (second row) George Harding, Logan Cain, Alva Wirt, Jesse Moorman, Clem Quesy, and Glenn Noel; (third row) Jim Davis, Charley Martin, Everett Rhoads, Charley Hodson, Gene Frye, Ward Hutchins, and Claude Johnson. (Courtesy of Redfield Museum.)

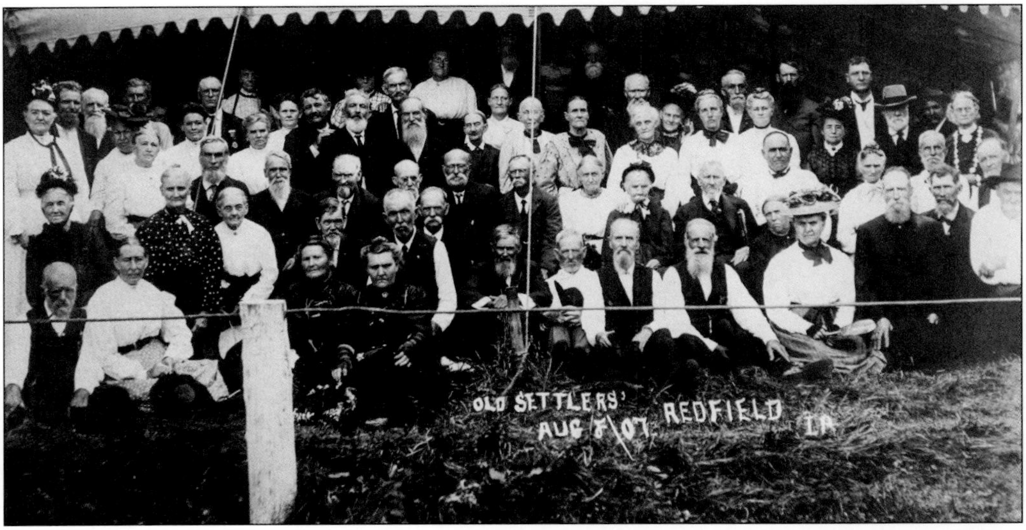

Redfield's Old Settlers. The Dallas-Guthrie Old Settlers Association was organized in 1895. One must have lived in Dallas County prior to 1870 (later amended to 1890) to be eligible for membership. The organization's purpose was that "old pioneers might meet and talk over the incidents of bygone days." Members like these in August 1907 enjoyed picnics near Hanging Rock, band concerts, and five-minute talks by the old settlers. (Courtesy of Redfield Museum.)

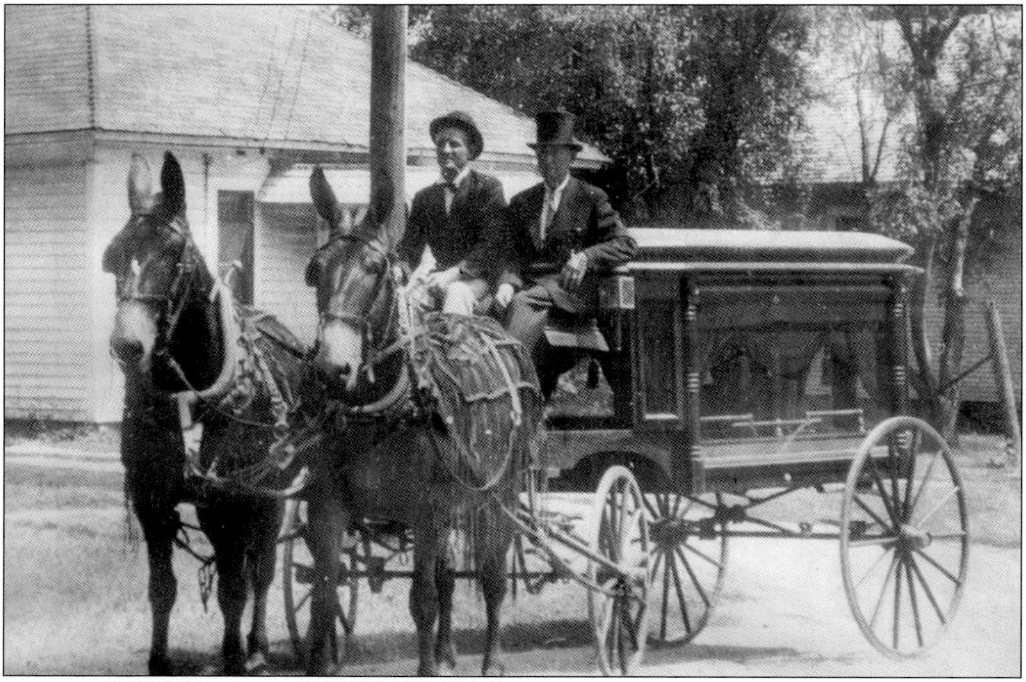

The Last Ride. The ornate hearse that served families in the Redfield area was provided by funeral director Hammie DeFord. Karl Martin is the mule driver. DeFord served the area from 1917 to 1965 as both funeral director and coroner. When someone died, he was called upon to determine the cause of death. If he thought a crime had been committed, DeFord took the evidence to the county attorney, and he was often called as a witness in court. (Courtesy of Adel Historical Museum.)

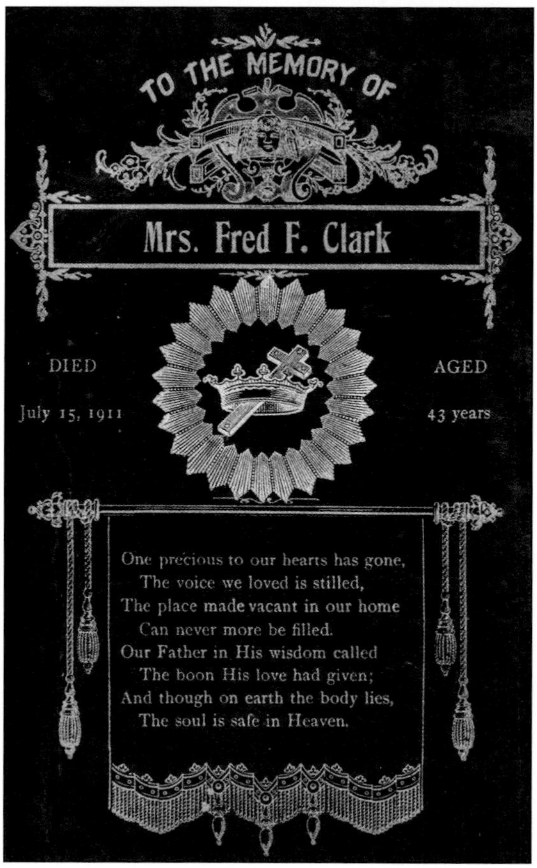

Gone but Not Forgotten. Memorial cards like this one for 43-year-old Mrs. Fred Clark, who died in 1911, were common in the late 19th and early 20th centuries, especially from 1895 to 1915. Printed on thick card stock, memorial cards were ordered and received after the loved one's funeral service. They were designed to be kept in the family photo album as a keepsake to memorialize the deceased. (Courtesy of Redfield Museum.)

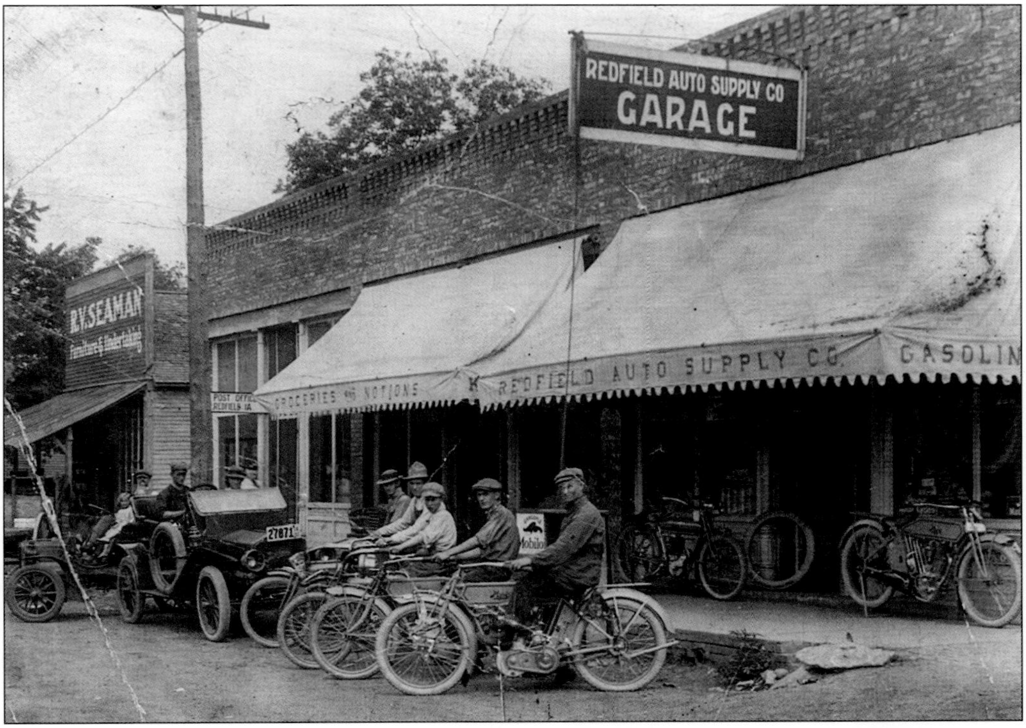

Motorcycles, Cars, and More. Around 1913, the Redfield Auto Supply Company was a dealership for Pope motorcycles and various automobiles. The car in front is a 1911 Parry, while in back is an REO two-cylinder vehicle from the early 1900s. Behind the cars, notice the shop of R.V. Seaman. Undertaking was a common side business for furniture makers, since they made coffins as well as furniture. (Courtesy of Redfield Museum.)

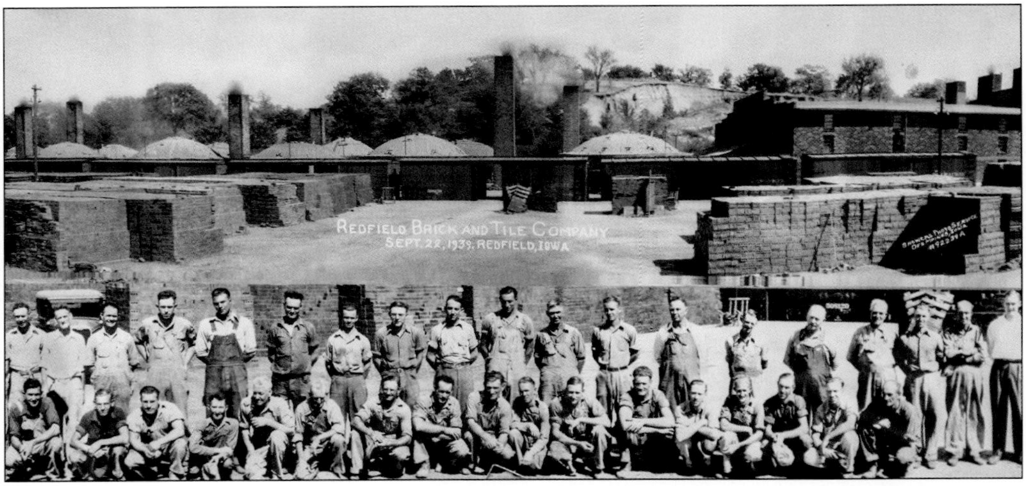

Brick and Tile. Due to Redfield's location near the river and rich clay deposits, brick and tile manufacturing has thrived since the 1870s, providing jobs for generations of families. Before the 1940s, these businesses typically operated from April to November. In the winter, men found work cutting ice from the Raccoon River. There are beehive kilns in this September 22, 1939, photograph of the Redfield Brick and Tile Company. (Courtesy of Redfield Museum.)

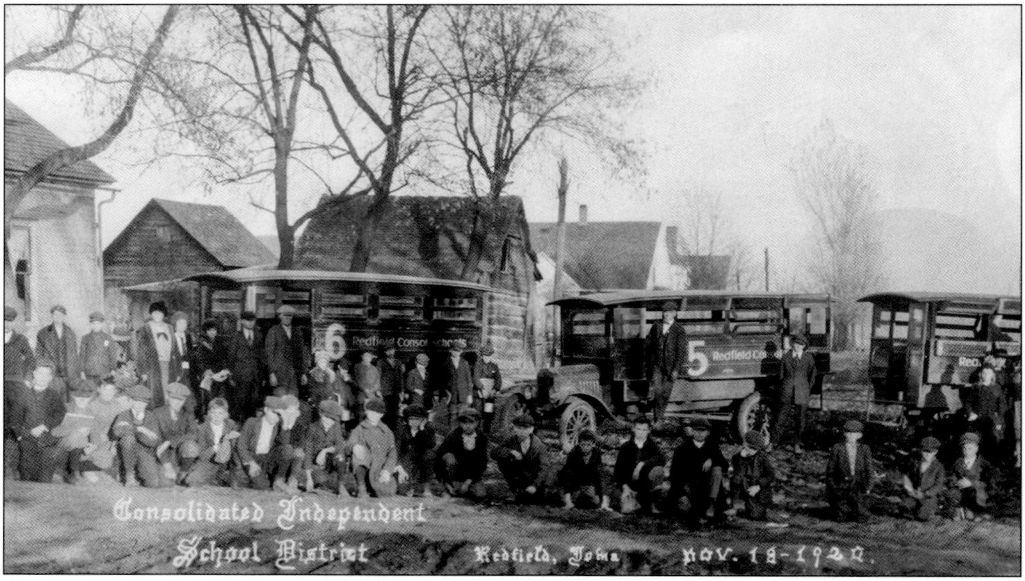

CONSOLIDATED SCHOOL. The first known school in the area was built in Wiscotta, south of Redfield. The earliest Redfield school was a log cabin, followed by a frame schoolhouse and a brick schoolhouse. By March 1922, students began attending the new Redfield Consolidated School. This November 1920 photograph shows the district's motorized school buses. In that era, it was not uncommon for high school students to serve as bus drivers. (Courtesy of Redfield Museum.)

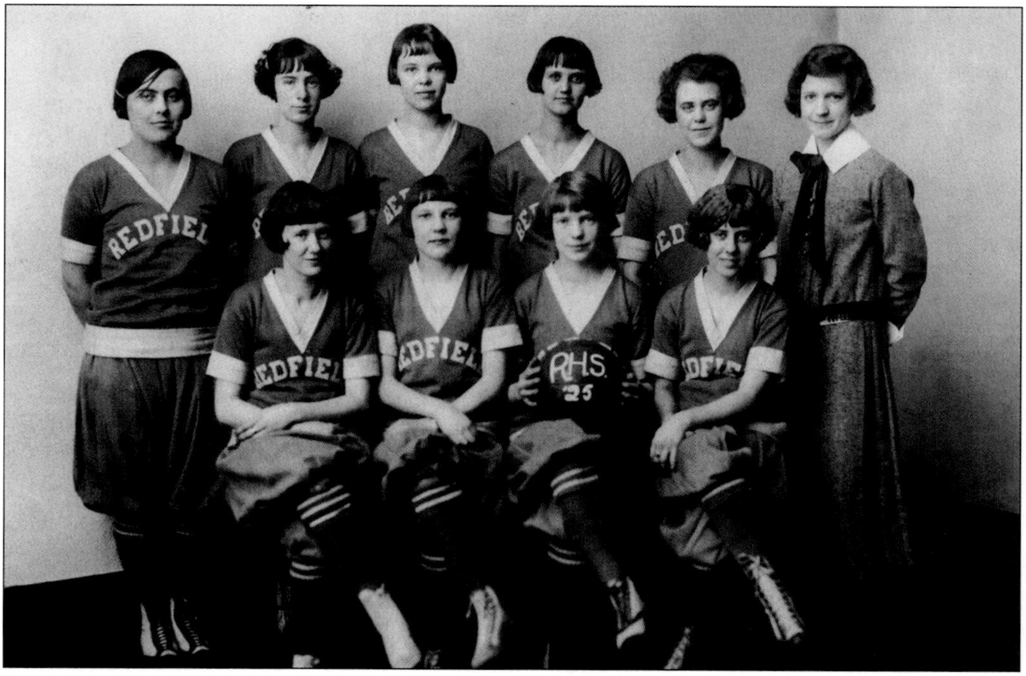

PLAY LIKE A GIRL. Iowa was one of the few states in the 1920s where girls' high school basketball was played. A girls' state basketball tournament was established in 1920, and the sport thrived in rural schools like Redfield. Iowa's larger schools did not share this enthusiasm. Many people at the time believed it was harmful for girls to engage in "strenuous" activities like basketball. (Courtesy of Adel Historical Museum.)

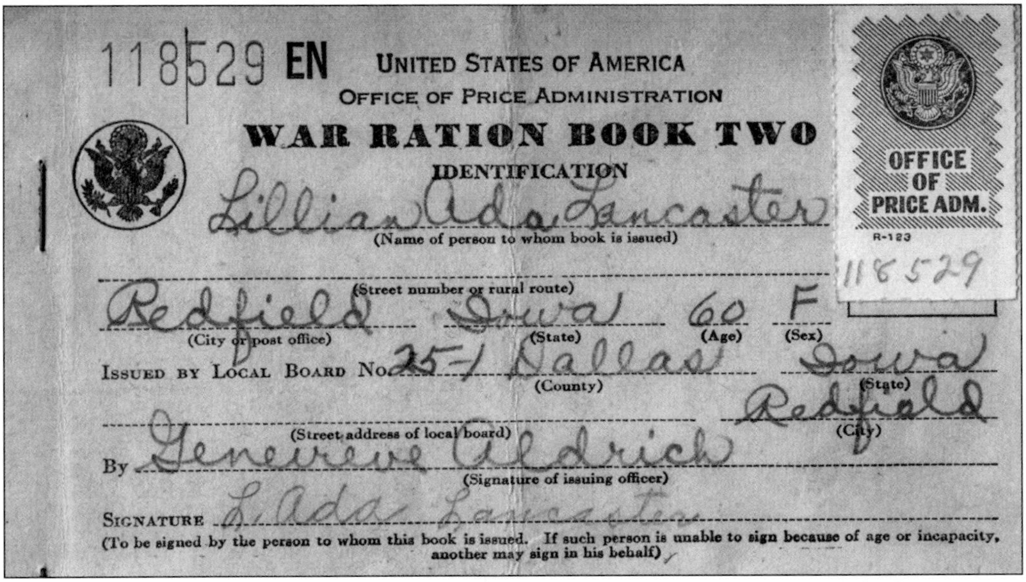
118529 EN
UNITED STATES OF AMERICA
OFFICE OF PRICE ADMINISTRATION
WAR RATION BOOK TWO
IDENTIFICATION
Lillian Ada Lancaster
(Name of person to whom book is issued)
(Street number or rural route)
Redfield (City or post office) Iowa (State) 60 (Age) F (Sex)
ISSUED BY LOCAL BOARD No. 25-1 Dallas (County) Iowa (State)
(Street address of local board) Redfield (City)
By Genevieve Aldrich (Signature of issuing officer)
SIGNATURE L. Ada Lancaster
(To be signed by the person to whom this book is issued. If such person is unable to sign because of age or incapacity, another may sign in his behalf)
OFFICE OF PRICE ADM.
R-123
118529

WORLD WAR II RATION BOOK. During World War II, the US government established a rationing system to more fairly distribute foods in short supply. Every American (including Lillian Lancaster of Redfield) was issued ration books containing stamps for rationed items like sugar, meat, cooking oil, and canned goods. Once a person's ration stamps were used up for the month, he or she could not buy any more of that food. (Courtesy of Redfield Museum.)

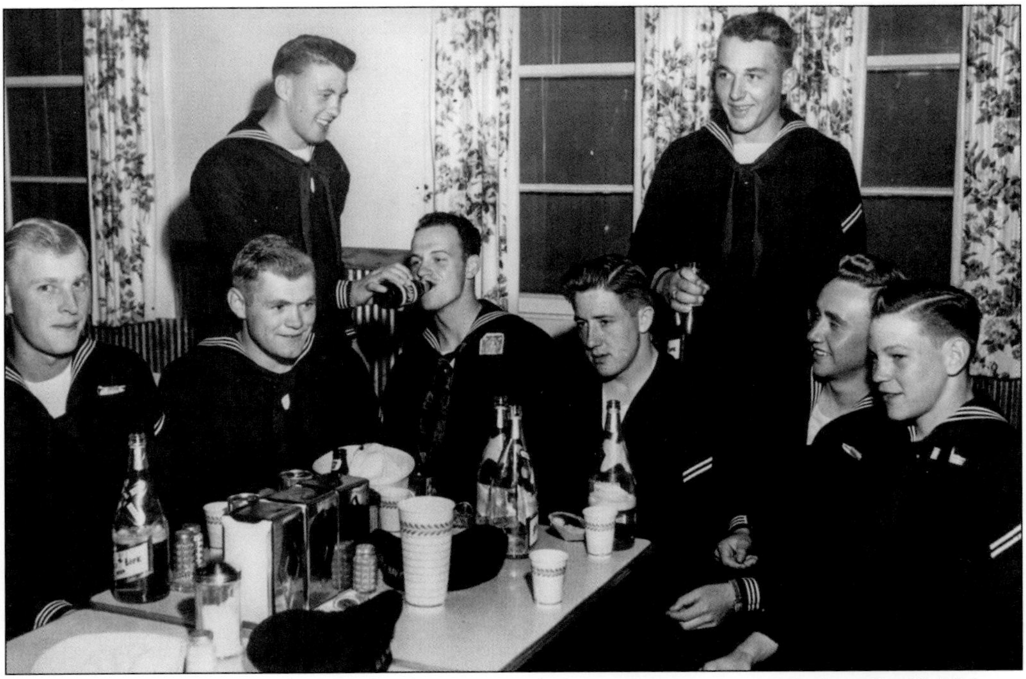

SAILORS FROM REDFIELD. Thousands of Iowans, including many young people from Redfield, have served in all branches of the US military throughout American history. This 1951 photograph of US sailors in Washington State shows five Redfield men—Richard Bales (standing left), Darrell Stapes (standing right), Henry Kester, Ronald Simpson, and Kenneth Lamb—along with Robert Hester, who was from Earlham. (Courtesy of Redfield Museum.)

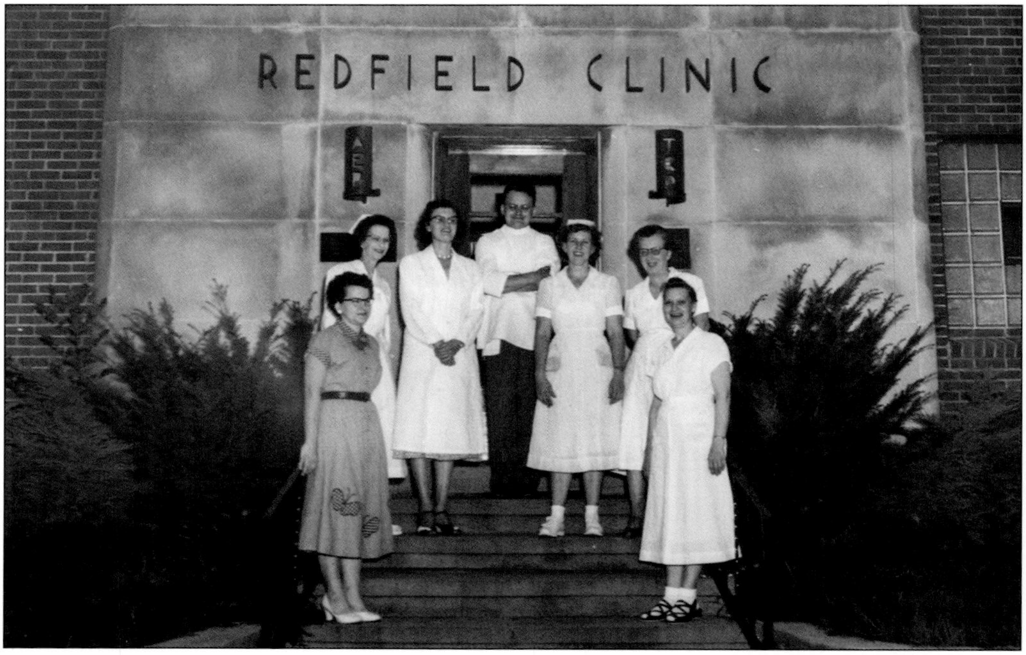

REDFIELD CLINIC. Medical professionals served Redfield from the mid-1800s. Dr. Macy Maulsby came to Linden to farm, but demand for physicians prompted him to move to Redfield. The pioneer doctor traveled on horseback to serve patients up to 40 miles away. In 1947, Drs. T.C. and Arline Peace (shown in the center) built Redfield's hospital/clinic, which was sold in 1972 to the Des Moines College of Osteopathic Medicine. (Courtesy of Redfield Museum.)

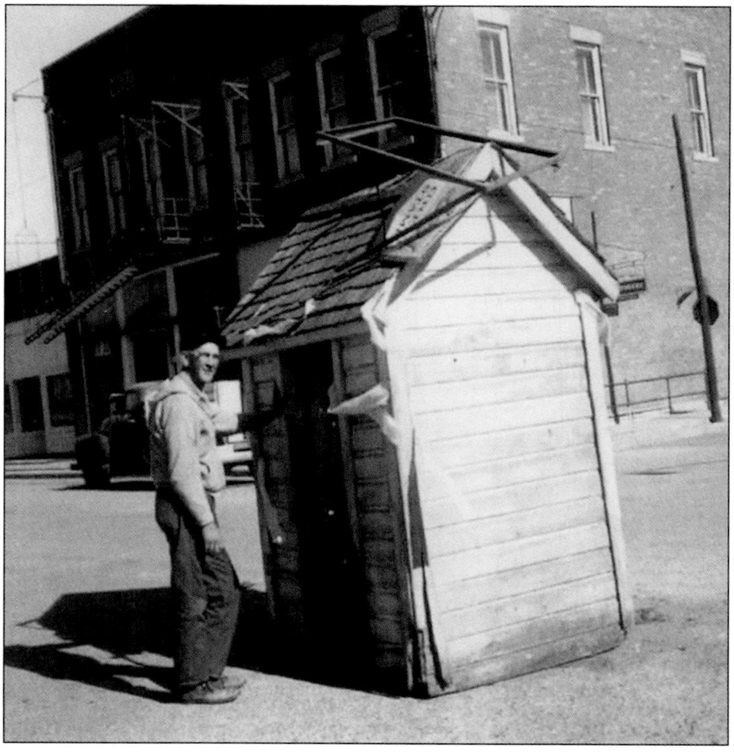

THE GREAT OUTHOUSE CAPER. There was a time when toppling outhouses was the ultimate Halloween prank in Iowa's rural communities. While indoor toilets and septic systems were becoming more common, outdoor toilets located strategically downwind from the house remained a daily necessity for some people. This outhouse, shown with Lawrence "Pappy" Hurst, was not toppled, but it was relocated to the intersection of First Street and Thomas Street in Redfield. (Courtesy of Redfield Museum.)

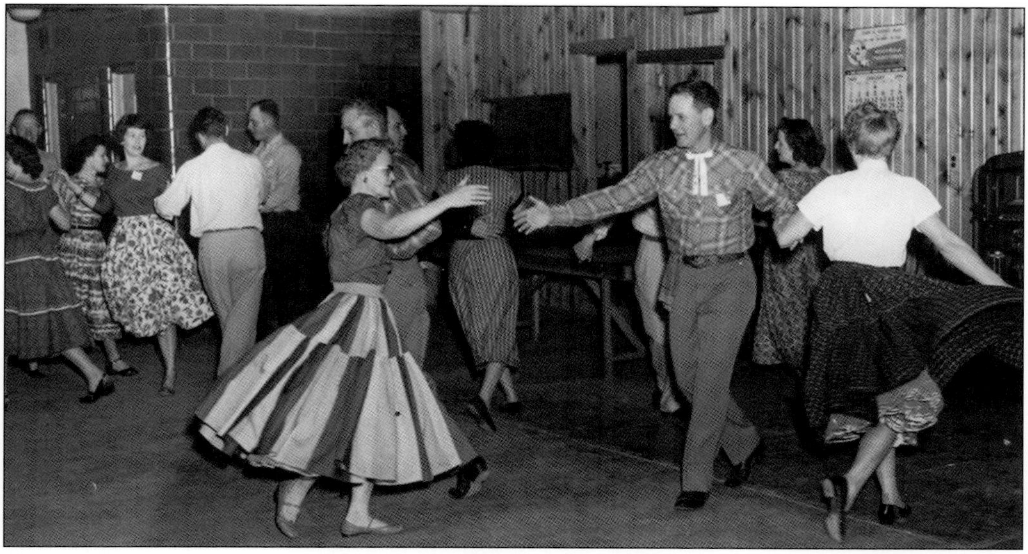

Swing Your Partner and Do-Si-Do. Square dancing was popular in rural communities for decades. While square dancing fell out of favor during the Jazz Age, auto manufacturer Henry Ford's interest in reviving the dances of his youth gave it a new lease on life in the 1920s and beyond. A square dance caller provides the choreography cues for the dancers, including this group in Redfield around 1949. (Courtesy of Redfield Museum.)

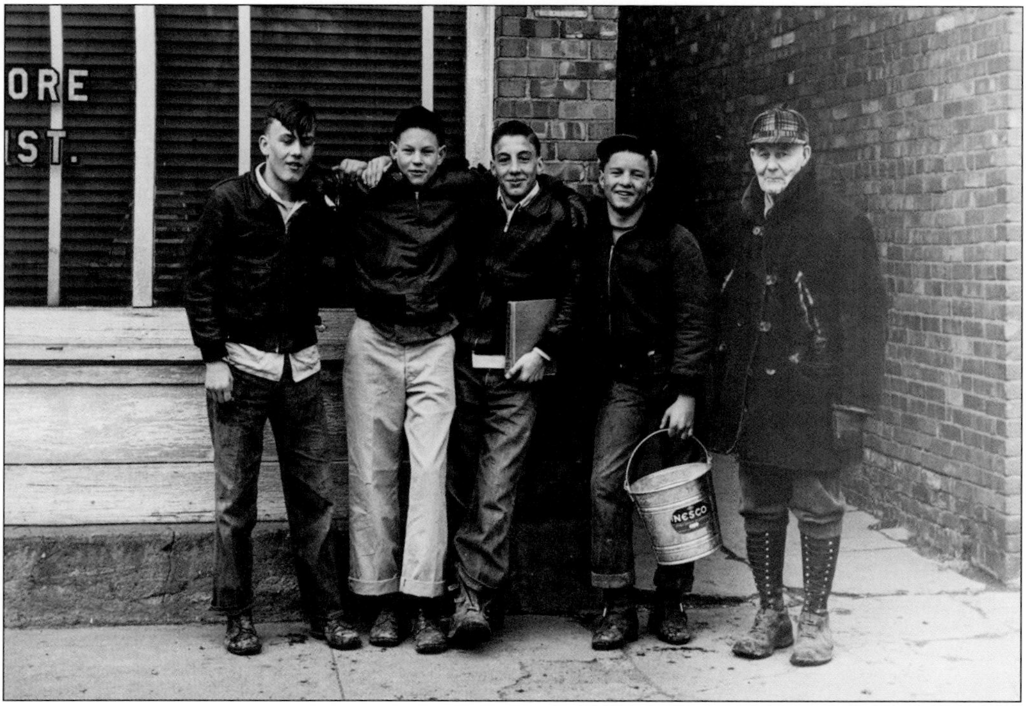

Small-Town Justice. These juvenile offenders, (from left to right) Merle Stapes, Henry "Hank" Kester, Lloyd Stapes, and Carrol "Butch" Christensen, are accompanied by Redfield's town marshal, "Jim Boozle" Cunningham, in the late 1940s or early 1950s. The boys are on punishment duty and are cleaning windows they had supposedly spat on. The building behind the group is still standing, although part of the roof has fallen in. (Courtesy of Redfield Museum.)

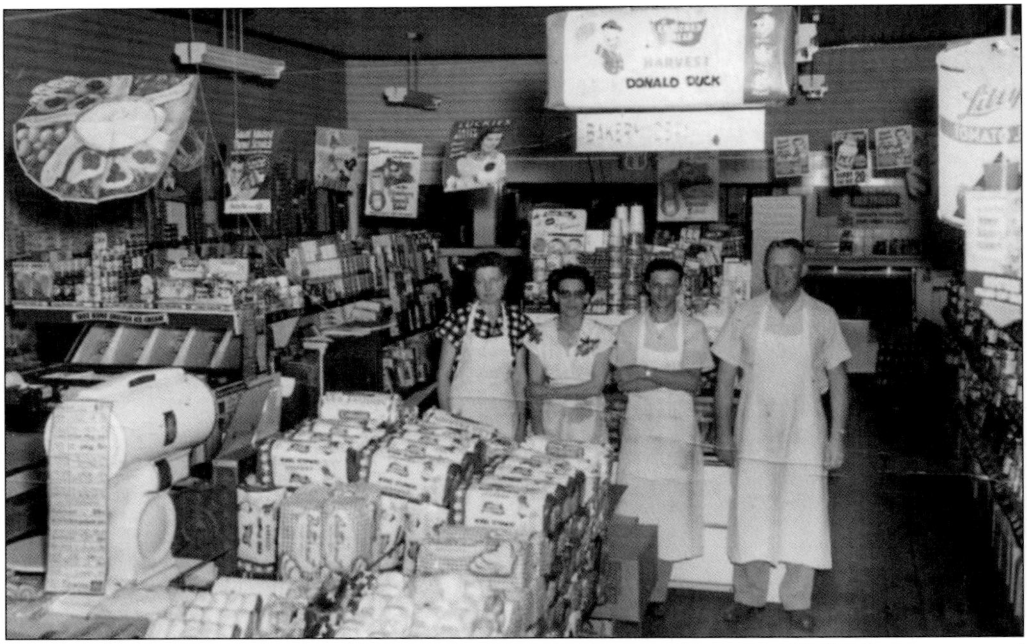

Donald Duck Bread. This interior shot of Towns Super Valu in Redfield shows a typical small-town Iowa grocery store, complete with advertising ranging from Lucky cigarettes to Libby's Tomato Juice to Donald Duck bread. Donald Duck was one of the most licensed Disney characters of the time. In the early 1950s, American grocery shoppers could find many Donald Duck–branded foods, from root beer to "Cheese Quackers" to bread. The Redfield store's staff seen here includes, from left to right, Mary Spillers, Tops Leeper, Dickie Martin, and Lyle Towns. (Courtesy of Redfield Museum.)

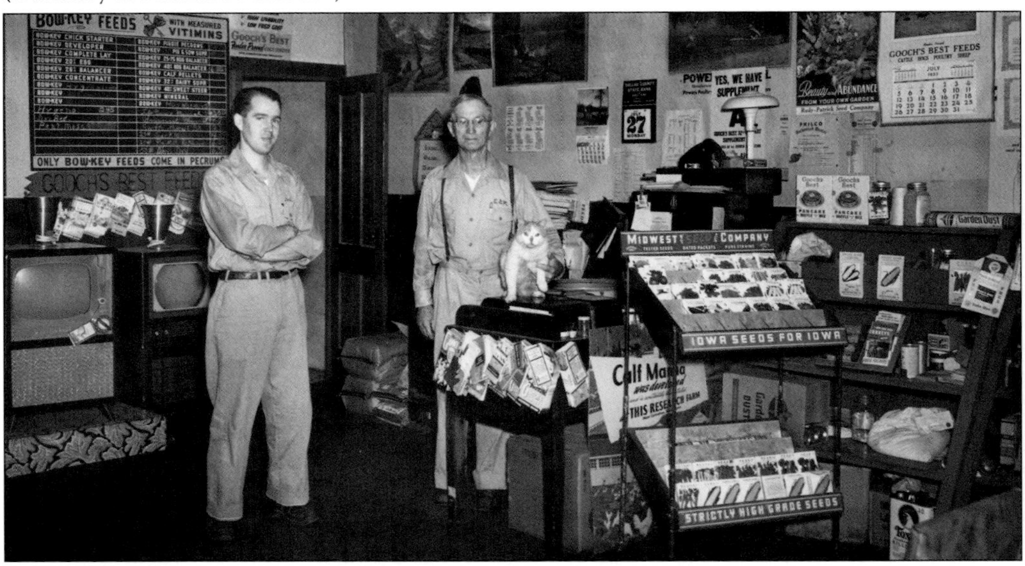

Glimpse inside the Feed and Seed Store. This photograph was taken on July 27, 1953, in a store in Redfield where one could buy feed for hogs, cattle, and chickens from brands like Gooch's Best Feeds. Pet food, along with packets of seeds for vegetable gardens, was also available. A television set is behind the employee named Dale (on the left), and the employee on the right holds a cat. (Courtesy of Redfield Museum.)

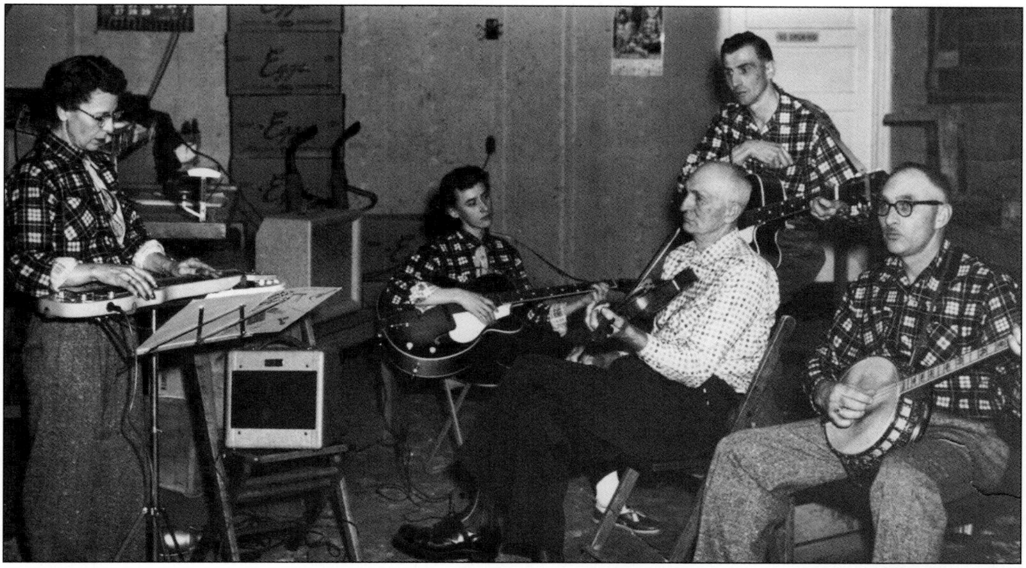

JAM SESSION. Iowa's small towns were often blessed with many talented musicians. In Redfield, folks sometimes gathered at the produce and egg station for informal jam sessions. Shown from left to right are Oma Reynolds (Jesse Reynold's wife) on the steel guitar, Wanda Chase, Ross Reynolds (Jesse Reynold's father) on the fiddle, Mel Chase (Wanda's husband), and Jesse Reynolds. This gathering likely took place at First Street and Taylor Street. (Courtesy of Redfield Museum.)

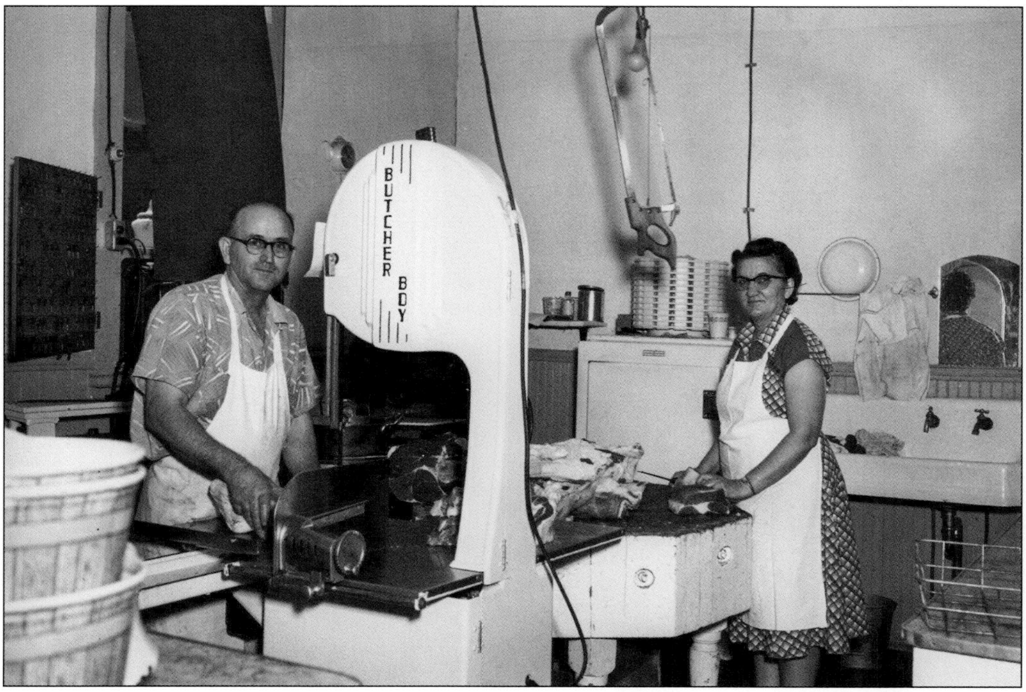

REDFIELD LOCKER. Fresh, homegrown meat processed locally has been an Iowa tradition for generations. The Redfield Locker plant was established in 1938 by Dick Patty in connection with his feed and produce business. The business was sold many times through the years. E.R. and Lela Griffith (shown here) purchased the locker in 1951 and sold it to Willard and Betty Griffith in 1969. (Courtesy of Redfield Museum.)

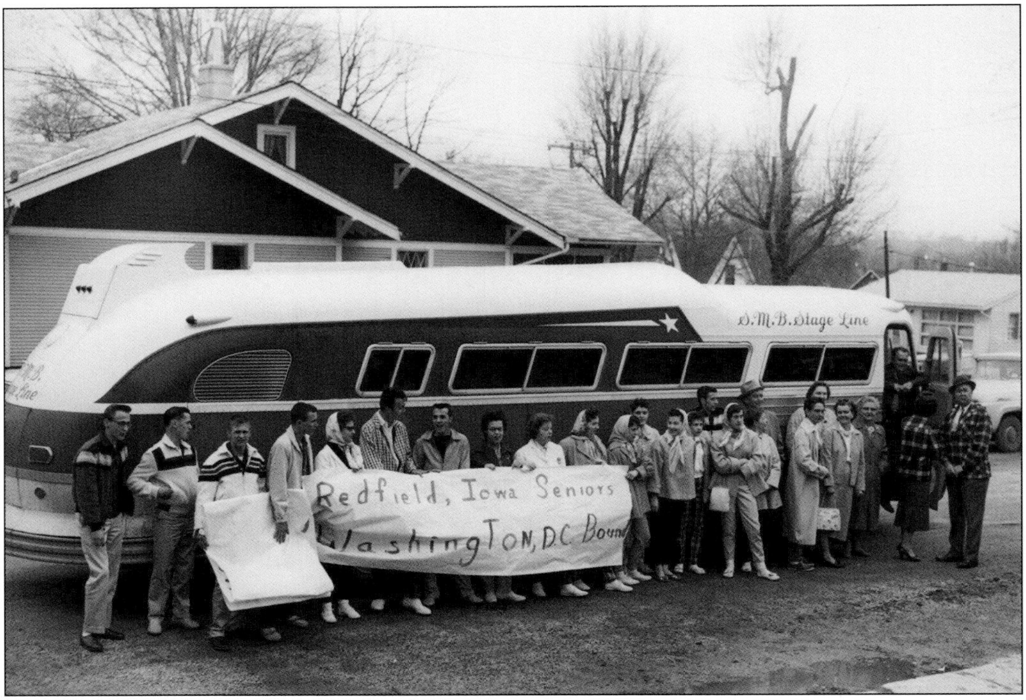

REDFIELD SENIOR TRIP. Redfield's high school seniors are bound for Washington, DC, for this class trip in the spring of 1959. Class members hosted bake sales and other fundraisers to pay for the trip, which was a highlight of the school year. Destinations varied through the years but helped students learn about the wider world beyond Iowa. Some small, rural Iowa schools still carry on this tradition. (Courtesy of Redfield Museum.)

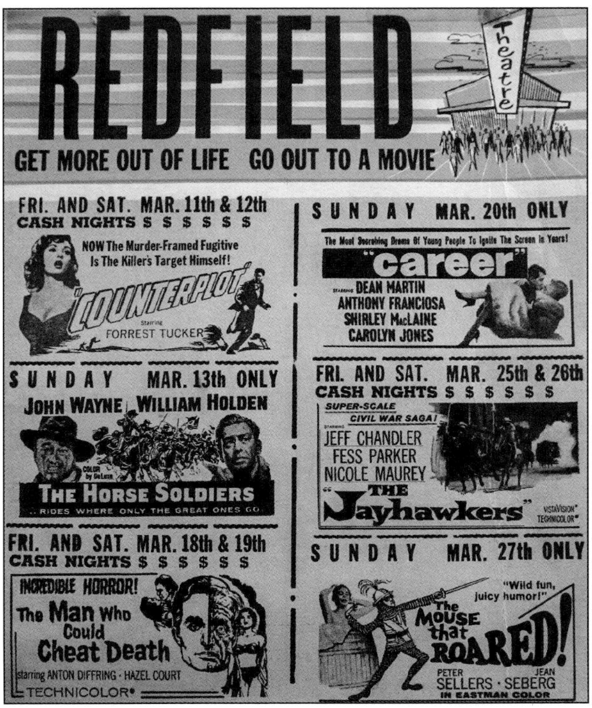

MOVIES IN REDFIELD. With the slogan "Get more out of life, go to a movie," the Redfield Theater encouraged people of all ages to catch a show at the local theater. In 1959, admission ranged from 30¢ to 65¢. Evening shows were available, along with Sunday matinees at 2:00 p.m. Iowa native John Wayne stars in *The Horse Soldiers*, which was only shown on Sunday, March 13, 1959, at the Redfield Theater. (Courtesy of Redfield Museum.)

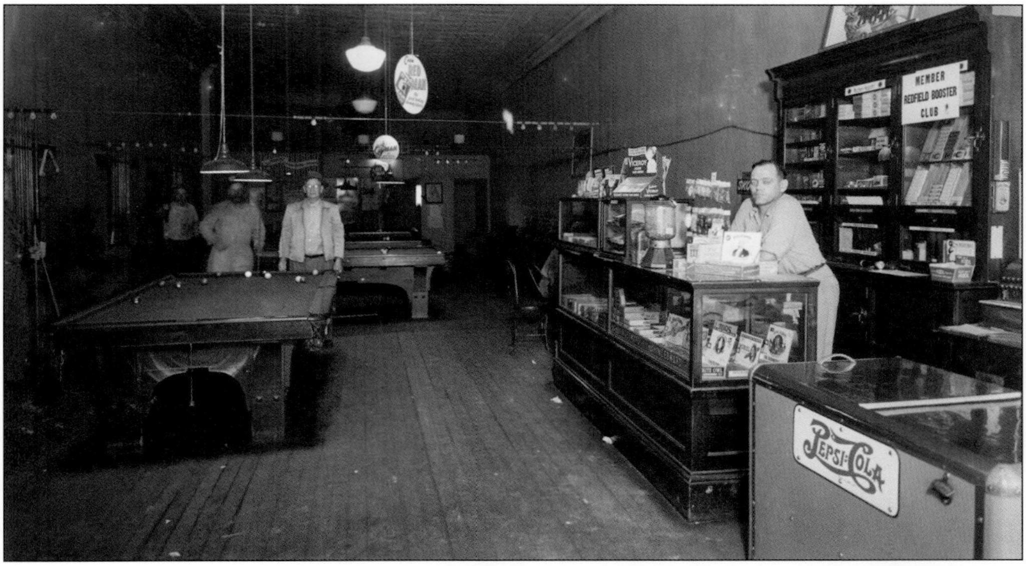

Pool Hall. For many years, pool halls and taverns were almost exclusively a man's domain. In Redfield, Phil Beane (shown here) ran the local pool hall, which was often thick with smoke and might have a pitch game in progress. There are Red Man chewing tobacco signs, King Edward cigars, Tums antacids on the counter, and a Redfield Booster Club member sign. (Courtesy of Redfield Museum.)

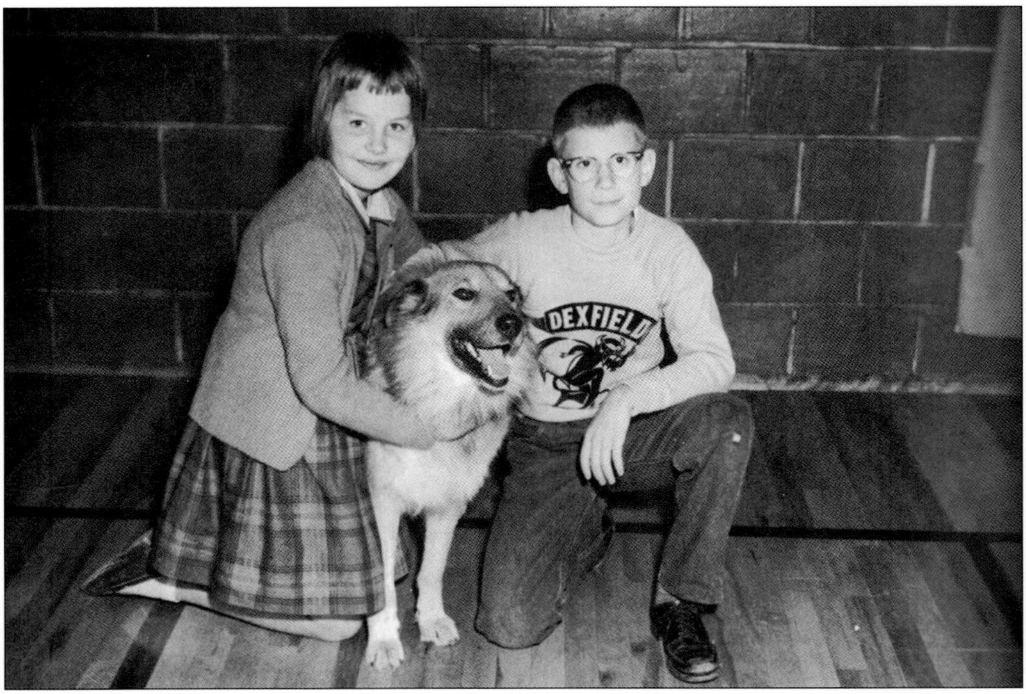

Hobo the Dog. "Always faithful" describes Hobo, a beloved dog who lived across from the Redfield school in the 1960s. Hobo never missed a day of school, led the football team onto the field, and made sure all the students arrived safely inside the building each morning. Hobo is shown in the 1964 Dexfield *Trident* yearbook with Teresa Piatt and Rick Cummins, who were in fourth or fifth grade. (Courtesy of Redfield Museum.)

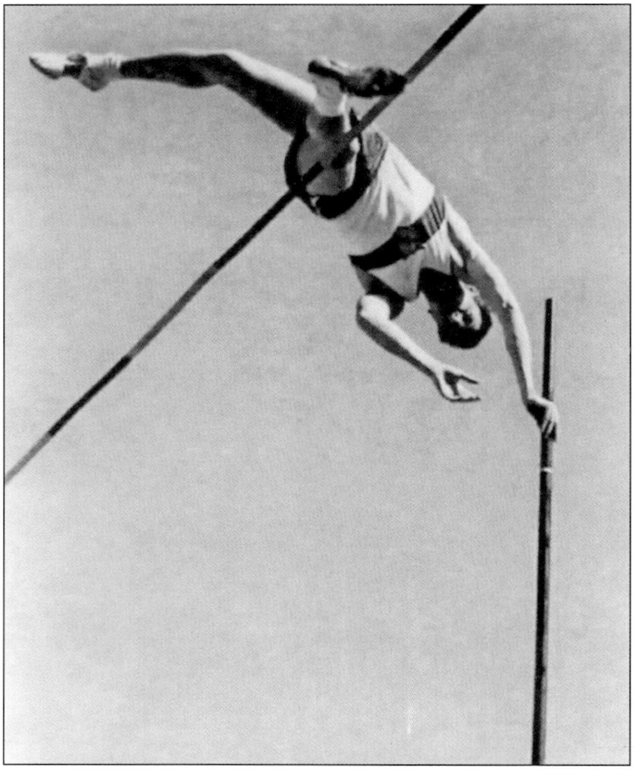

Rex Harvey, Decathlete and Engineer. Rex Harvey of Redfield began participating in track and field at the age of 12. He is shown pole-vaulting during the spring 1970 track-and-field season at Iowa State University, where he earned his mechanical engineering degree. Harvey, an Air Force veteran, developed 15 patents, mostly for commercial aircraft and supercomputers. Harvey was also a 1976 Olympic trials finalist and has completed 161 decathlons. (Courtesy of Iowa State University.)

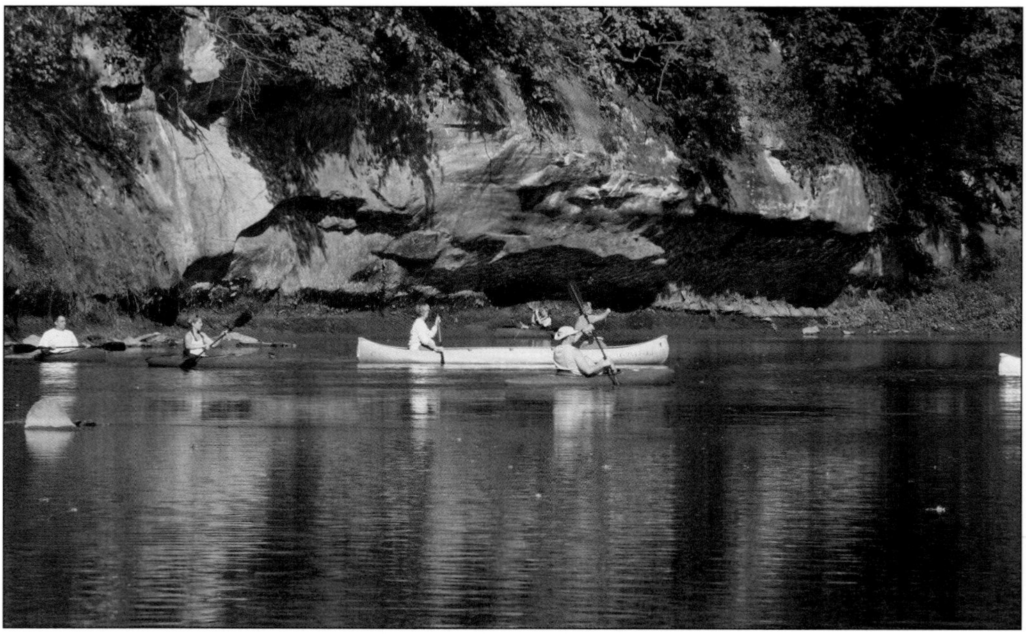

Hanging Rock. It is said that Native Americans used to place their dead in the trees at Hanging Rock, a massive outcropping of sandstone and limestone along the Raccoon River south of Redfield. A local landmark for centuries, the area just downstream of Hanging Rock was forded by wagon trains heading west in the mid-1800s. Today, canoers and kayakers enjoy seeing Hanging Rock on their river journeys. (Courtesy of Dallas County Conservation.)

Three

Dexter
The Original One-Horse Town

Drive into Dexter, and it seems like a typical Iowa small town, with a Casey's convenience store, café, library, and other assorted shops. Drive to the north edge of Dexter and head out into the country, however, and a set of historical markers reveal this is no ordinary place.

Located in southwest Dallas County near the borders of three other counties (Guthrie, Adair, and Madison), Dexter is famous for the 1933 capture of some members of the Barrow Gang (although Bonnie and Clyde escaped) and Pres. Harry Truman's visit to the 1948 National Plowing Match. Much of this history is on display at the Dexter Museum and is also well documented on stone markers north of town, near the location of the former Dexfield Park, one of Iowa's first amusement parks.

The stories do not end there, though. Dexter was founded in 1868 and quickly found itself growing into a thriving town filled with businesses ranging from washing machine manufacturers to hog oilers and every industry in between. In fact, Dexter once had an industrial base rivaling Perry, a much larger community in northern Dallas County. Dexter was also the home of Dexter Normal College, which flourished until 1896, when it was consolidated with the public school system. By 1900, Dexter reached its peak population of 795, according to the US Census Bureau, although the population was closer to 600 by 2010.

Dexter has always enjoyed a prime location near some of the most important routes through the area, from the early-20th-century Great White Way to the modern Interstate 80. For westbound travelers, Dexter was a stopping point on a main route to Council Bluffs and points west. For eastbound travelers, Dexter became the doorway to Dallas County. Drew's Chocolates, which has thrived in Dexter since the 1920s, has developed a loyal customer base in part by serving travelers passing through the area.

The town of Dexter's namesake was a famous racehorse. Dexter, dubbed "the king of the turf," was a celebrated trotter in the 1865–1870 era. Dexter is proud to be known as the original one-horse town.

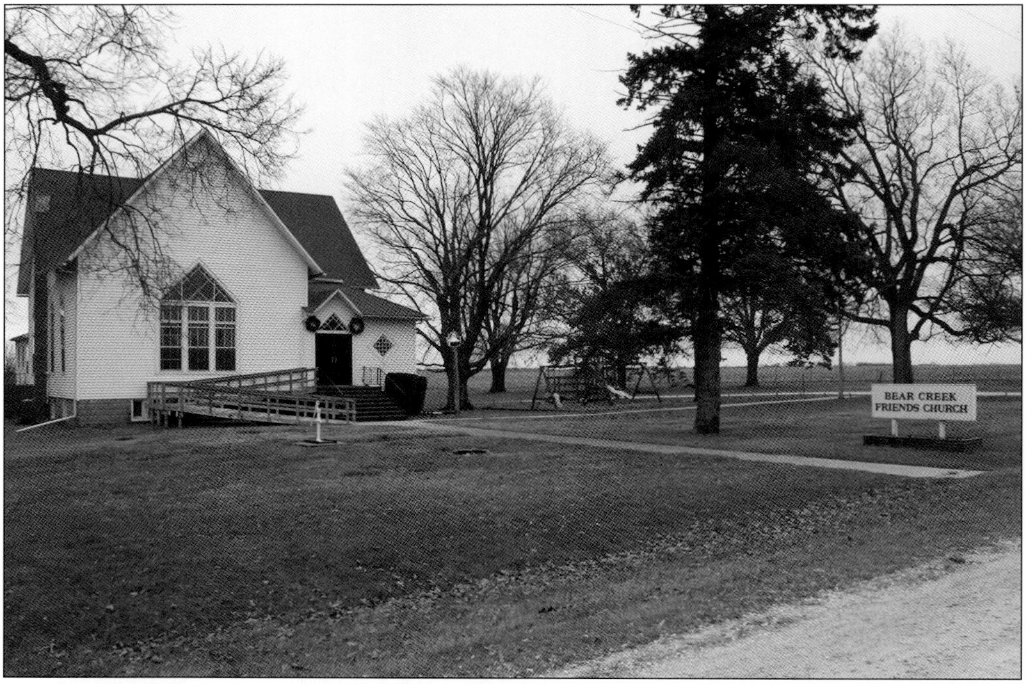

QUAKER DIVIDE AND FUGITIVE SLAVES. Fugitive slaves in 1850s Iowa sometimes traveled the Underground Railroad to the "Quaker Divide" northeast of Dexter. Many local members of the Society of Friends (Quakers) supported antislavery efforts. Their Bear Creek Church, which still serves the community, is shown here. Some residents, like Harmon Cook, were conductors on the Underground Railroad. His story is recorded in the 1914 *History of the Quaker Divide* published by the Dexter Sentinel. (Author's collection.)

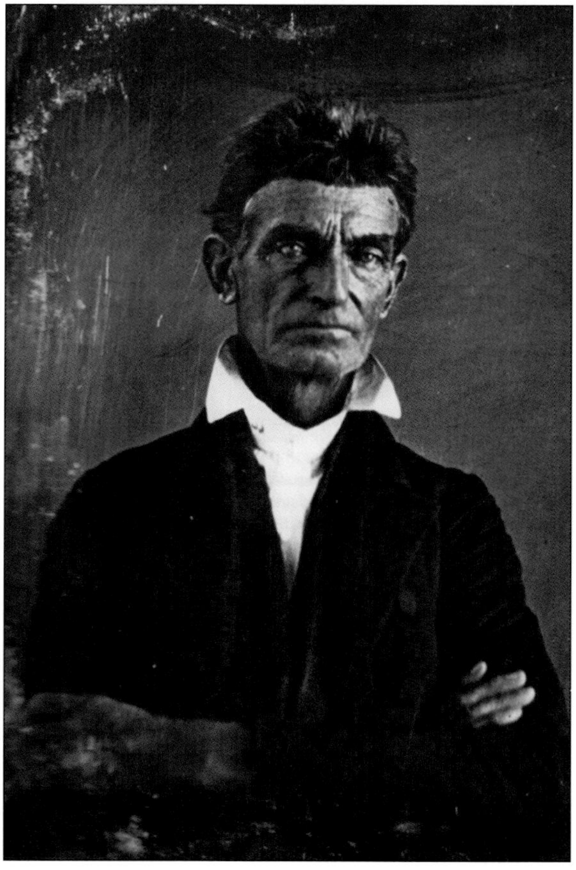

JOHN BROWN IN DALLAS COUNTY. One line of the Underground Railroad crossed the Raccoon River in southern Dallas County. When abolitionist John Brown was in the Dexter-Redfield area before his 1859 raid at Harper's Ferry, Virginia, he admonished Harmon Cook, an Underground Railroad conductor who almost got caught going to Des Moines. "Young man, never do so rash a thing as to talk and laugh out loud on the way." (Author's collection.)

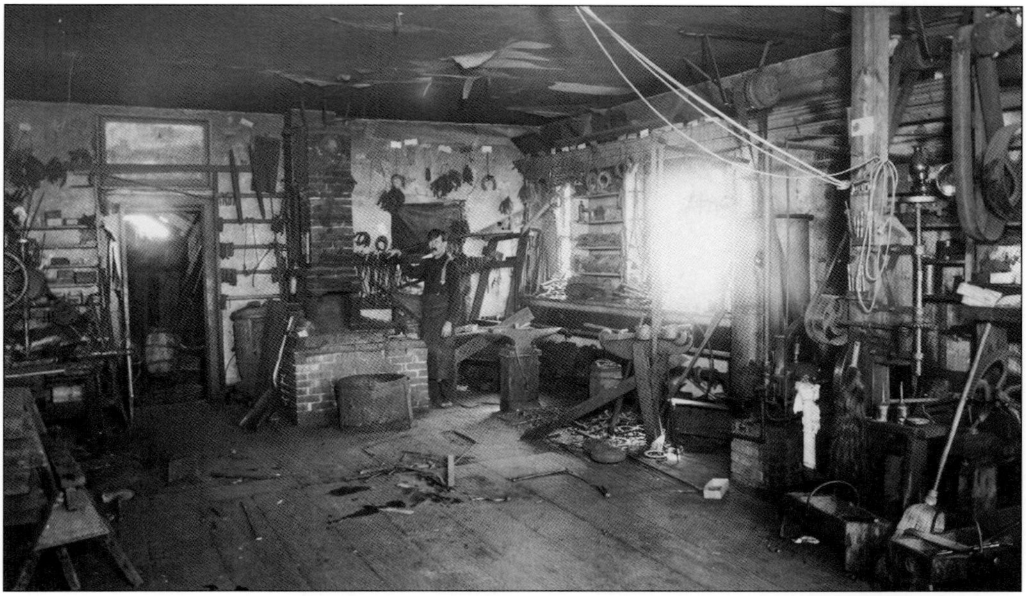

Blacksmiths Forged the Essentials of Life. Blacksmiths were skilled craftsmen who provided an essential service for the pioneers of Dallas County. Shops like the Welch blacksmith shop in Dexter made tools from hammers to farm equipment and also repaired equipment. Blacksmiths' skills were also essential to transportation, providing horseshoes and metal components for wagons, carriages, and sleighs. Blacksmiths sometimes made toys for local children, as well. (Courtesy of Dexter Museum.)

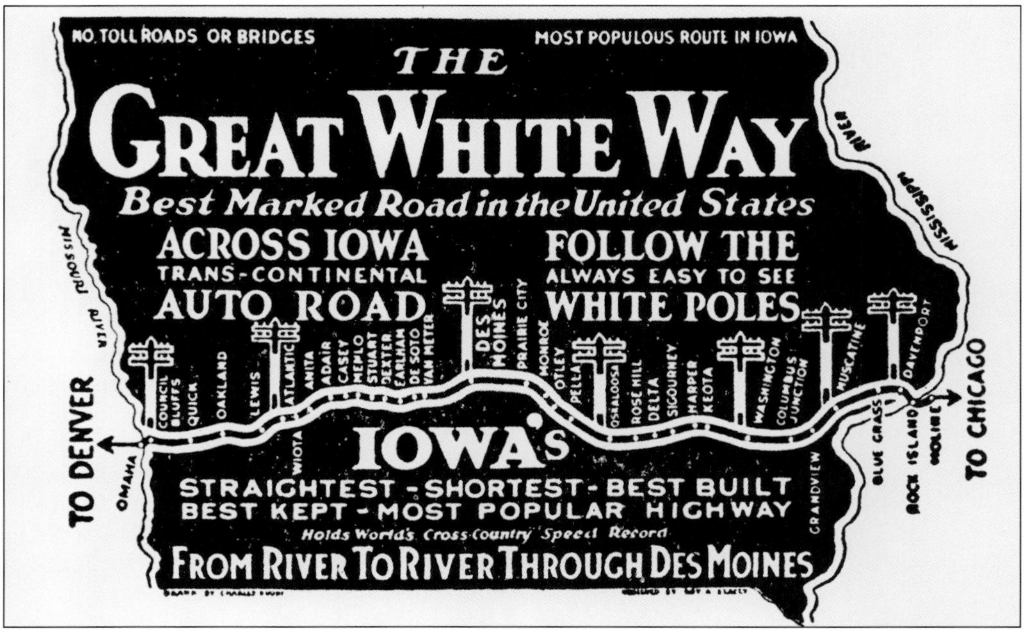

Great White Way. The automobile age spurred the development of the Great White Way, also called the White Pole Road, between Des Moines and Atlantic. Poles were painted with a six-foot band of white to mark the route, which passed through Dexter, De Soto, and Van Meter in Dallas County. The route extended to Council Bluffs by 1910 and east to Davenport by 1912. (Courtesy of Liz Gilman.)

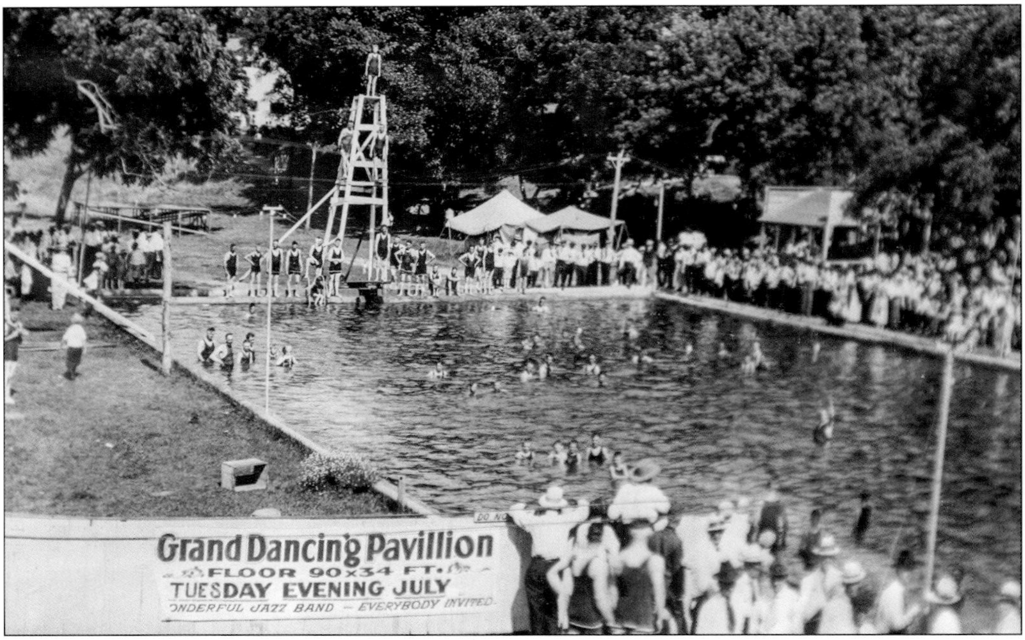

HEALING WATER AT DEXFIELD PARK. Opened in 1915, Dexfield Park became one of Iowa's largest amusement parks. It was located a few miles north of Dexter and opened every summer for a number of years. Dexfield Park's large cement swimming pool was fed by nearby Marshall Springs. The water was said to have healing qualities for arthritis sufferers. A long line of drinking fountains south of the pool allowed people to consume this water. (Courtesy of Dexter Museum.)

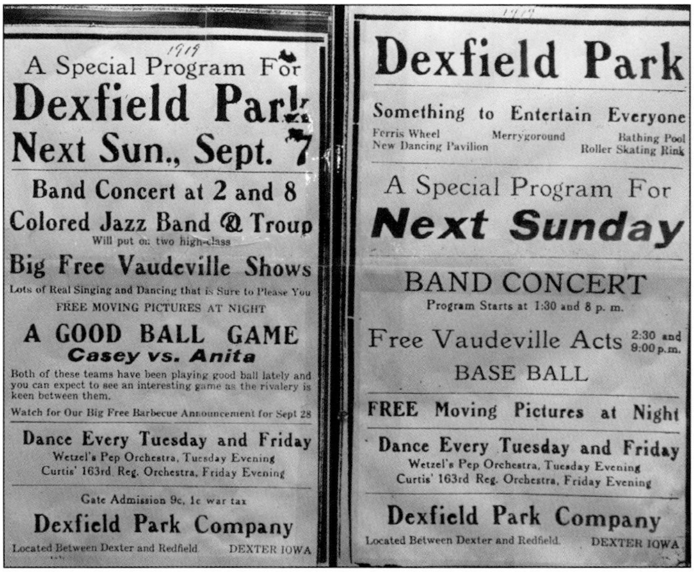

FUN AND GAMES AT DEXFIELD PARK. More than 4,000 people flocked to Dexfield Park on Sunday summer afternoons to enjoy baseball games, dancing, vaudeville shows, movies, roller-skating, picnics, and more, as shown in this 1919 advertisement. A victim of the Great Depression, the park closed permanently after the summer of 1932. In July 1933, the Barrow Gang (including Bonnie and Clyde) was involved in a shoot-out at Dexfield Park. (Courtesy of Dexter Museum.)

COME TO THE CHAUTAUQUA. Theodore Roosevelt called Chautauqua "the most American thing in America." From July 14 to 21, 1916, people came to Dexter for Chautauqua lectures from Prof. C.W. Wassam, "whose enthusiasm is as contagious as the measles," according to advertisements; performances by Maud Schearer and her Shakespearian Players and the Metropolitan Singers; and other entertainment and education. The Chautauqua circuit, which thrived from the late 1800s through the 1920s, brought culture to small-town America. (Courtesy of Dexter Museum.)

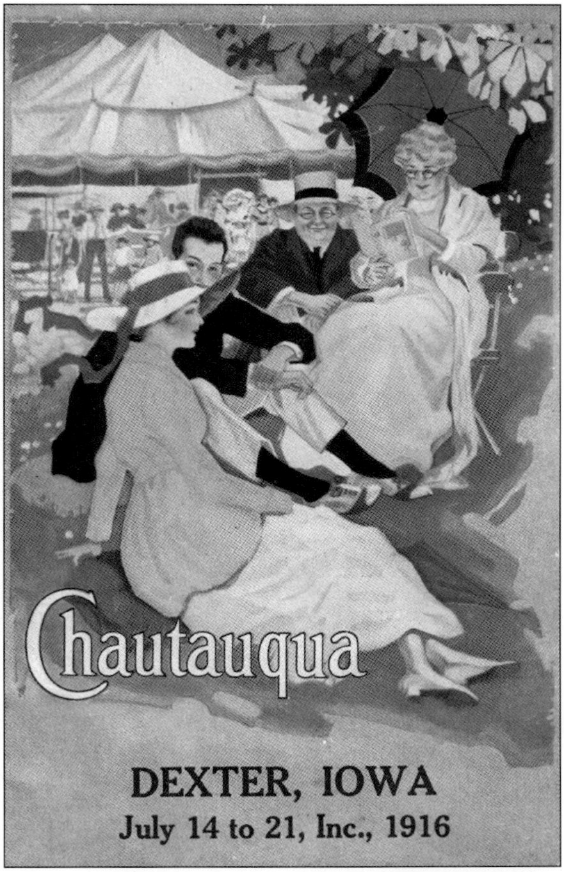

ROUNDHOUSE. The Dexter Community House, or "Roundhouse," was built in 1916. Citizens pledged $5 shares to build the 100-by-68-foot elliptical building, which includes a box office and stage. The $10,000 Roundhouse was designed by Maj. Matthew Leander King, grandfather of Hollywood actor Nick Nolte. According to local lore, cars were driven up ramps onto the roof to prove the strength of the seemingly unsupported dome. The building is still used today. (Author's collection.)

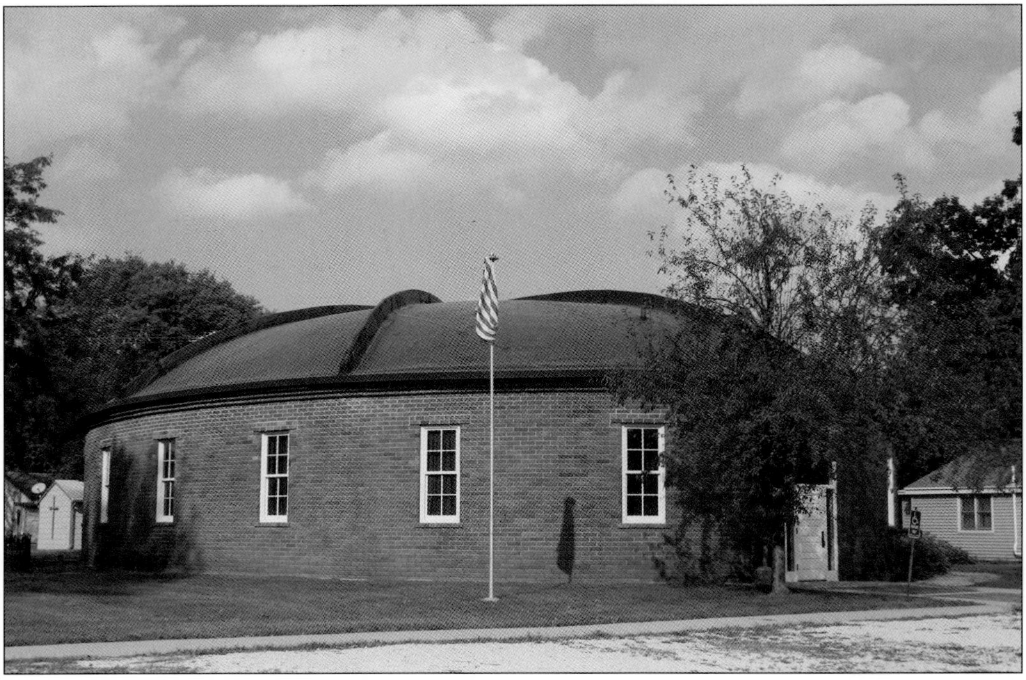

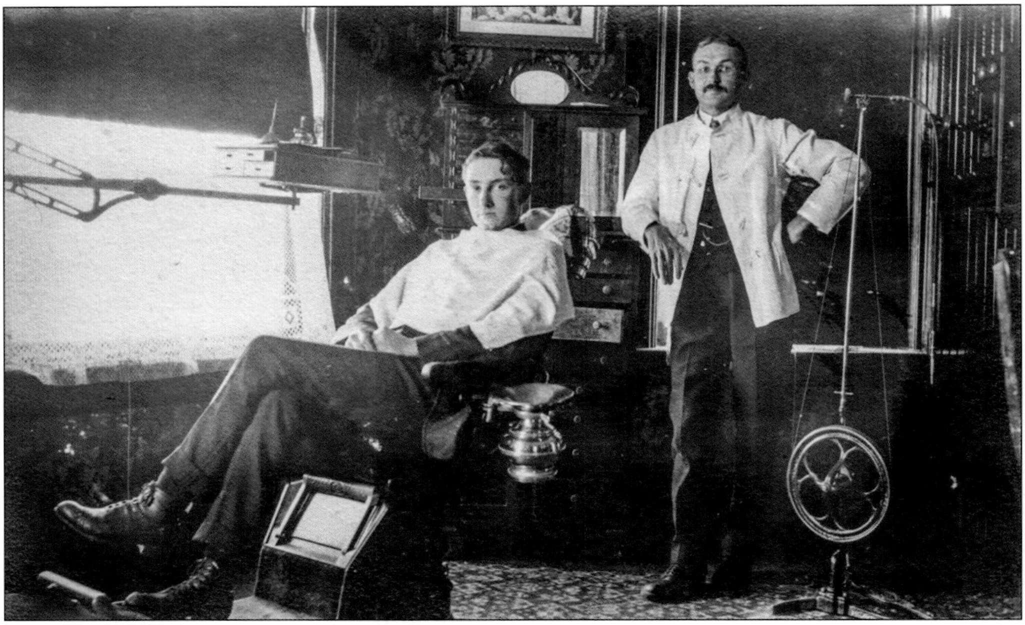

Dexter Dentist. Dr. Wilbur J. Hemphill was an early-20th-century dentist and prominent businessman in Dexter. Dr. Hemphill has a foot-pedal-powered drill in his office. (Courtesy of Dexter Museum.)

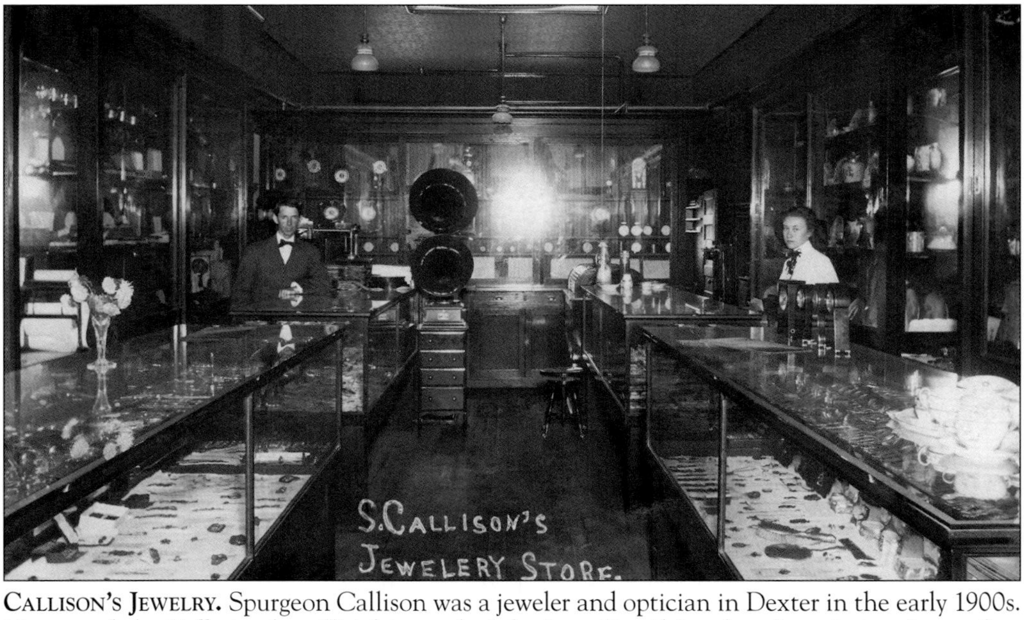

Callison's Jewelry. Spurgeon Callison was a jeweler and optician in Dexter in the early 1900s. He started the *Bulletin*, the official journal of the Iowa Retail Jewelers Association. It was first published in Dexter, with Callison as the editor. In 1908, the National Association of Retail Jewelers adopted the *Bulletin* as its official paper at its convention in Cincinnati, Ohio. (Courtesy of Dexter Museum.)

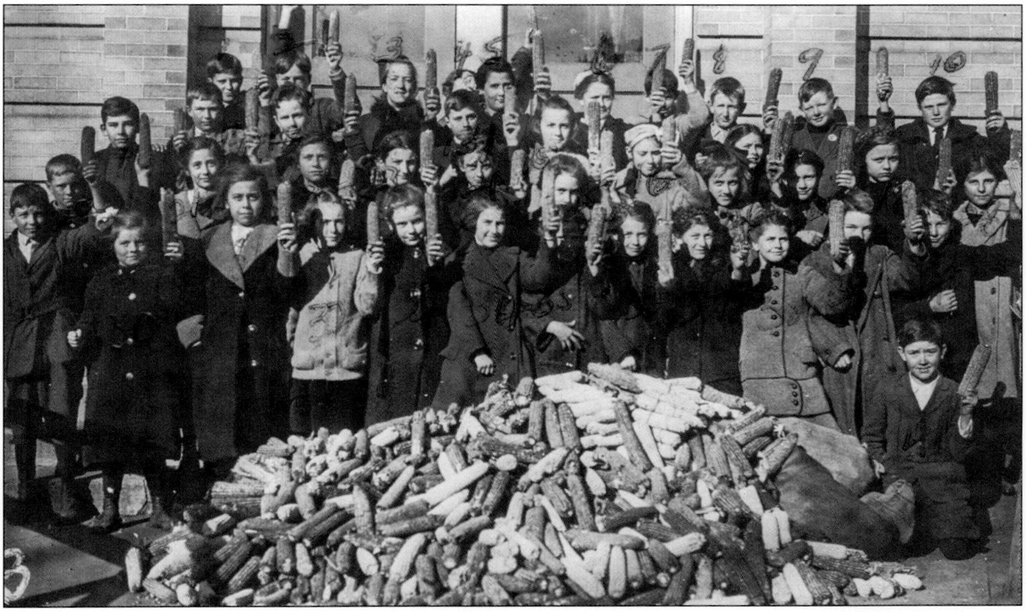

Corn for Belgium. Dexter children brought corn to school in 1915 to send to Belgium during World War I. Famine threatened seven million people in beleaguered Belgium, which depended on imports for most of the nation's food. Fellow Iowan and future US president Herbert Hoover helped feed millions of people through the Commission for the Relief of Belgium, earning him praise as "the Great Humanitarian." (Courtesy of Dexter Museum.)

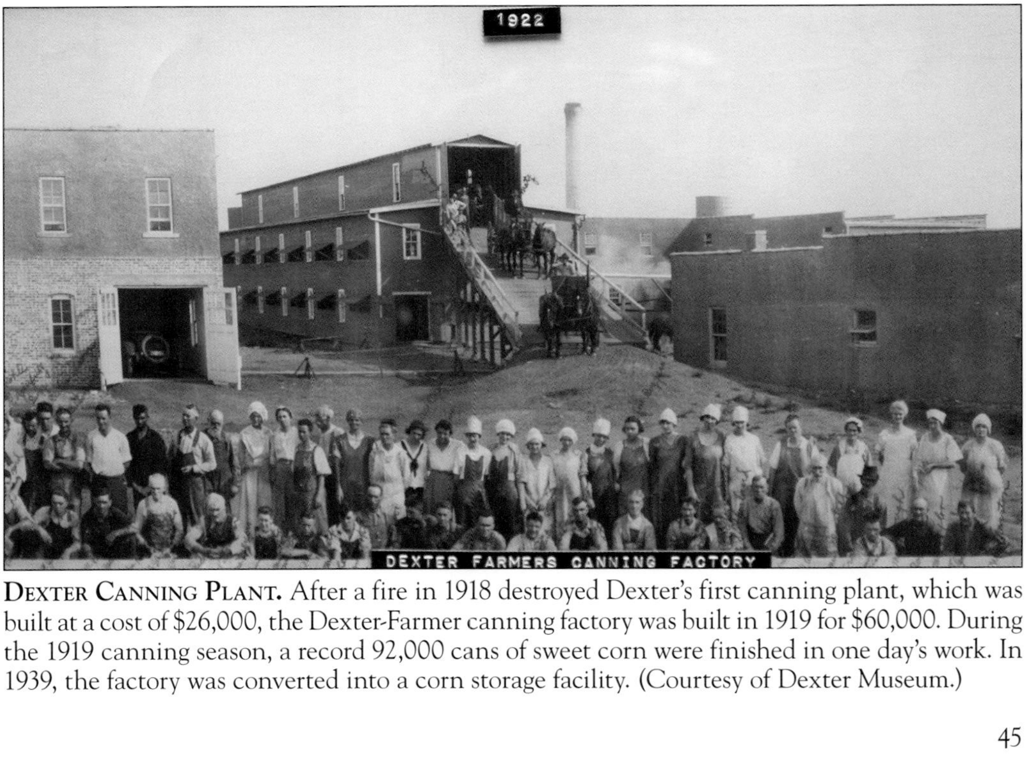

Dexter Canning Plant. After a fire in 1918 destroyed Dexter's first canning plant, which was built at a cost of $26,000, the Dexter-Farmer canning factory was built in 1919 for $60,000. During the 1919 canning season, a record 92,000 cans of sweet corn were finished in one day's work. In 1939, the factory was converted into a corn storage facility. (Courtesy of Dexter Museum.)

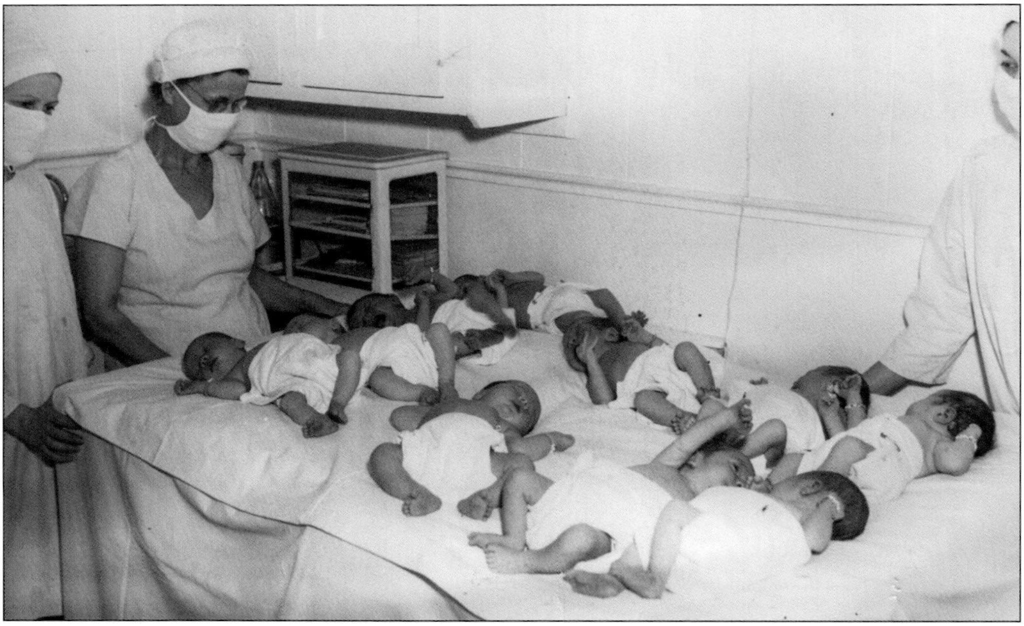

POSTWAR BABY BOOM. Here is what Baby Boomers looked like at the hospital in Dexter on June 30, 1949. Mary Pickett (second from right), a registered nurse, and her colleagues are shown here caring for 10 of Dexter's newest residents. (Courtesy of Dexter Museum.)

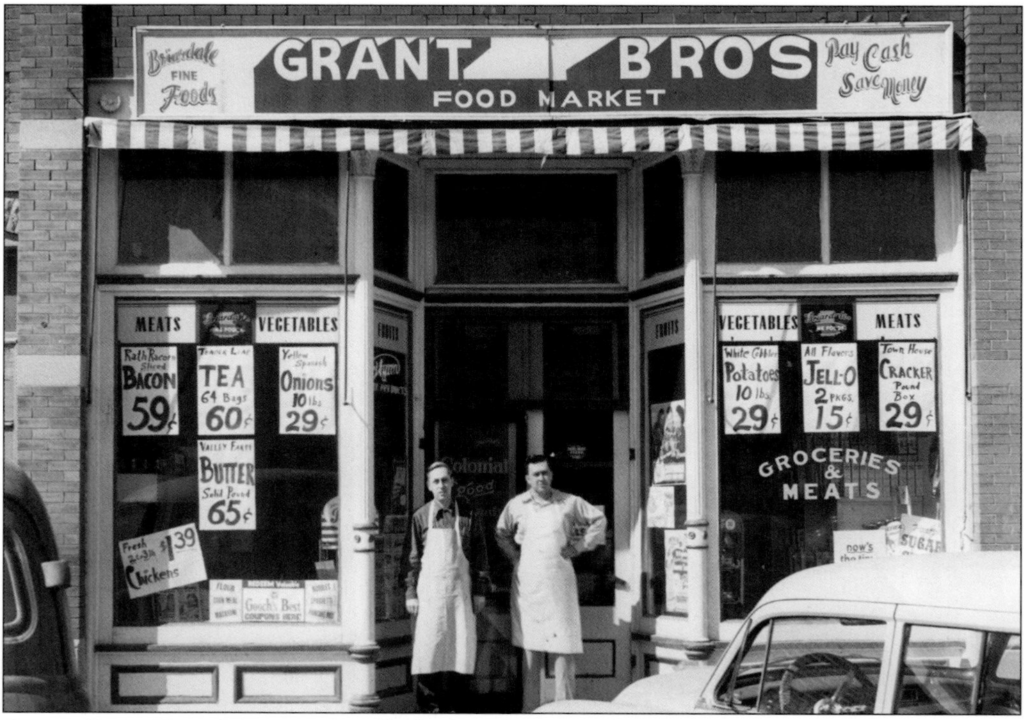

GRANT BROS. FOOD MARKET. Orville (left) and Raymond Grant take a break from their work at Grant Bros. Food Market in Dexter. The 1954 grocery prices include 10 pounds of potatoes for 29¢, bacon for 59¢, one pound of butter for 65¢, fresh two-to-three-pound chickens for \$1.39, and two packages of Jell-O for 15¢. (Courtesy of Dexter Museum.)

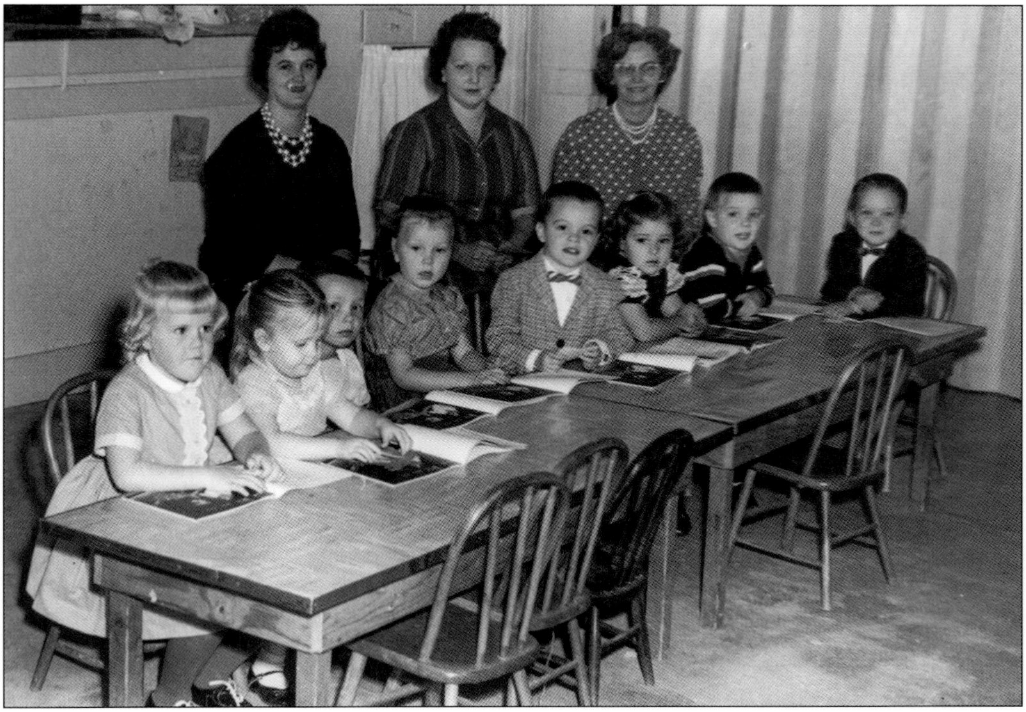

Methodist Sunday School. The nursery Sunday school at the Dexter Methodist Church in 1962 includes teachers (from left to right) Eleanor Stiles, Kay Stanley, and Martha Webb, the primary department superintendent. The children include (from left to right) Becky Wahlert, Susan Paullin, an unidentified visitor, Jeri Lynn Stanley, Timmy Stiles, Michelle Lenocker, Jim Anctil, and Tony Dickson. (Courtesy of Dexter Museum.)

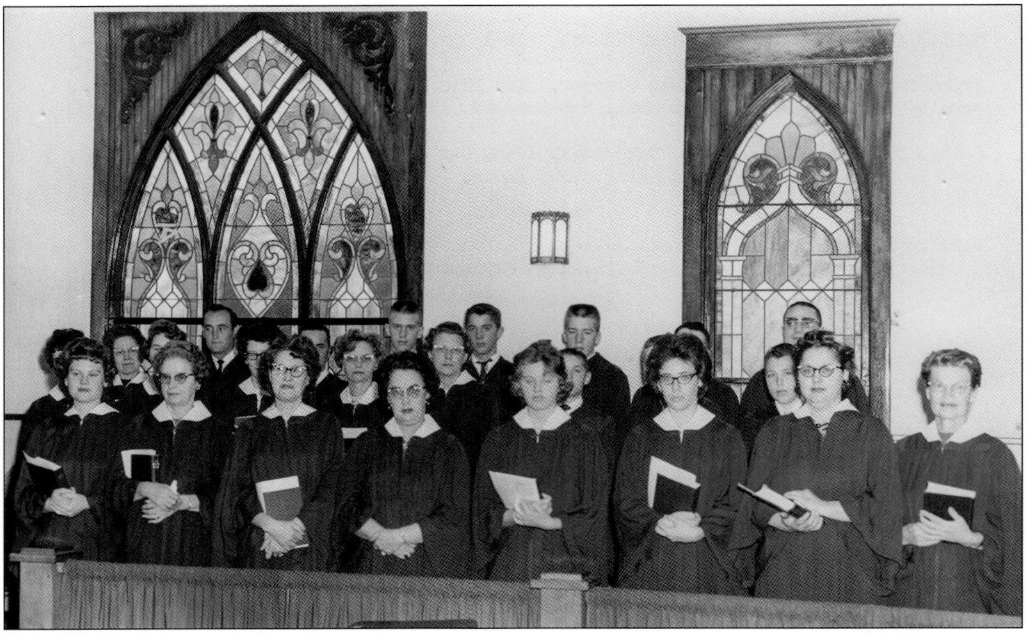

Make a Joyful Noise. Sunday worship services at the Dexter Methodist Church in 1961 included the senior choir. (Courtesy of Dexter Museum.)

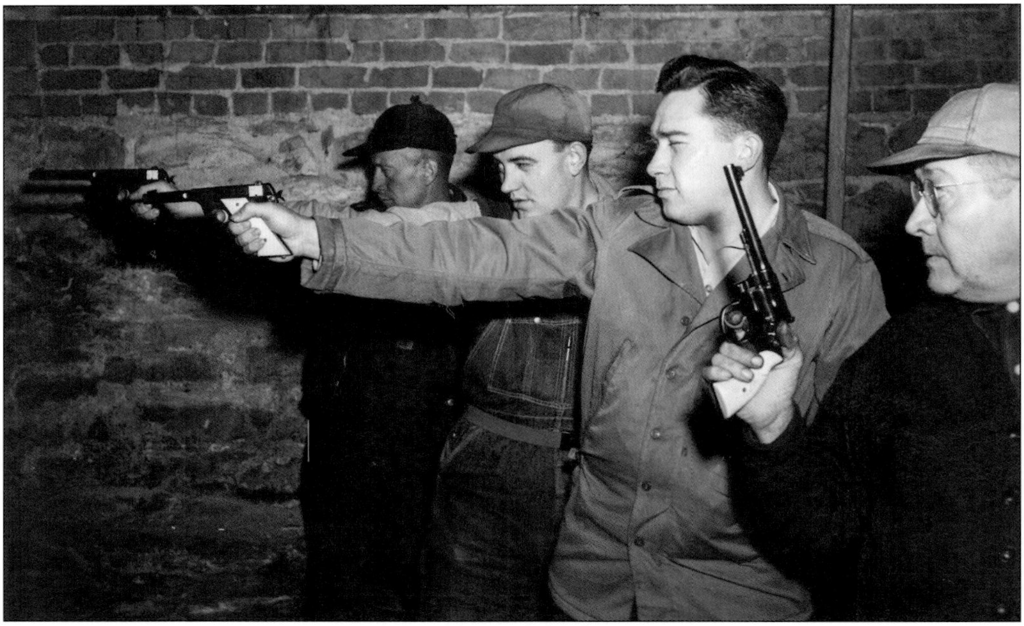

DEXTER GUN CLUB. Members of the Dexter Gun Club practiced shooting in the basement of a building that now houses the Dexter Library on Marshall Street. From left to right are John Baldwin, Clyde Campbell Jr., Raymond Grant, and town marshal John Love, who served from 1933 to 1965 and played an active role in the capture of Barrow Gang members at the 1933 Dexfield Park shoot-out. (Courtesy of Dexter Museum.)

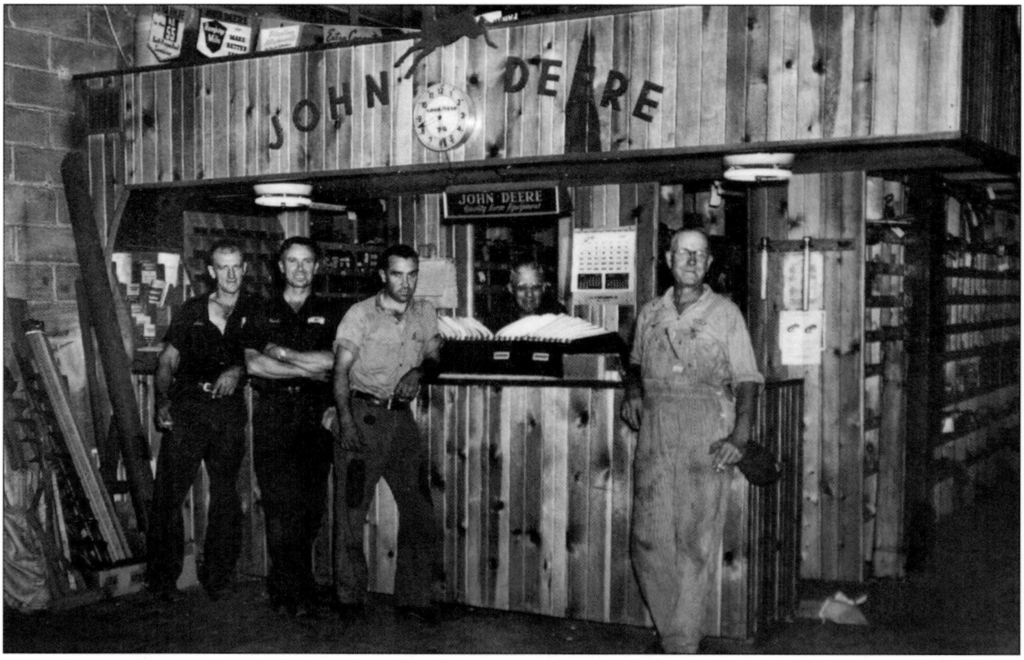

JOHN DEERE DEALERSHIP. Agriculture has been a vital part of the Dexter economy for generations. Implement stores like this John Deere dealership in Dexter in the 1950s served farmers throughout the area. Shown are, from left to right, Clell Sellers, Earl Gleason, Dorr Davis, Harry Smith, and Floyd Craven. (Courtesy of Dexter Museum.)

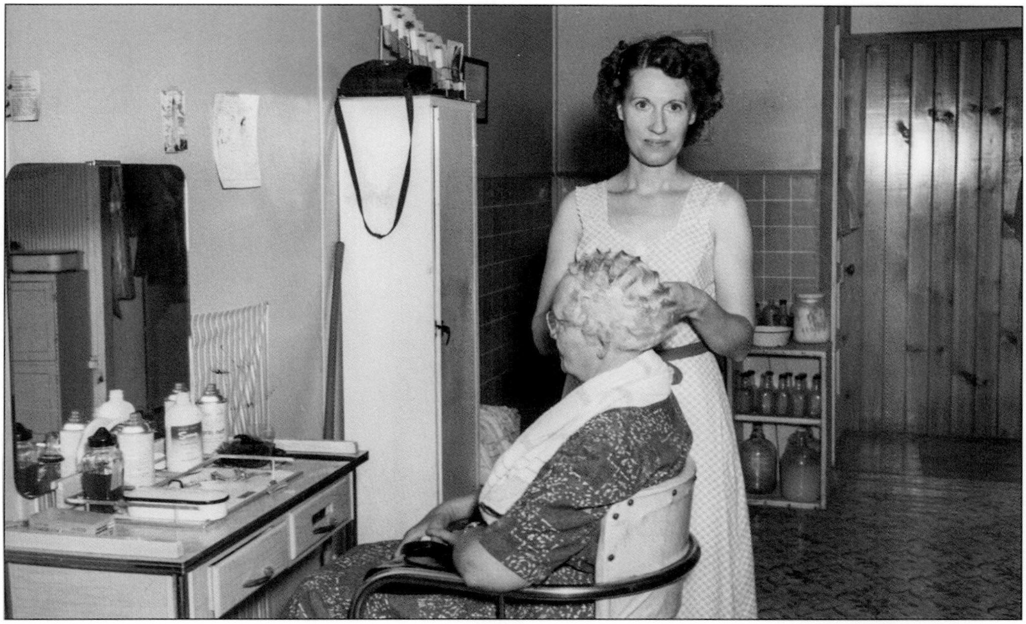

Maxine Hadley's Beauty Shop. Maxine Schell Hadley ran a beauty shop in Dexter after serving with the Waves (Women Accepted for Volunteer Emergency Service) in World War II. In July 1933, Hadley unknowingly walked into the Barrow Gang's campsite with her fellow Girl Scouts during an early-morning hike at Dexfield Park. Hadley had no idea who the surprised campers were who returned the girls' "good morning" greetings. (Courtesy of Dexter Museum.)

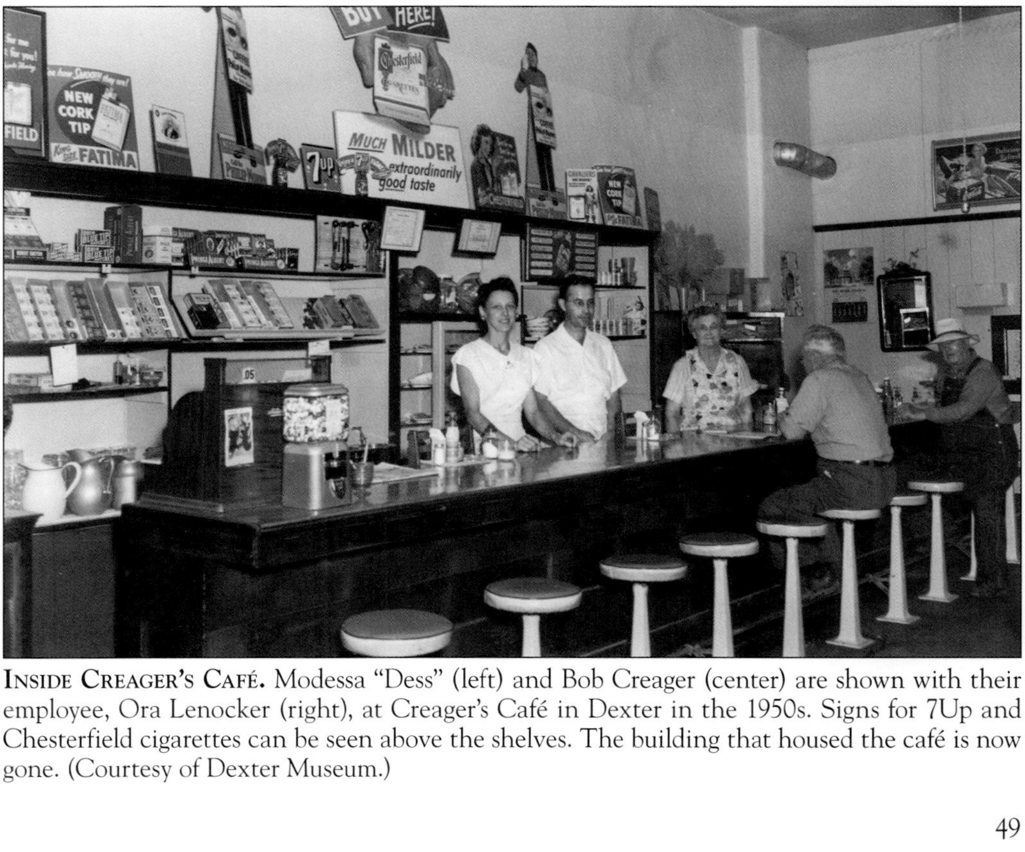

Inside Creager's Café. Modessa "Dess" (left) and Bob Creager (center) are shown with their employee, Ora Lenocker (right), at Creager's Café in Dexter in the 1950s. Signs for 7Up and Chesterfield cigarettes can be seen above the shelves. The building that housed the café is now gone. (Courtesy of Dexter Museum.)

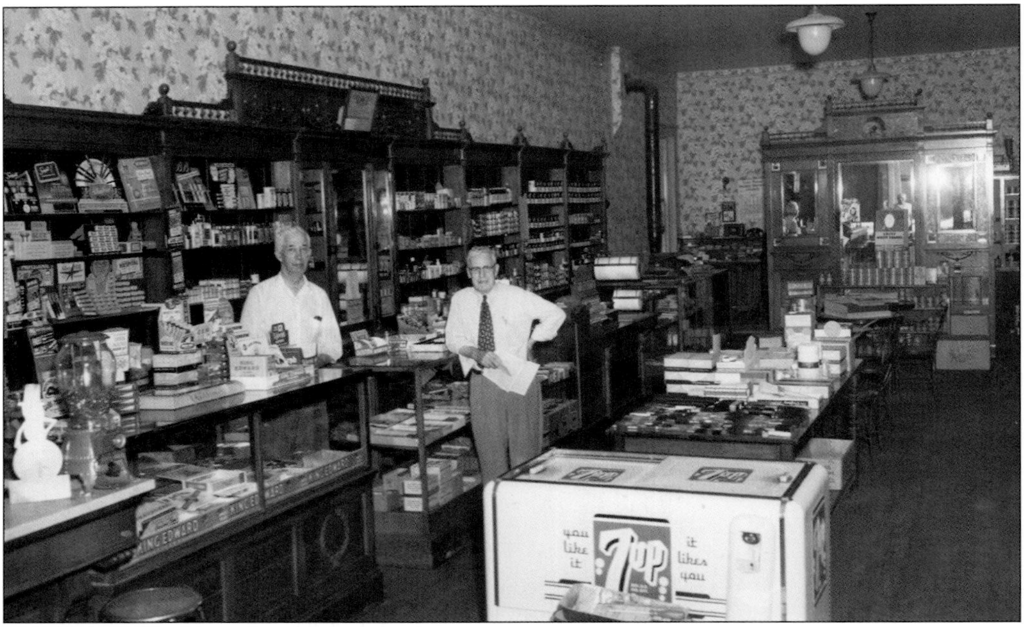

Dexter Drugstore. Drugstores were common in small towns across Iowa well into the 1950s and 1960s. This photograph shows Bill Stanley in front of the counter in his Dexter drugstore along with Beach Landers behind the counter, where razor kits, King Edward cigars, and other items are displayed for sale. (Courtesy of Dexter Museum.)

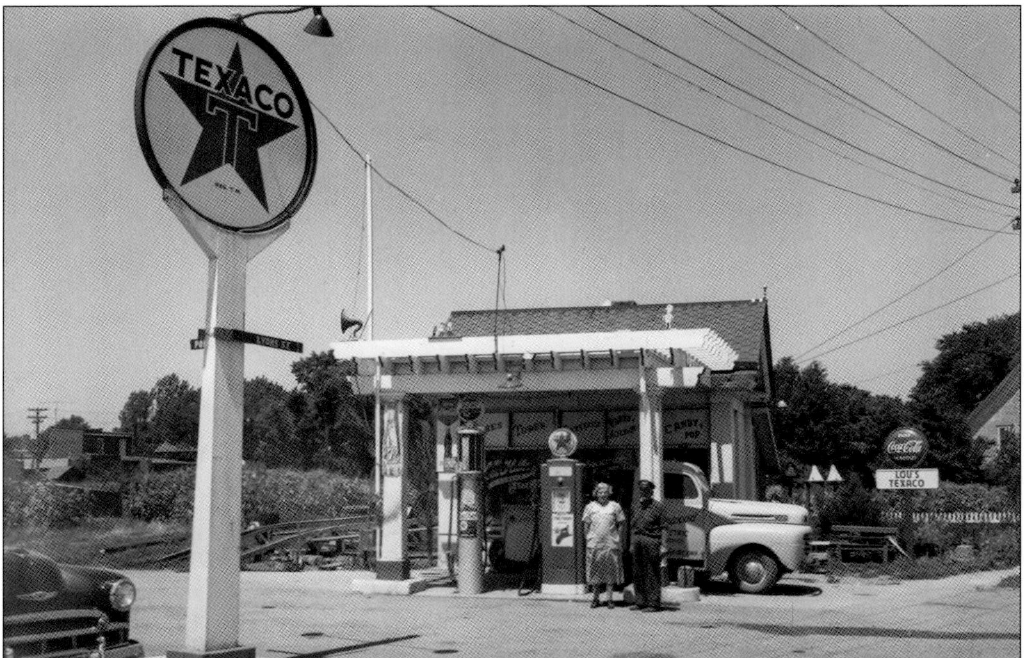

Texaco Station. With its prime location near the highly traveled White Pole Road and later Interstate 80, Dexter could support several filling stations. Shown here are Cora and Lou Hill at their service station, about a block southeast of Main Street. There were at least seven gas stations in Dexter at the time. (Courtesy of Dexter Museum.)

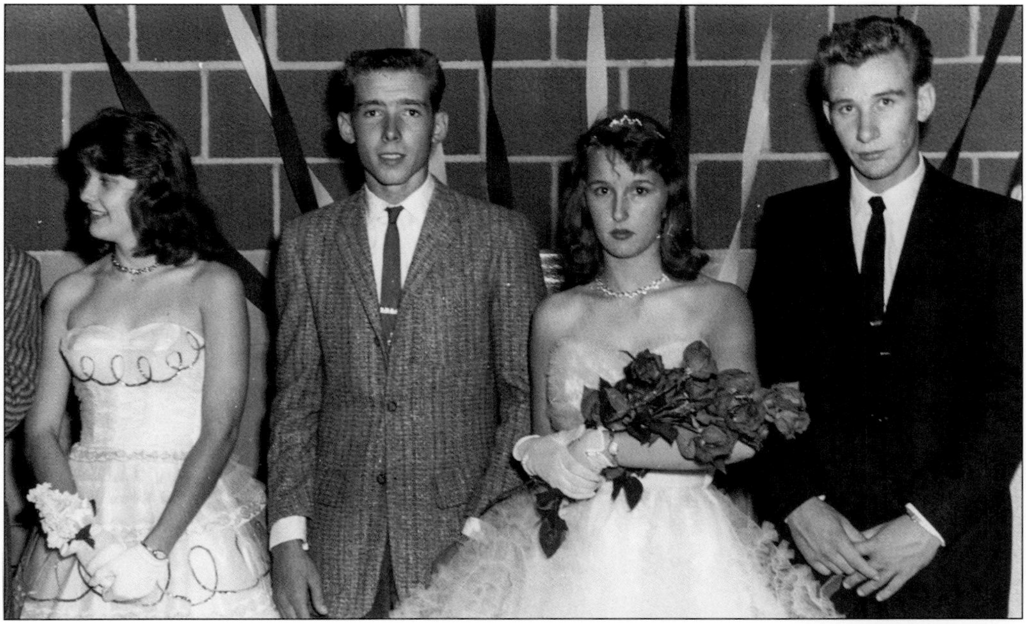

Homecoming, 1959. From left to right are Margaret Pierce Morrison, attendant; Jerry Carrico, football team captain; Barbara McMenamin Marks, homecoming queen; and Dennis Simpson, football team captain. Not shown is Sandy Christensen Smeltzer, who was also an attendant. In 1960, the first class of students graduated from Dexfield High School following the consolidation of Dexter and Redfield. (Courtesy of Dexter Museum.)

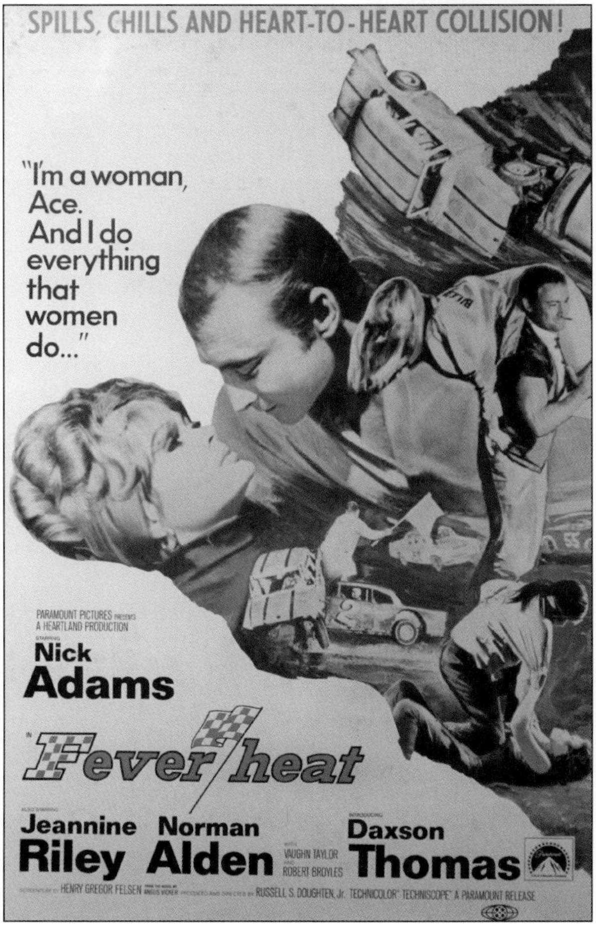

Hollywood in Dexter. Parts of the 1968 movie *Fever Heat* were filmed in Dexter. Forty locals had bit parts or drove race cars, and a large number are in the racetrack crowd scenes. Ace Jones (Nick Adams), an ex–stock car racer, pulls into a small-town Iowa garage and meets Sandy (Jeannine Riley). When Ace shows Sandy he can help collect debts owed by racers, the two become business partners and more. (Courtesy of Dexter Museum.)

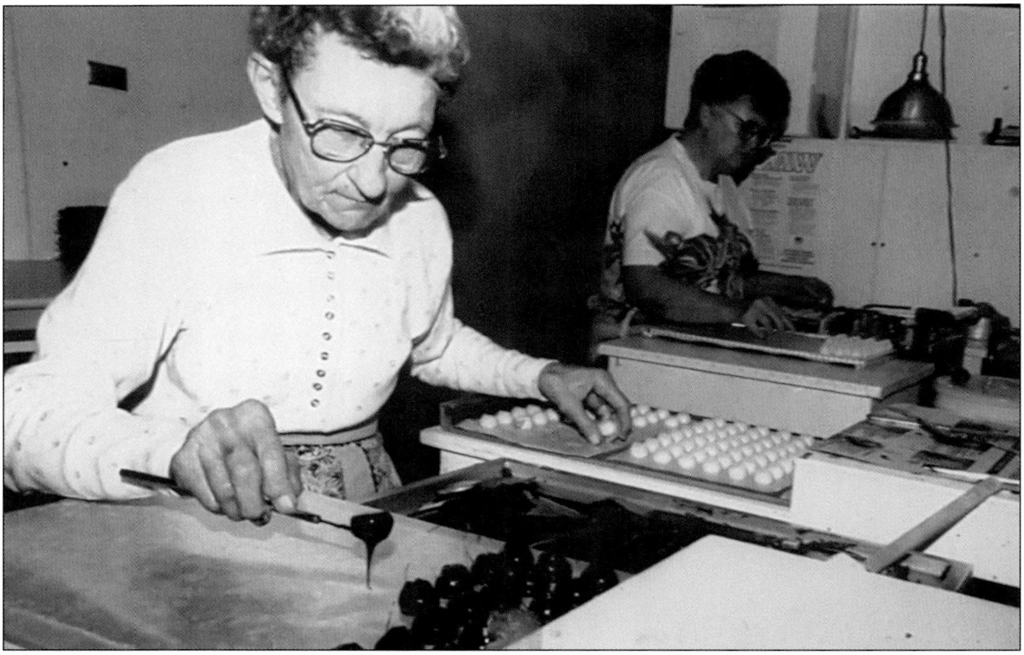

Drew's Chocolates. Helen Drew opened a candy business in Dexter in 1927 after obtaining recipes from relatives in New Hampshire. Longtime employees included Vivian Clausen (right) and Betty Lenocker, who started working at the candy shop at age 18 and continued working there part-time after retiring at age 65. Drew's still uses original recipes and equipment. The shop's employees also fork-dip the delicious candies. (Courtesy of Drew's Chocolates.)

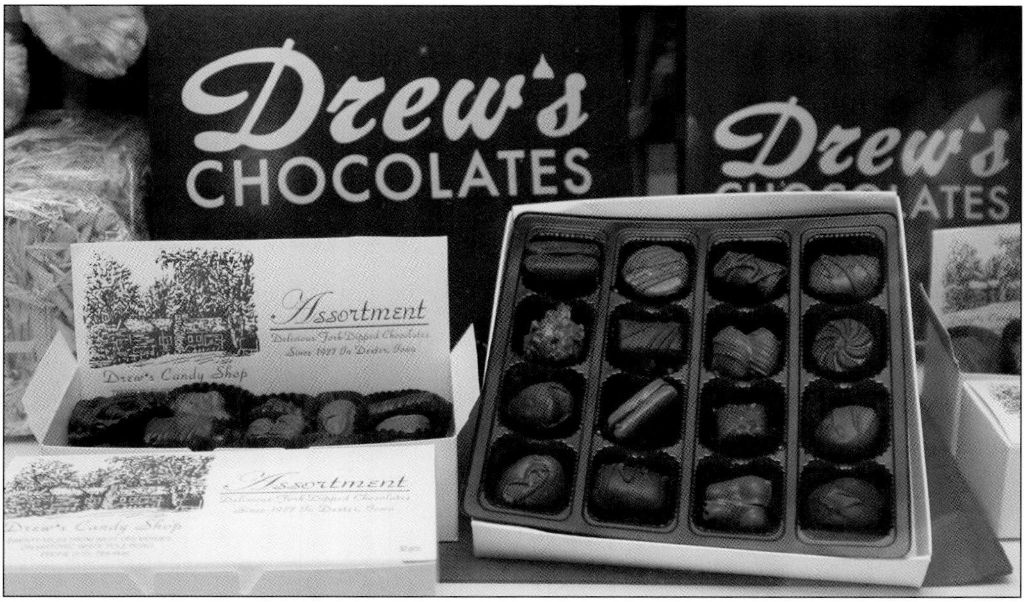

A Sweet Taste of Dexter. Drew's Chocolates have been savored by generations of customers across the country. One of the shop's top-selling items is the deluxe assortment, which includes chocolate-dipped creams and more. For some families, no Christmas celebration or Valentine's Day is complete without Drew's Chocolates. Some customers stop by the shop, while others rely on mail order to receive their favorite Drew's Chocolates. (Author's collection.)

Four

Dallas Center
Nurtured by Banking and Agriculture

Described as "quietly progressive" by the City of Dallas Center, this quiet community in the heart of Dallas County boasts a rich heritage in agriculture and is home to companies that lead the world in animal and plant genetics, from Stine Seed to Hy-Line International. Dallas Center's history will forever be linked to the Brenton family, who invested in farmland and grew a strong banking enterprise in the area for generations.

Founded in 1869, Dallas Center grew from 133 people in 1870 to more than 1,600 by 2010, according to US Census data. When Dr. James Brenton and his family moved to Dallas County from Indiana in 1853, Dallas Center was not even a spot on the map.

Dallas County had only been established six years earlier, in 1847, and the region was almost the end of the pioneer frontier. On October 13, 1853, the Brenton family arrived in Adel Township and settled halfway between Adel and what would become Dallas Center. They moved onto an 80-acre farm purchased from the US government for $1.25 an acre and built a log cabin. A true pioneer, James Brenton became the first country doctor west of Des Moines.

Brenton's descendants would grow the family's roots in the Dallas Center area even deeper, buying more land, expanding their crop and livestock farms, and entering the world of banking, making Brenton a distinguished name in Iowa and the country.

Today, the Brenton family's legacy lives on in the 140-acre, nonprofit Brenton Arboretum, which was founded by Buz Brenton in 1997. The land is part of the original homestead acquired by Dr. James Brenton and his son, William Henry, soon after they arrived in Iowa in 1853 by covered wagon. An ever-expanding collection of more than 2,200 trees and shrubs representing 468 species, hybrids, and cultivars is showcased at the Brenton Arboretum, whose mission is to bring joy to all through the beauty and knowledge of the natural world of trees.

The arboretum is one more way Dallas Center helps people enjoy a small-town quality of life, all within 20 miles of the Greater Des Moines community.

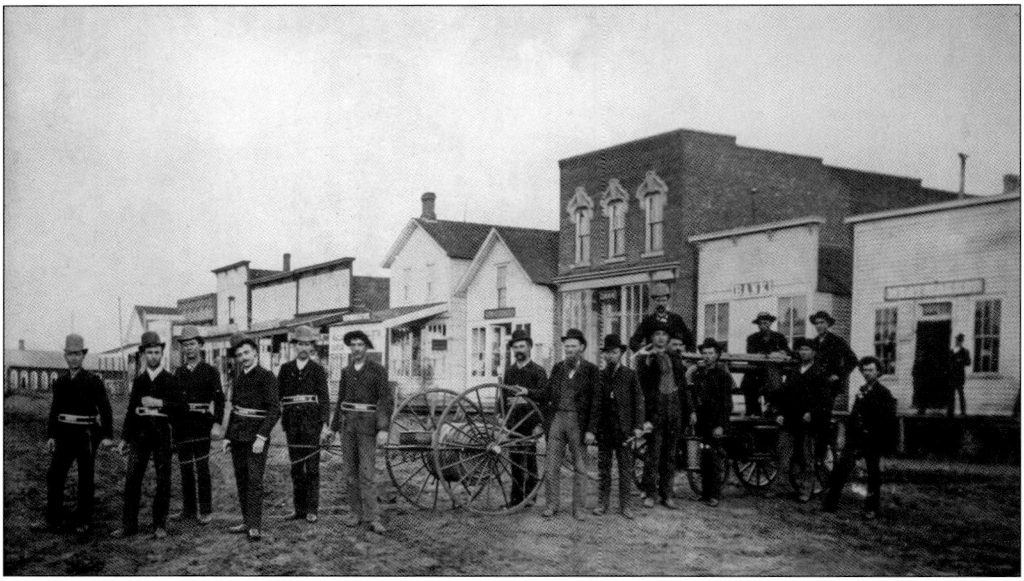

DALLAS CENTER'S FIREFIGHTERS. Dirt streets were common when Dallas Center's first volunteer fire department posed for this c. 1890 photograph. The group includes, from left to right, Michael Dignan, G.H. Loring, Thomas Behan, F.L. Loring, E.S. Everett, Alvin Lane, Harry Roberts, T.K. Nazarene, E.J.M. Stevens, Ed S. Van Duzen, J.A. Richmond, P.A. Becker, Abe L. Hammond, Charles H. Whitteberry, Cal Wise, John Hoff, and James T. Cumming. (Courtesy of Roy R. Estle Memorial Library, Dallas Center.)

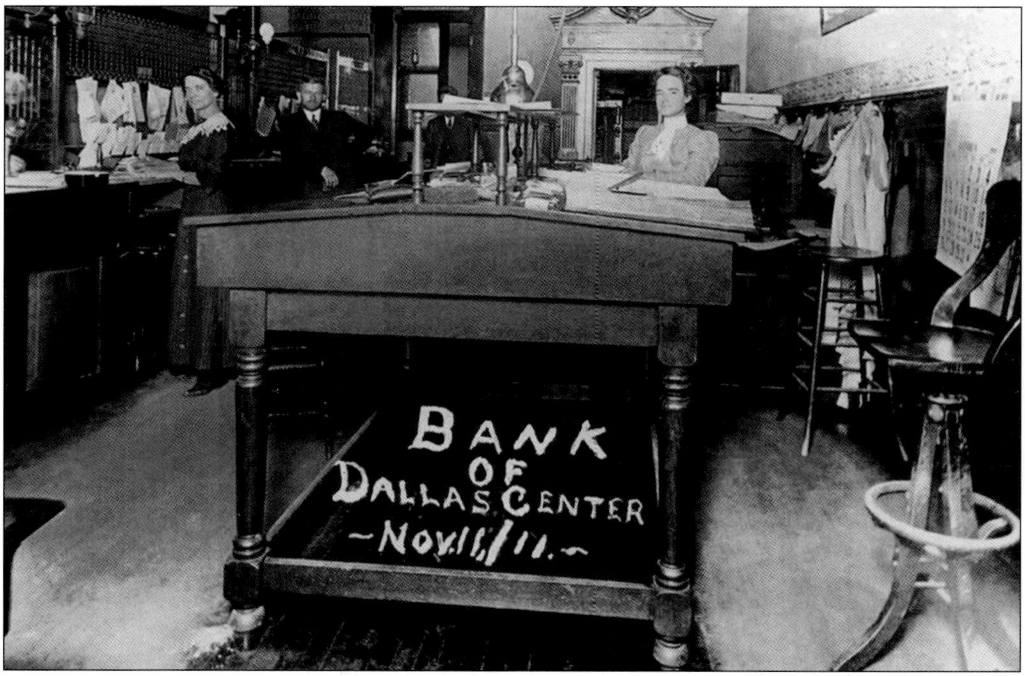

BRENTON BANK. Unlike those in other states, most Iowa banks developed as country banks, and their business was primarily agricultural credit. In the spring of 1882, William Brenton took his first formal steps into the world of banking in Dallas County. Here is a rare glimpse inside the Brenton family's Bank of Dallas Center in 1911. (Courtesy of Brenton family.)

BRENTON HOME. Pioneer farmer and banker William Brenton built this home in Dallas Center around 1879. Brenton's generosity extended to Kate Shelley, a teenager who crossed the Des Moines River over a 700-foot-long bridge one stormy night in July 1881 to warn a passenger train about a washed-out bridge down the tracks. Brenton bought Shelley to Dallas Center to receive the schooling she wanted to become a teacher. (Courtesy of Brenton family.)

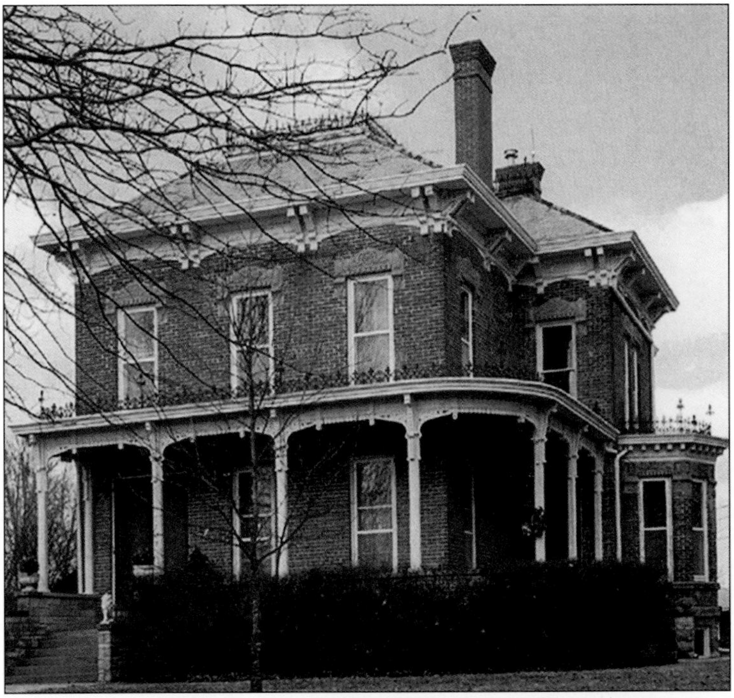

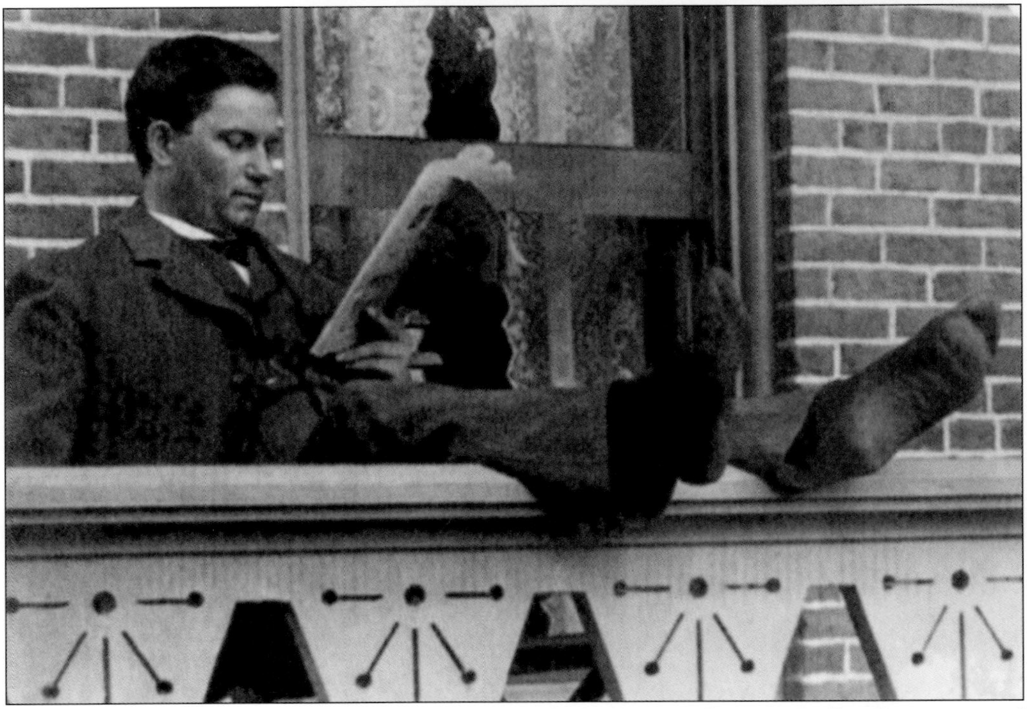

CLYDE TAKES A BREAK. Clyde Brenton relaxes outside the Brenton home in Dallas Center around 1900. Brenton, who was born in 1868 on his parents' farm 3.5 miles southwest of Dallas Center, loved banking and business. While the Bank of Dallas Center's assets in 1907 totaled more than $568,800, the Brentons' farmland was still more profitable. "The Brentons at heart have always been and still are farmers," Clyde noted. (Courtesy of Brenton family.)

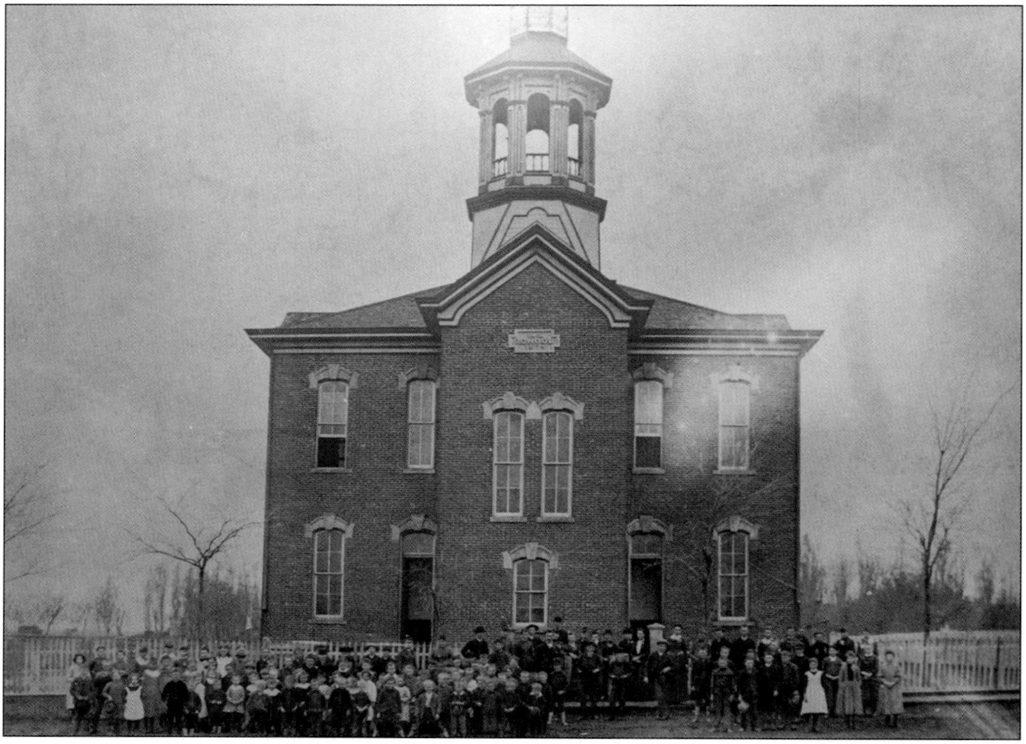

SCHOOL DAYS IN DALLAS CENTER. A commitment to high-quality education runs deep in Dallas County, including Dallas Center. This brick school was built in 1874. Dallas Center now includes two modern school buildings for elementary and middle school students who are enrolled in the Dallas Center–Grimes School District. (Courtesy of Roy R. Estle Memorial Library, Dallas Center.)

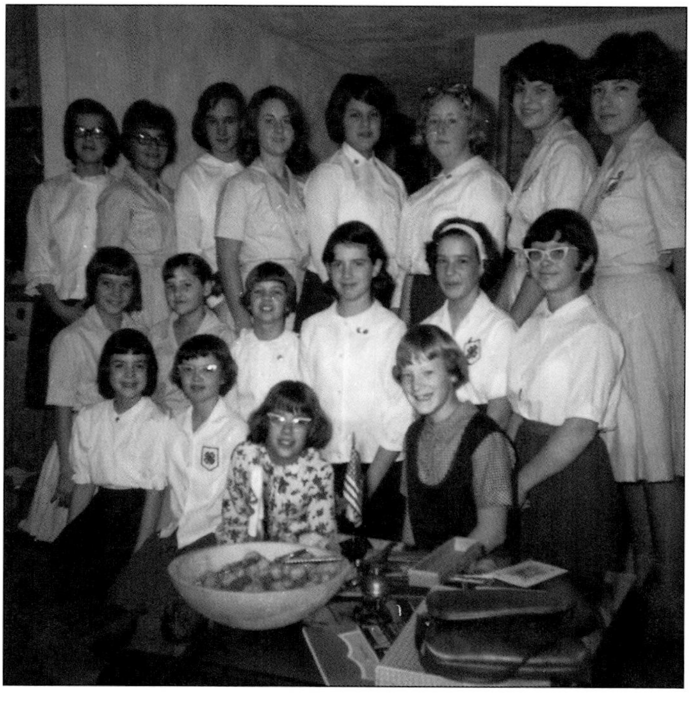

SUGAR GROVE 4-H CLUB. In 1917, a 4-H club led by Mrs. A.J. Hayes (Mary) was founded at Sugar Grove No. 9, a one-room country school near Dallas Center. This group evolved into the Sugar Grove Sunshine 4-H Club, which Lorna Grow has served as a leader for 50 years. Sugar Grove Sunshine 4-H members are shown here in 1966–1967. (Courtesy of Lorna Grow.)

Hy-Line Poultry. Founded in 1936, Hy-Line International developed the world's first hybrid egg-laying chicken produced on a commercial scale. Henry A. Wallace (left), 33rd vice president of the United States (1941–1945), conducted genetic selection research on his father's Iowa farm, where he discovered the potential of hybrid vigor to revolutionize agriculture. Hy-Line International is the world leader in layer poultry genetics, with research and development and production offices near Dallas Center. (Courtesy of Hy-Line International.)

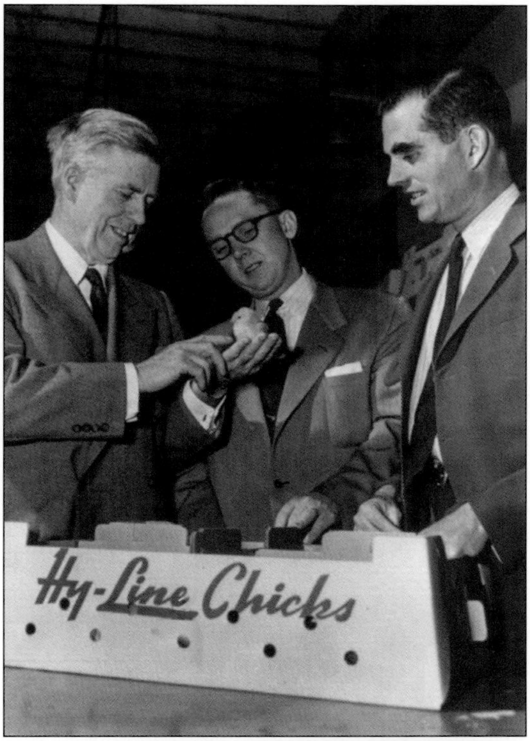

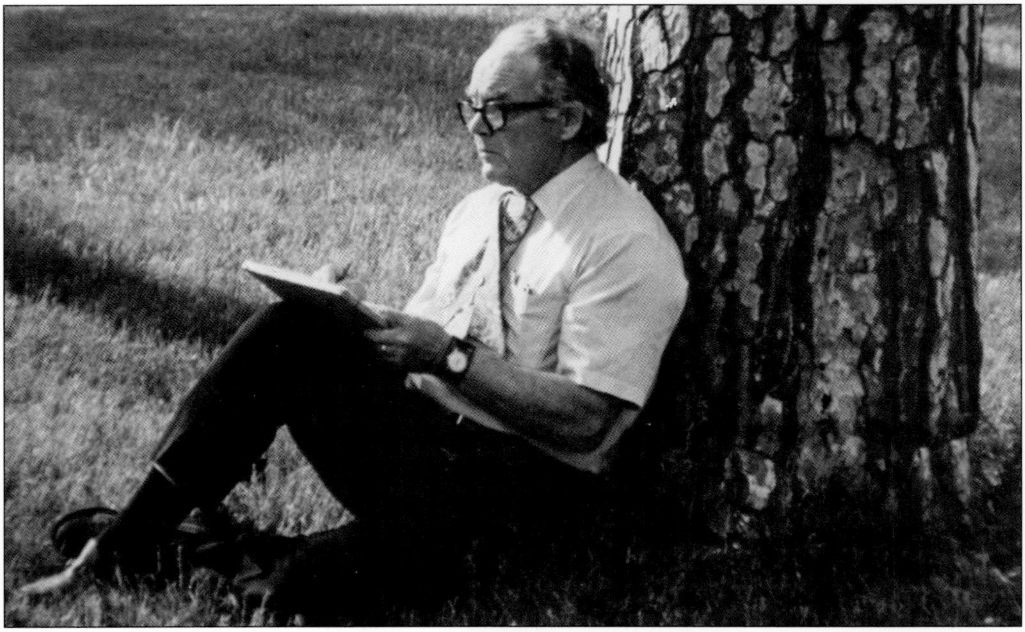

Bill Wagner's Legacy of Preservation. William "Bill" Wagner (1915–2001) was an internationally renowned architect and longtime Dallas Center resident who dedicated his life to historic preservation. His preservation work is reflected in many of Iowa's iconic buildings, including the Terrace Hill governor's mansion in Des Moines, West Branch's Herbert Hoover National Historic Site, the Dallas County Courthouse, and more. "I believe buildings have soul," he said. (Courtesy of Dallas County Conservation.)

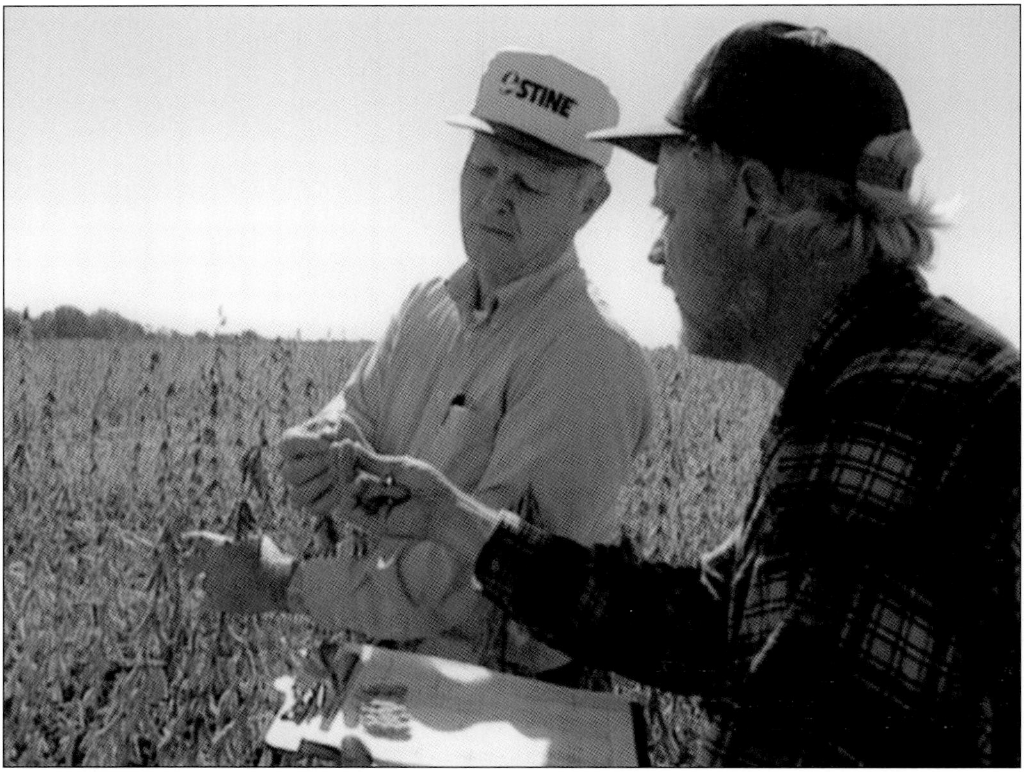

Harry Stine, Ag Entrepreneur. Harry Stine (left) owns Stine Seed, the largest private seed company in the world. He has been called the king of soybean genetics and continues to seek innovations that improve agricultural productivity. Entrepreneurship and innovation are second nature to Stine, whose grandparents settled in Dallas County in the late 1800s. In 2015, Stine was the only Iowan to make *Forbes*'s billionaires list. (Courtesy of Stine Seed.)

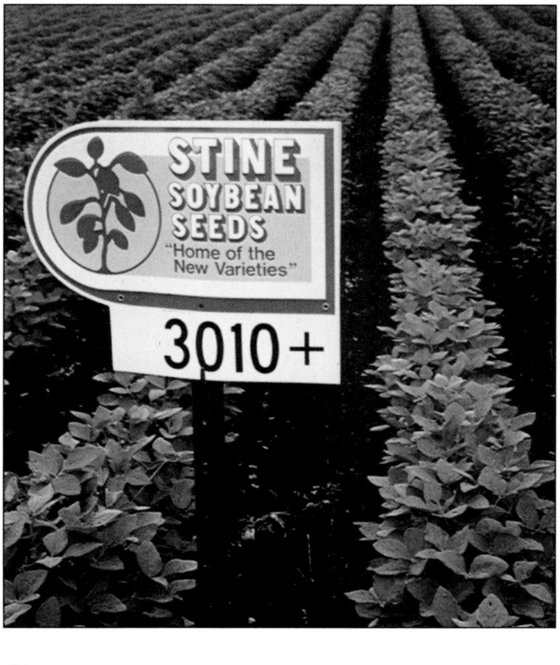

Soybeans Revolutionize Agriculture. Soybeans are a relatively new crop in American agriculture, first appearing on Iowa farms around World War II. In the late 1960s, Harry Stine and four other investors founded Improved Variety Research, a soybean breeding organization that was the first private soybean research and development firm in the United States. Since then, Stine Seed has developed some of the world's most valuable agricultural products. (Courtesy of Stine Seed.)

Five

Van Meter
Baseball, a Mystery, and More

Located just south of Interstate 80, Van Meter could be easy for casual observers to overlook unless they know the small town's claims to fame—Van Meter was home to one of America's most beloved professional baseball pitchers and continues to live with a century-old paranormal mystery.

Founded in 1870 and named in honor of pioneer businessman Jacob Van Meter, president of Van Meter Milling Company, Van Meter grew from 376 people in 1880 to 1,016 by 2010, according to US Census data. Abundant natural resources and rich farmland expanded the town's economic base, which included coal mining, brick and tile manufacturing, and agriculture.

One of Van Meter's most famous native sons, Bob Feller, grew up on a farm northeast of Van Meter where his father, Bill, focused on raising hogs, wheat, corn, and a ballplayer. The Fellers listened to broadcasts of Chicago Cubs baseball games on Des Moines' WHO Radio, where a fledgling sportscaster named Ronald Reagan was building his career. When Bob Feller was 12, his father built Oakview Park, complete with bleachers and scoreboard, on the family farm. The Fellers developed their own team at this original "field of dreams," where neighboring teams were invited to play.

Bob Feller, whose dazzling fastball made him a national celebrity at 17 and propelled him to the Hall of Fame as one of baseball's greatest pitchers, never forgot his Iowa roots. While he spent his entire professional baseball career with the Cleveland Indians and remained in Ohio, he returned time and again to Van Meter.

Another well-known figure also appeared in Van Meter repeatedly, although the infamous Van Meter Visitor came under the cover of darkness and disappeared as mysteriously as it arrived in 1903. This strange legend stemmed from accounts by a respected Van Meter businessman who reported seeing a winged monster that terrorized the town for several nights. Described as half human and half animal, the creature had enormous bat wings and a blinding light shooting from its horn. Courageous residents chased the creature to a local mine shaft, where it disappeared, never to be seen again. Nearly 114 years later, the mystery remains unsolved.

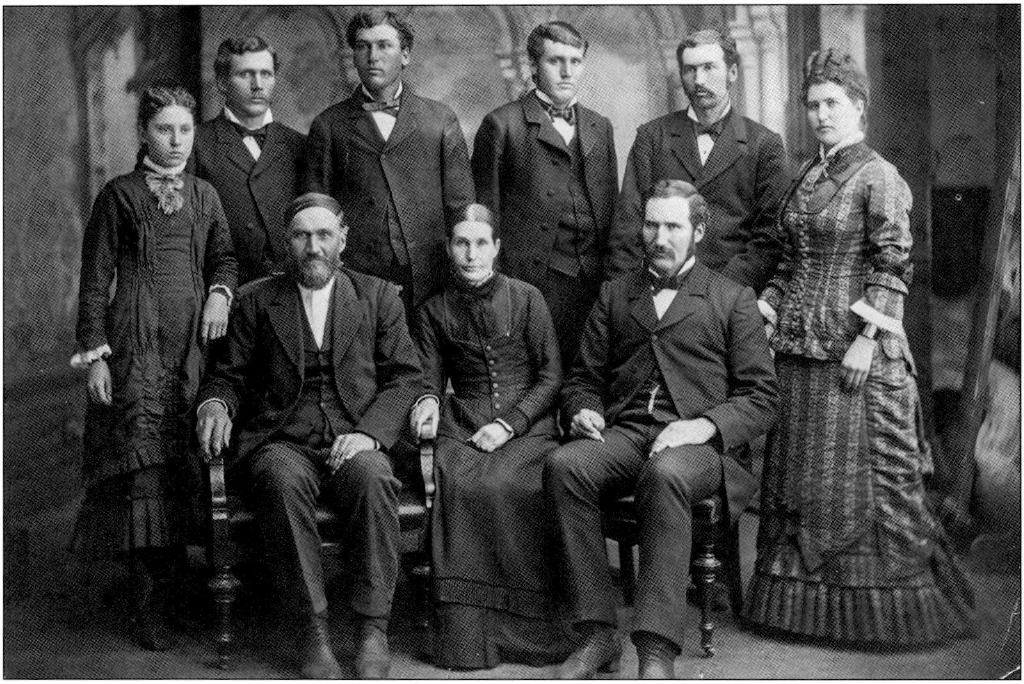

Go West, Young Man. Lured by the appeal of the frontier, 23-year-old Ohio native Nathan Moore traveled by steamboat to Keokuk, Iowa, and then walked to Dallas County, where he built the first dwelling in the Van Meter area in 1846. When Moore and his wife, Elizabeth, wed in 1849, it was the second marriage performed in Dallas County. The couple raised seven children, and Nathan Moore died at the age of 90. (Courtesy of Van Meter Public Library.)

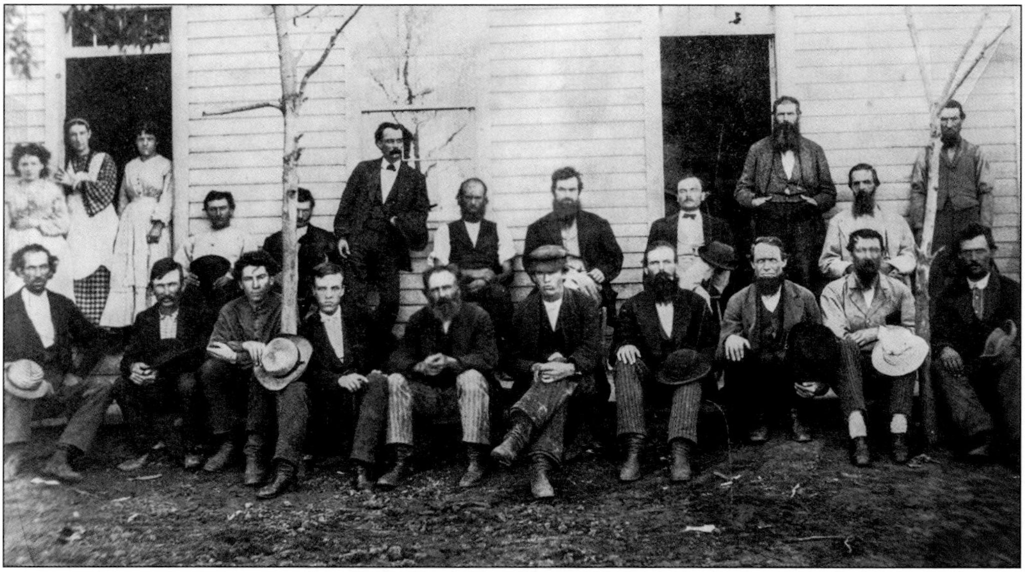

Pioneer Hotel. Van Meter's hotel, shown here in 1874, stood where Lander's Hardware was located years later. Some of the people shown include Peggy Thomas, Phoenix Briggs, L.W. Clayton, Mailand Little, Sam Akers, Tom Clayton, Alec Logan, Dan Briggs, Miss Duke McCoy, Mrs. Logan Simpkins, Logan Doty, George Briggs, Miles White, Phil Hunt, Jake Van Meter, H.C. Clayton, Charles McCoy, William Jennings, and Bill Shull. (Courtesy of Van Meter Public Library.)

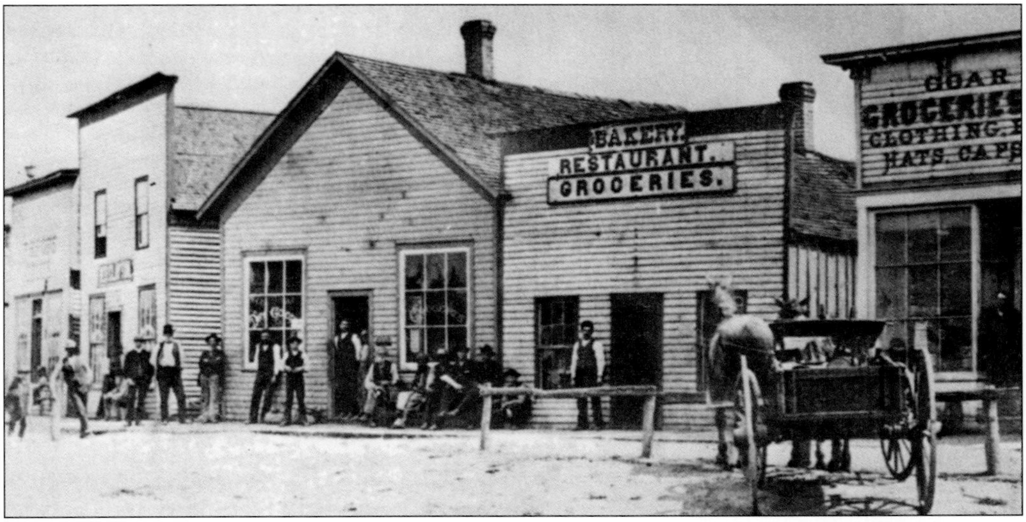

Van Meter in the 1880s. When Van Meter was founded in 1870, the Civil War had ended only five years earlier, the first transcontinental railroad was recently completed, and Iowa was experiencing major growth. Van Meter (shown here in the 1880s) was named for J.R. Van Meter, a pioneer flour miller who later led the community into its coal-mining period. Businesses in early Van Meter included a bakery, dry goods store, restaurant, general store, and more. (Courtesy of Van Meter Public Library.)

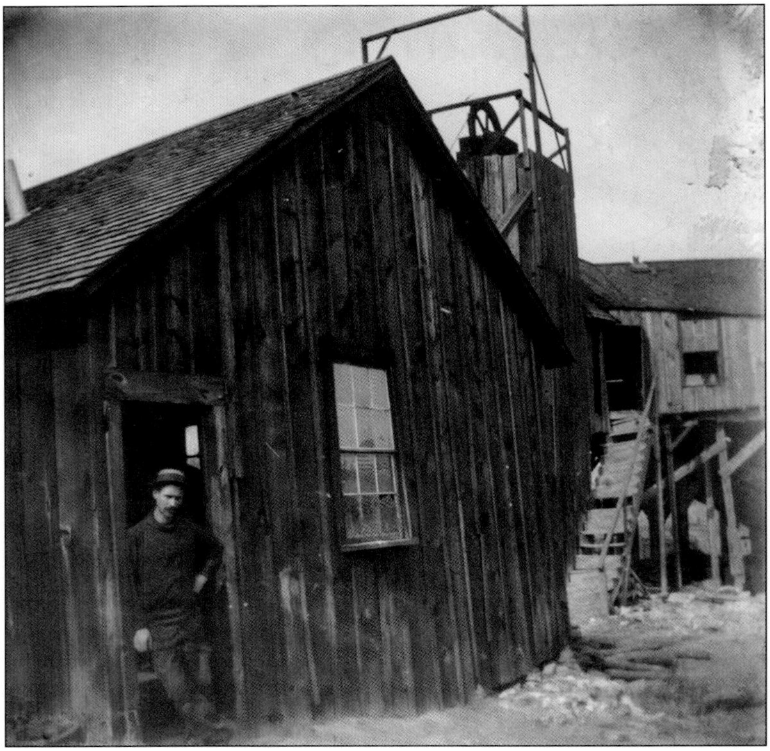

Mining Put Van Meter on the Map. Numerous coal veins were located around Van Meter. In 1878, Boag & Van Meter sunk a 257-foot-deep shaft to a three-foot vein. The mine was sold to the Chicago Coal Company, whose managers in 1879 included J.L. Platt, president; John Walker, superintendent; John Honicker, clerk; and Ira Hall, weigh boss. When the miners went on strike in 1902, the owners closed the mine permanently. (Courtesy of Van Meter Public Library.)

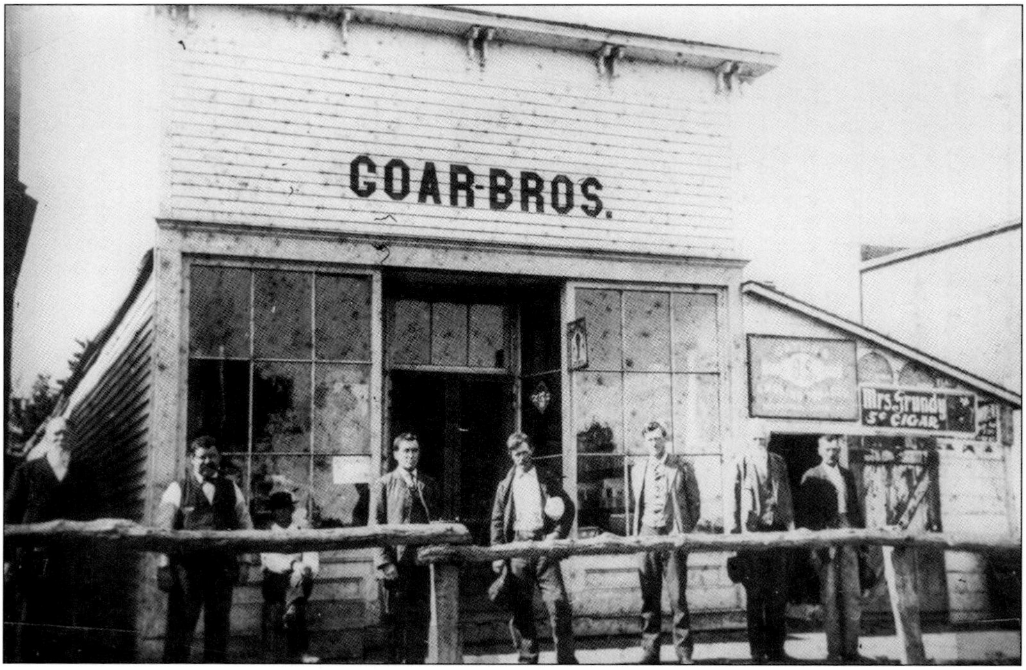

MEN OUTSIDE THE GOAR GENERAL STORE. Wooden hitching posts are in front of the Goar Bros. Store in Van Meter, where customers could purchase 5¢ cigars and other items. The men shown are, from left to right, a Mr. Clayton, Marty Mehan, Frank Johnson, Elmer Goar, Charley McCoy, Jim E. Goar, Eli Goar, and Alic Montgomery. (Courtesy of Van Meter Public Library.)

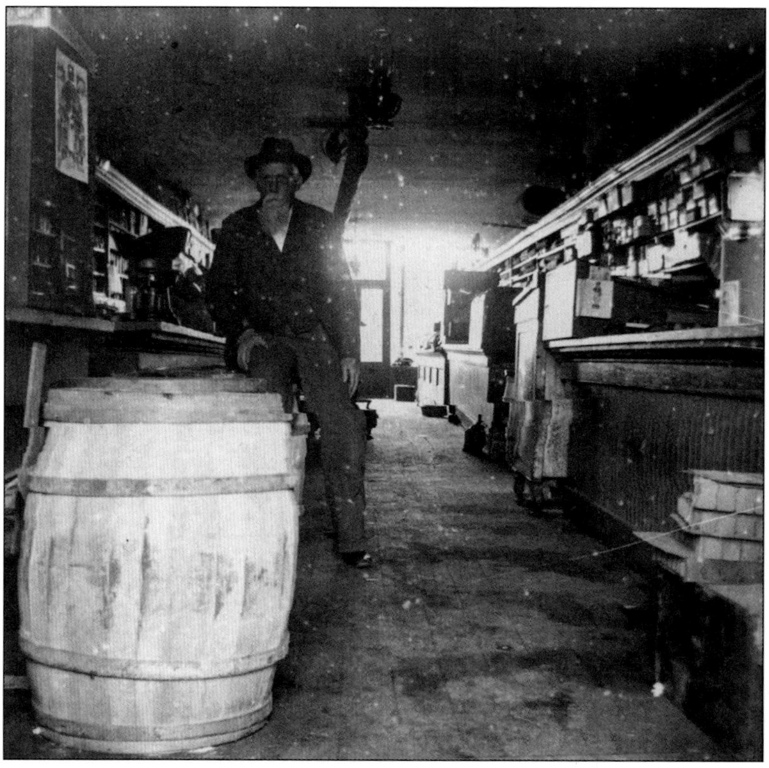

SUPPLIES BY THE BARREL. Eli Goar is shown inside the Goar Bros. Store in Van Meter. Many supplies were shipped and sold in wooden barrels. A kerosene lantern hangs from the ceiling. Goar's well-appointed store provided many essentials for the community, from groceries to clothing and hats. Goar was a leading merchant for 23 years in Van Meter, where he also founded the Van Meter Bank. (Courtesy of Van Meter Public Library.)

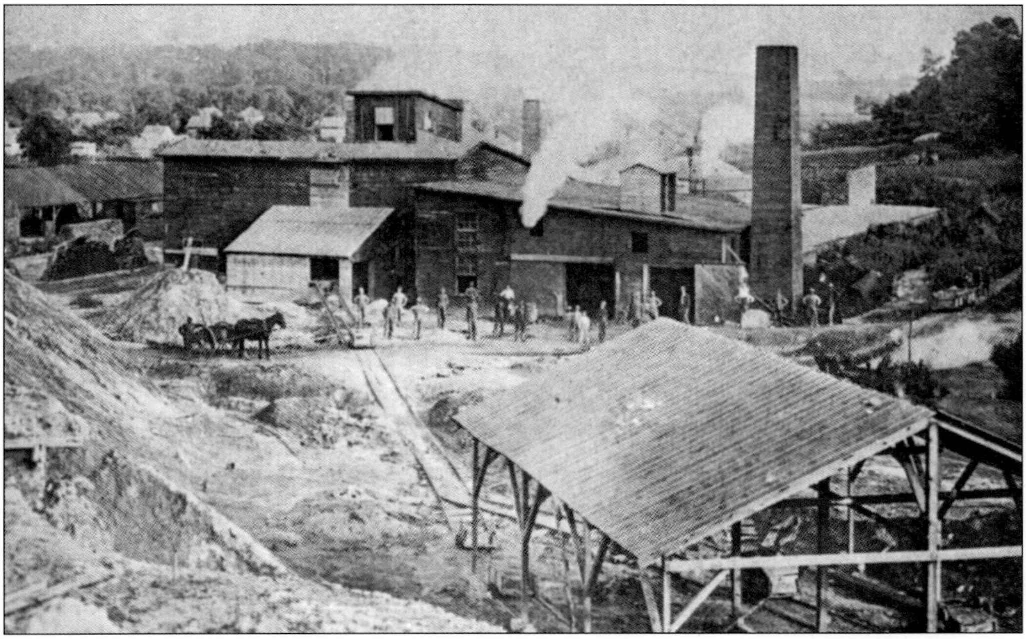

Platt Brothers Brick and Tile. Nature favored the landscape around Van Meter, providing the raw materials for the manufacture of brick and tile. In 1893, entrepreneurs built on the success of their coal mine near Van Meter to establish the Platt Pressed & Fire Brick Company. The plant used clay from the mine and surrounding bluffs to produce high-end brick and tile. (Courtesy of Van Meter Public Library.)

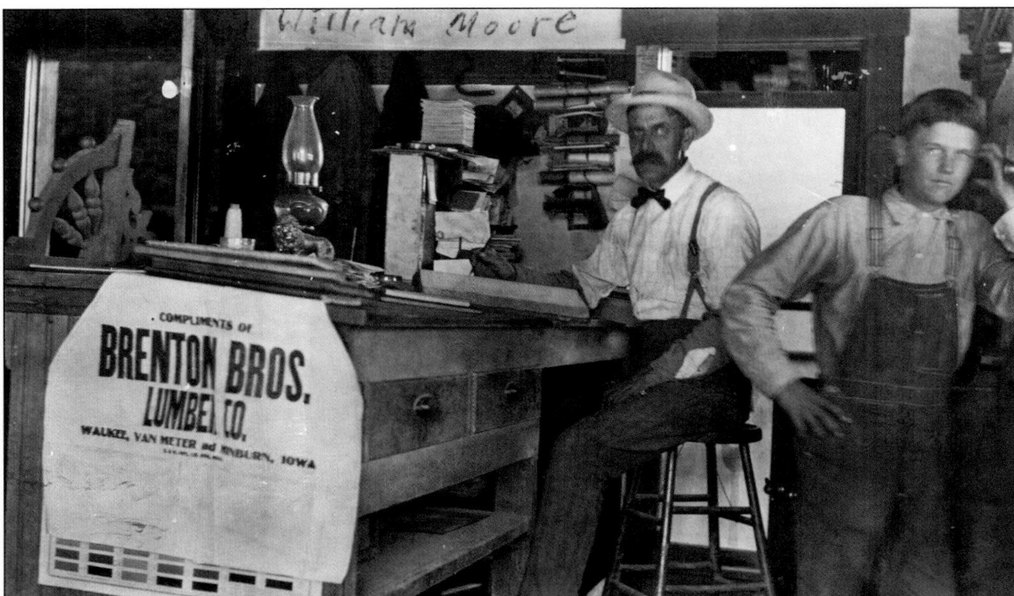

Brenton Bros. Lumber. The Brenton name has been well known throughout Dallas County for generations from banking to farming to other businesses. Van Meter resident William Moore (left) is shown in this early 1900s-era store, which displays a Brenton Bros. Lumber Co. sign. The Brentons had lumberyards in Van Meter, Waukee, and Minburn, along with grain elevators at Van Meter and Dallas Center. (Courtesy of Van Meter Public Library.)

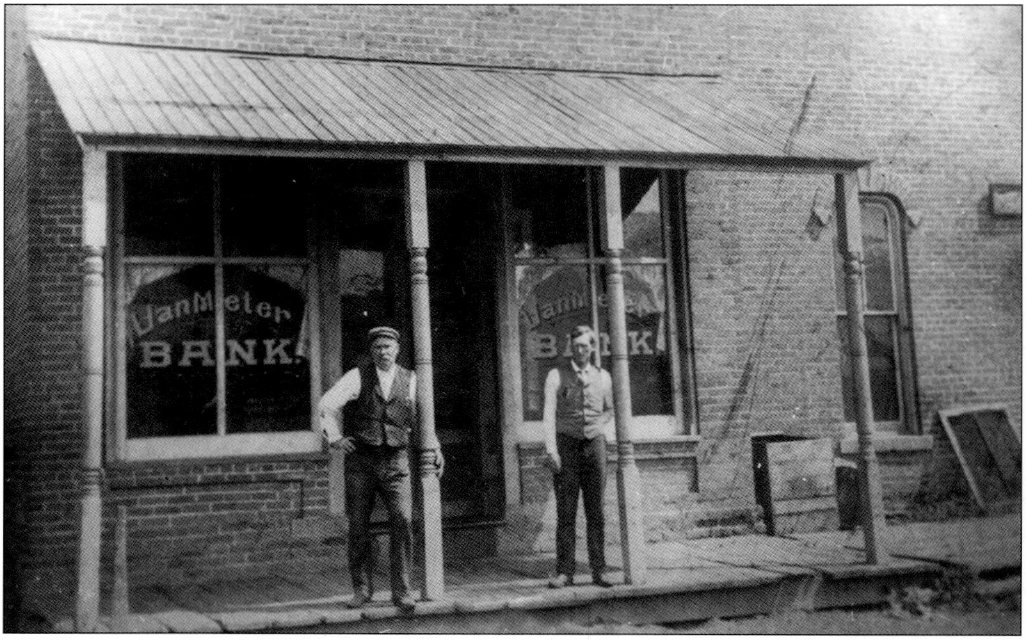

Van Meter Bank. The Van Meter Bank was organized on March 6, 1899, and was owned by the Goar brothers. The bank had capital of $10,000. The men shown here include L.W. Clayton (left) and Jim E. Goar. This picture was probably taken in 1901, when Clayton was admitted as an equal partner. The bank building on Grant Street now houses a law office. (Courtesy of Van Meter Public Library.)

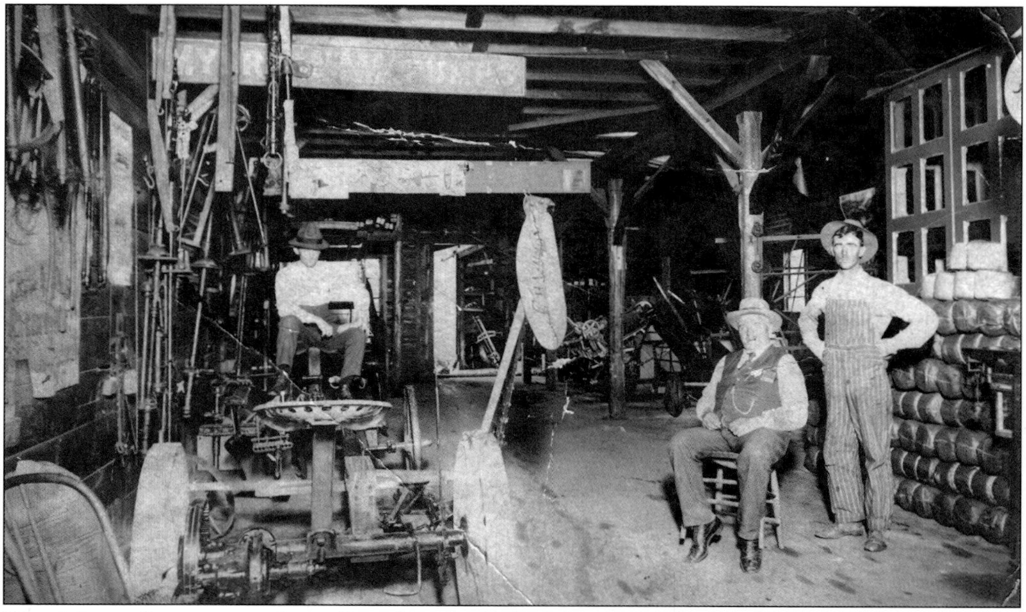

Van Meter Implement Shop. David T. Griffith is shown in the early 1900s in his Van Meter implement store with Will Hazen. After graduating from Capitol City Commercial College in 1896, Griffith worked in the grocery business in Earlham before moving to Van Meter. He purchased Charley McBride's share of an implement business, which was renamed Griffith Brothers. David and his brother, Ulysses, operated the business. (Courtesy of Van Meter Public Library.)

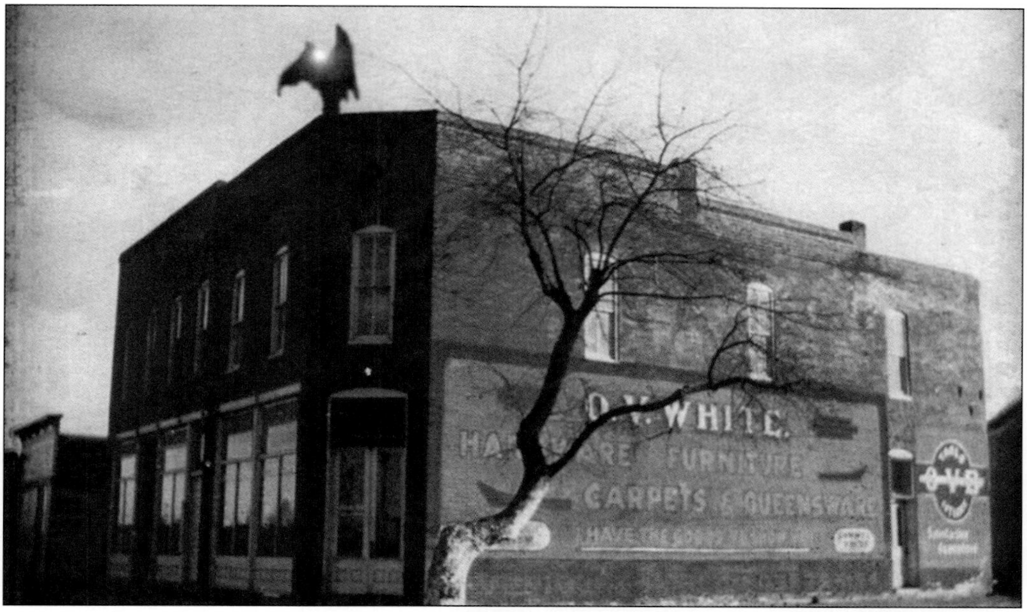

THE VAN METER VISITOR. This was the Fisher & White hardware store when co-owner Otto White encountered the mysterious Van Meter Visitor (represented here on top of the building in an artist's rendering) one night in October 1903. White saw an eight-foot-tall winged monster on a telephone pole. The monster shone a bright light into the businessman's apartment above the store, emanated a strong odor, and ran on all four feet before extending its wings and disappearing into a nearby coal mine. (Courtesy of Chad Lewis.)

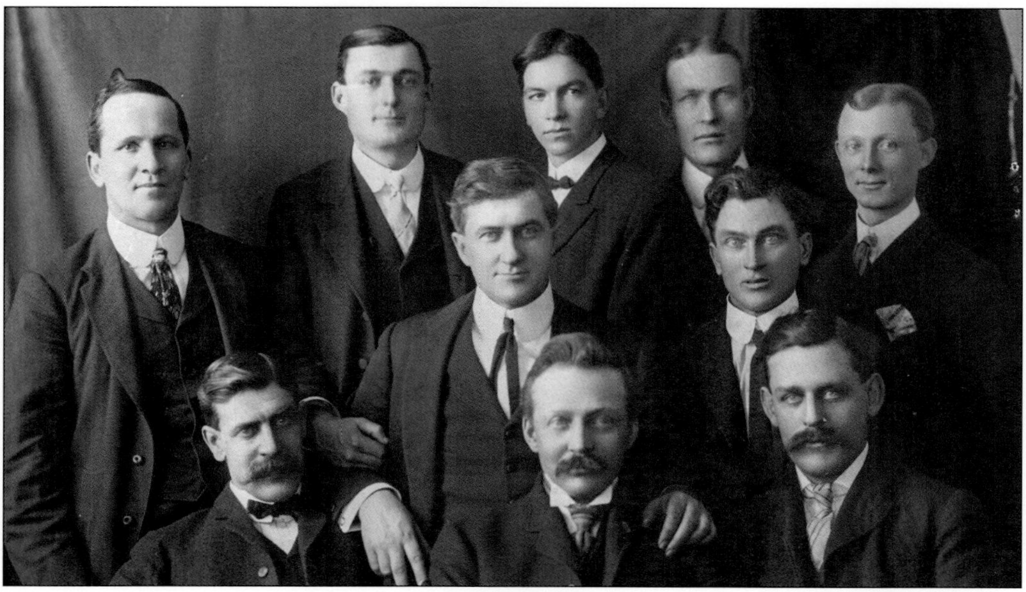

VAN METER'S BACHELORS. For several nights in the fall of 1903, many of these men reported multiple sightings of the Van Meter Visitor, a bizarre, giant batlike creature. This 1901 photograph includes "the handsome bachelors of Van Meter"; from left to right are (first row) William Moore, Ulysses "Uly" Griffith, and Ernest Trindle; (second row) Harry H. Phillips and Charlie A. England; (third row) Otto V. White, Howard T. Smith, Sidney Gregg, A.L. Jordan, and a Mr. Scott. (Courtesy of Van Meter Public Library.)

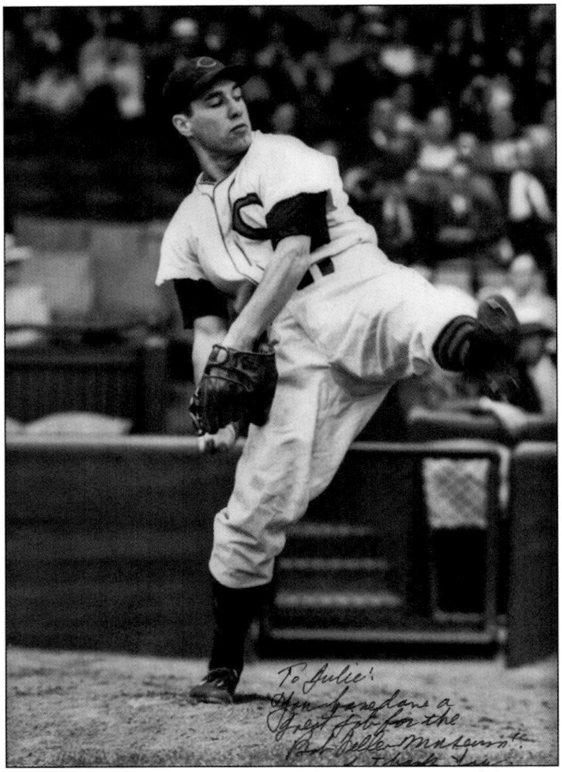

"Heater from Van Meter." Bob Feller, a farm boy from Van Meter, began pitching for the Cleveland Indians in 1936 at the age of 17. "Rapid Robert" was known for his devastating fastball and high strikeout totals. After his rookie season, Feller's graduation from Van Meter High School was broadcast by CBS Radio. Feller helped Cleveland clinch the 1948 World Series and was inducted into the National Baseball Hall of Fame in 1962. (Courtesy of Julie Bailey.)

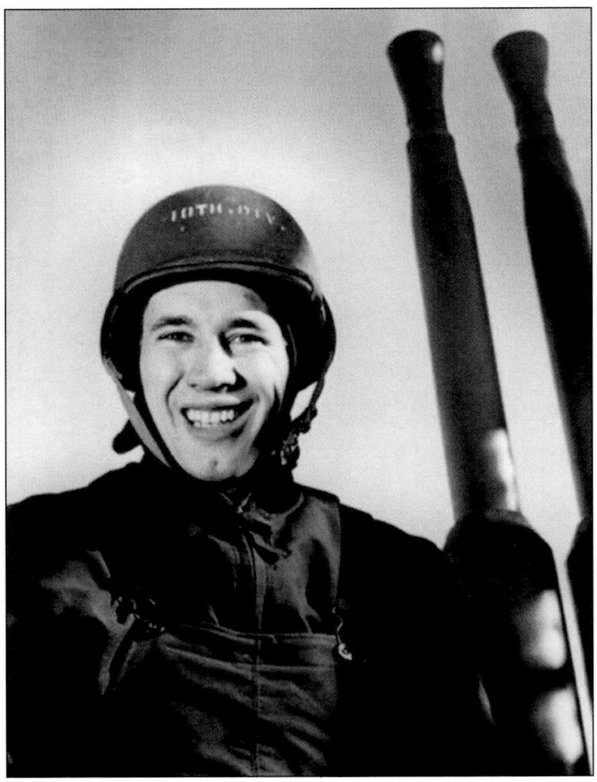

Feller Served in World War II. The day after the bombing of Pearl Harbor, Bob Feller (1918–2010) joined the US Navy and became major-league baseball's first player to enlist in World War II. Feller gave up nearly four seasons of baseball in the prime of his career but had no regrets, saying he was proud to serve on the USS *Alabama* and help America win the war. (Author's collection.)

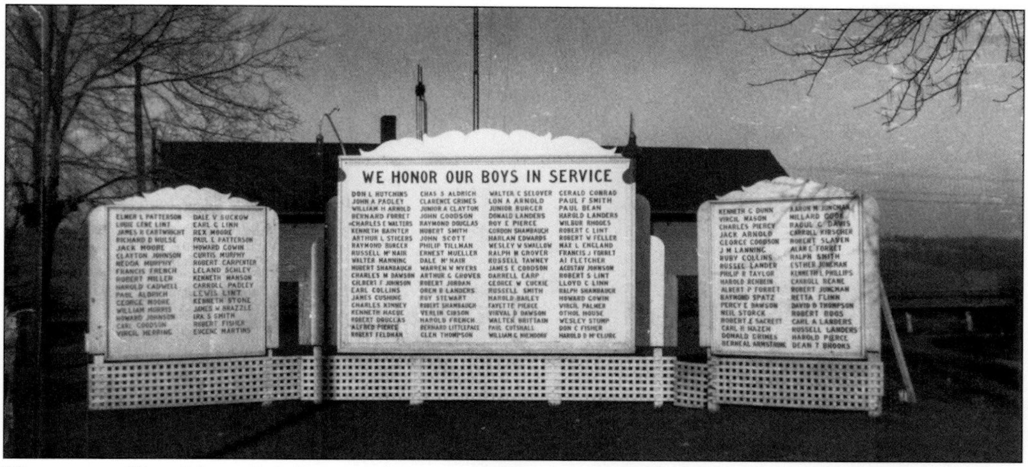

Honoring Van Meter's Military Men and Women. During World War II, small towns across Iowa, including Van Meter, displayed wooden honor boards listing the names of all the local men and women serving in the US military. Cleveland Indians pitcher and Van Meter native Robert W. Feller's name is listed in the middle board, about halfway down the right column. (Courtesy of Van Meter Public Library.)

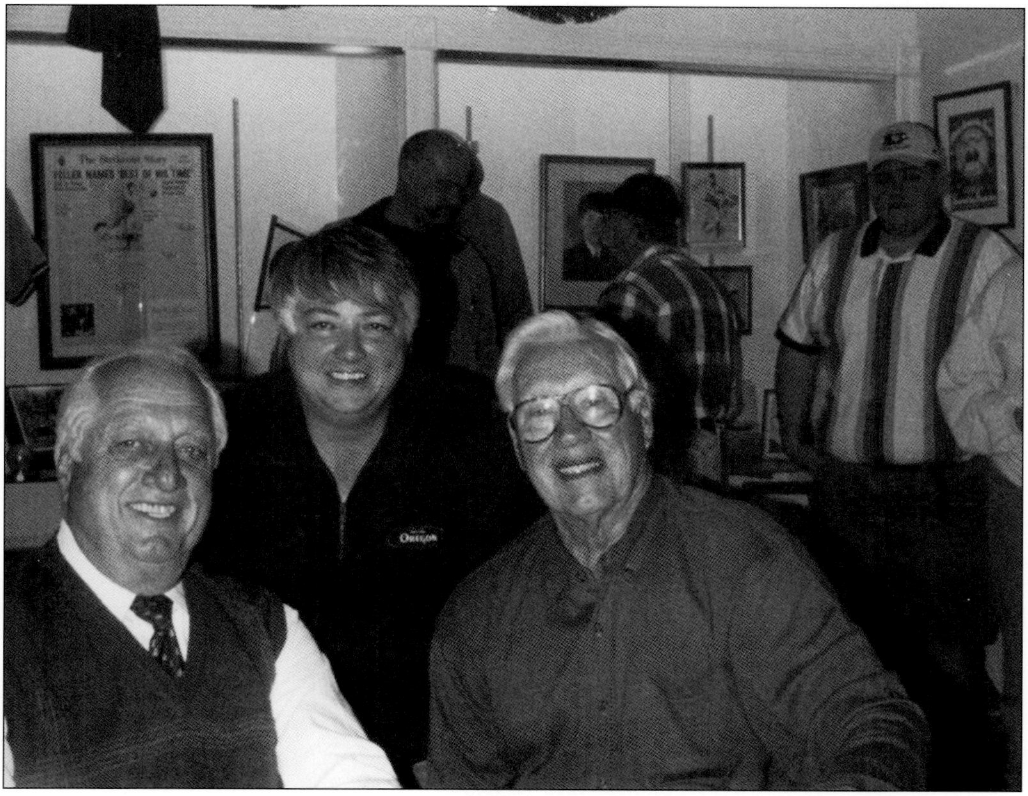

Celebrating Hall of Fame Legends. From the day it opened in 1995, the Bob Feller Museum in Van Meter became a draw for baseball fans. Every year, Feller invited famous retired ballplayers to the museum for fundraising events. Guests included fellow hall-of-famers like Stan Musial and Tommy Lasorda (left), shown with Bob Feller and Julie Bailey, former executive director of the museum, which closed in 2014. (Courtesy of Julie Bailey.)

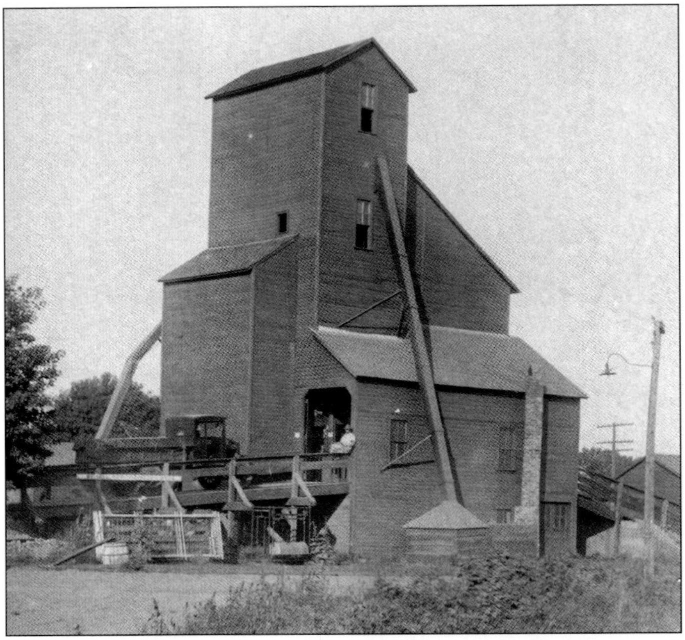

Delivering Grain to Van Meter. While a brick and tile plant, coal mining, and farming were among the major industries that drove Van Meter's economy around the beginning of the 20th century, only agriculture remains. Wooden elevators like this provided a convenient place for farmers to deliver their grain. Few wooden grain elevators remain in Iowa. (Courtesy of Van Meter Public Library.)

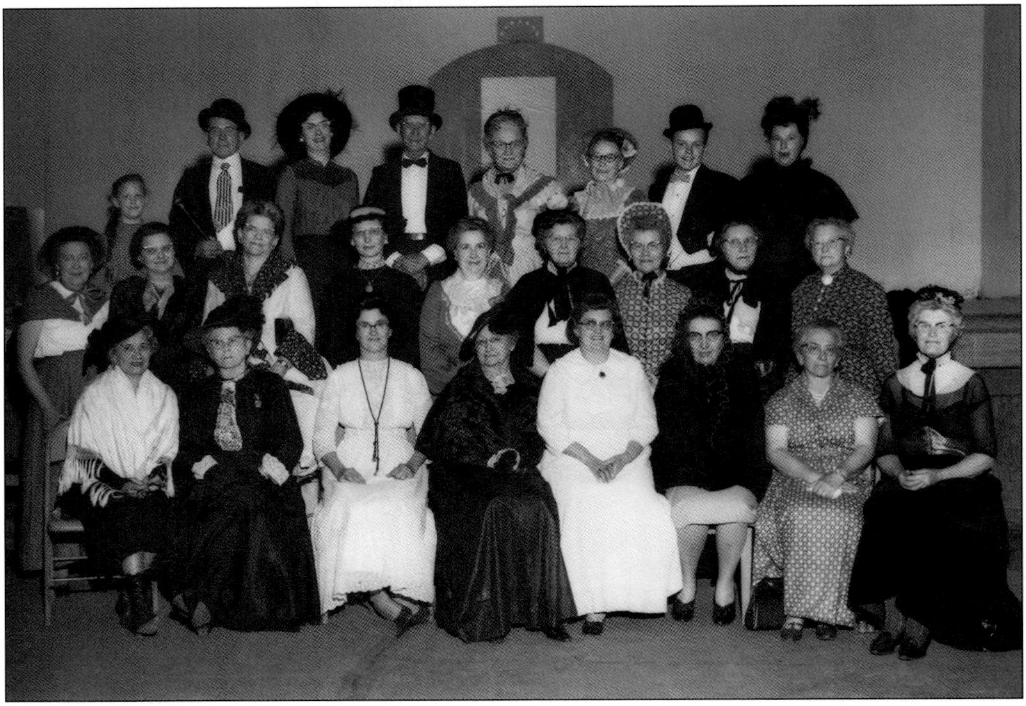

Van Meter Centennial Group. People dressed in period clothing for Van Meter Township's 1964 Historical Day, including (first row) Carmen Stone, Lois Jennings, Geneva Burgen, Bernice Stewart, Bonnie Feldman, two unidentified, and Mary Pritcherd; (second row) Marguerite Gutshall, two unidentified, Esther Radke, Helen Palmer, Garnet Switzer, Dora Sanders, Marie Jamison, and Opal Burger; (third row) Cate Jennings, Earl England, Willadene Schabilion, Roy Sanders, Mrs. Curtis Gregory, unidentified, Bill Jennings, and Hazel Lauterbach. (Courtesy of Van Meter Public Library.)

Rep. David Young. Republican David Young represents Iowa's Third District in the US House of Representatives. Growing up in Van Meter, this sixth-generation Iowan played Little League baseball and was a paperboy in town. Young was first elected to Congress in 2014 and won reelection two years later. Young introduced the No Veterans Crisis Line Call Should Go Unanswered Act in 2016. President Obama signed it into law on November 28, 2016. (Courtesy of davidyoung.house.gov.)

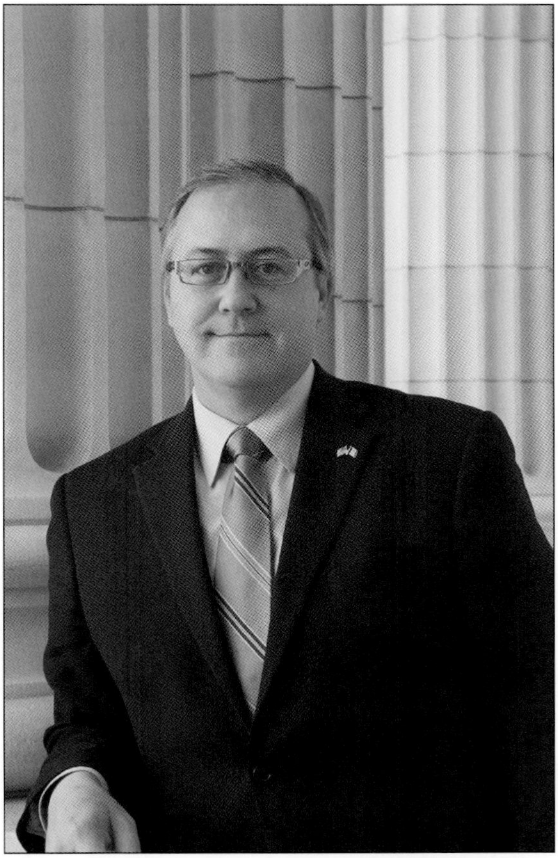

Iowa Veterans Cemetery. The Iowa Veterans Cemetery offers a picturesque setting in southern Dallas County along Interstate 80 near Van Meter. Following a ground-breaking ceremony on Veterans Day 2006, construction began the following year, with the dedication on July 3, 2008. The cemetery is slated to provide spaces for 81,000 burials. (Author's collection.)

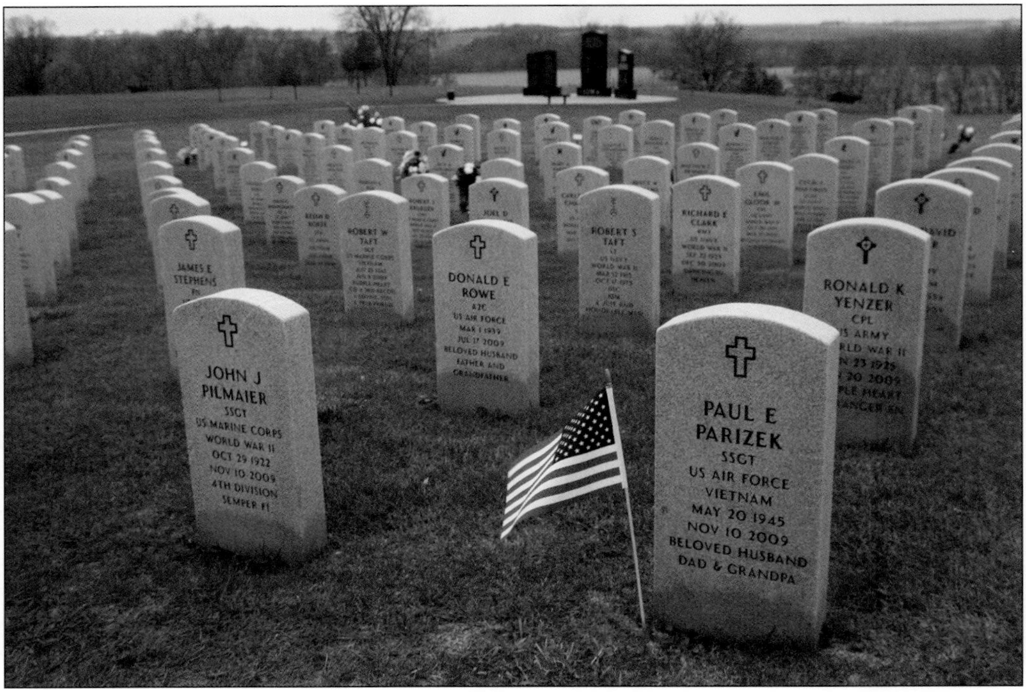

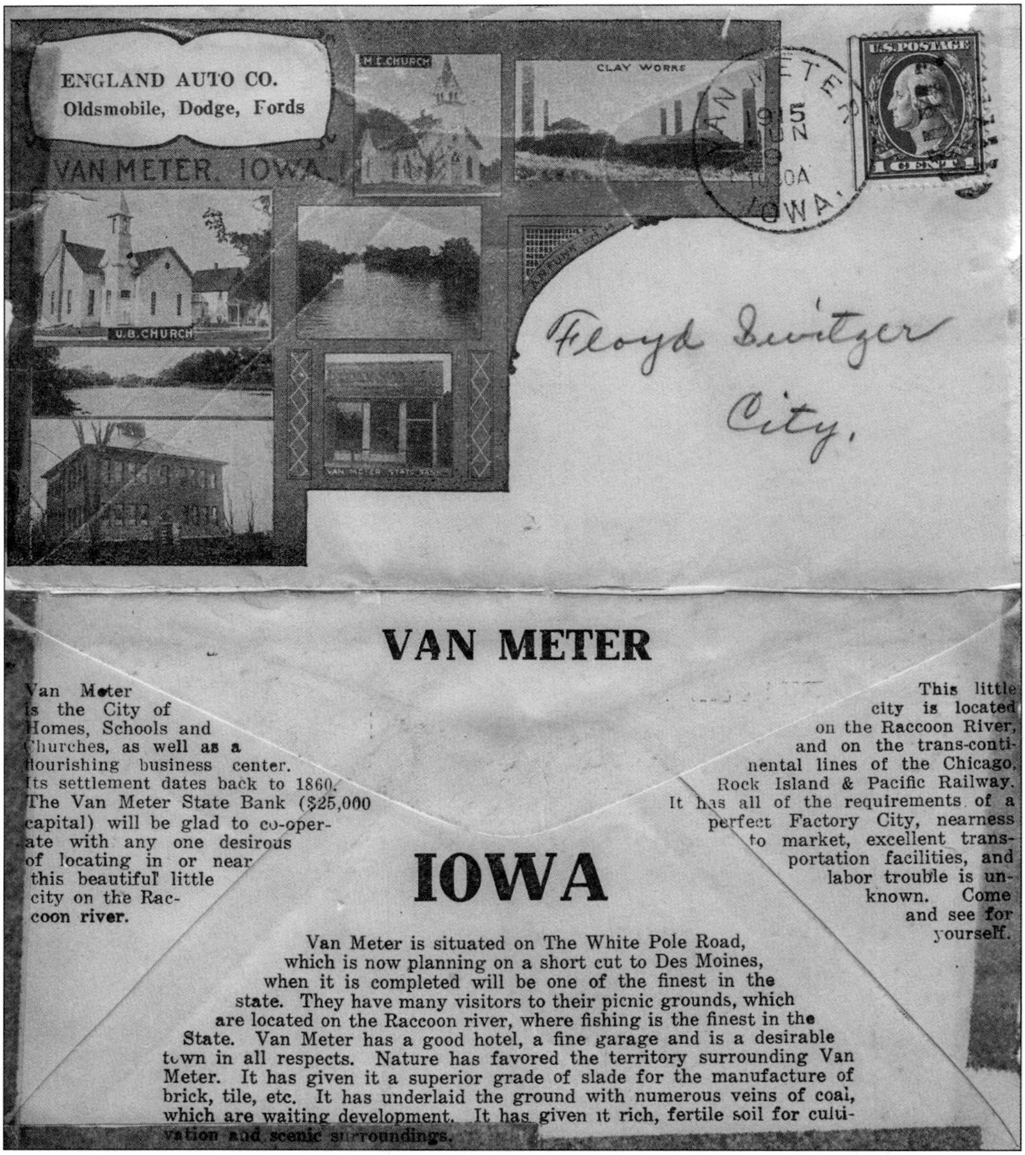

ENGLAND AUTO CO.
Oldsmobile, Dodge, Fords

VAN METER, IOWA

M.E. CHURCH

CLAY WORKS

U.B. CHURCH

VAN METER STATE BANK

Floyd Switzer
City.

VAN METER

Van Meter is the City of Homes, Schools and Churches, as well as a flourishing business center. Its settlement dates back to 1860. The Van Meter State Bank ($25,000 capital) will be glad to co-operate with any one desirous of locating in or near this beautiful little city on the Raccoon river.

This little city is located on the Raccoon River, and on the trans-continental lines of the Chicago, Rock Island & Pacific Railway. It has all of the requirements of a perfect Factory City, nearness to market, excellent transportation facilities, and labor trouble is unknown. Come and see for yourself.

IOWA

Van Meter is situated on The White Pole Road, which is now planning on a short cut to Des Moines, when it is completed will be one of the finest in the state. They have many visitors to their picnic grounds, which are located on the Raccoon river, where fishing is the finest in the State. Van Meter has a good hotel, a fine garage and is a desirable town in all respects. Nature has favored the territory surrounding Van Meter. It has given it a superior grade of slade for the manufacture of brick, tile, etc. It has underlaid the ground with numerous veins of coal, which are waiting development. It has given it rich, fertile soil for cultivation and scenic surroundings.

VAN METER LETTER, 1915. It cost a penny for the England Auto Company to send this unique correspondence on June 9, 1915. The envelope highlights Van Meter's many advantages, including a convenient location on the White Pole Road, a good hotel, a fine garage, and some of the best fishing in the state. The text states, "Van Meter is a desirable town in all respects. Come see for yourself." (Courtesy of Van Meter Public Library.)

Six

Perry
Northern Dallas County's Largest Town

Located in northern Dallas County, Perry came to life in 1869 and quickly became one of the largest towns not only in the county but also in the region.

After town founder Harvey Willis convinced a railroad surveyor to run the train through Perry, the town boomed almost overnight. As the community grew from a few hundred people to nearly 4,000 people by 1900, schools, churches, homes, and businesses also sprang up throughout the city, which was named after Colonel Perry, an official with the Des Moines Valley Railway.

As the town continued to boom, so did the population, which experienced steady growth until the 1980s. With a population of more than 7,700 residents in 2010, according to US Census data, Perry remains one of the largest towns in Dallas County, second only to Waukee.

The majestic, fully restored Hotel Pattee, built on Willis Avenue in 1913, showcases the unique heritage of Perry and Iowa, from the immigrant experience to hometown heroes. Throughout its history, Perry has hosted some of the biggest celebrities in America, from baseball legend Babe Ruth in 1922 to jazz trumpeter Louis Armstrong, who stayed at the Hotel Pattee in 1954 when he played at nearby Lake Robbins Ballroom.

Perry has long been a surprisingly diverse community. Railroad jobs attracted many African American families to Perry in years past. Some members of Perry's African American community established the Bethel Baptist Church, and others opened businesses, including a beauty salon. In recent years, meat processing jobs have attracted new residents from Mexico and elsewhere in Latin America, Africa, and beyond.

Diverse industries have helped Perry grow through the years, from manufacturing to food processing. In the early 1900s, Perry was home to a milk-condensing factory, the At Last Washing Machine Company, Perry Bottling Works, and more. Some industries have endured, including Osmundson Manufacturing Company, which has been producing disc blades, sweeps, plowshares, and other tillage tools for America's farmers since 1903, and Progressive Foundry, which supplies high-quality ductile iron castings.

Today, Perry remains a center of commerce where countless small-town stories past and present define families, generations, and the community.

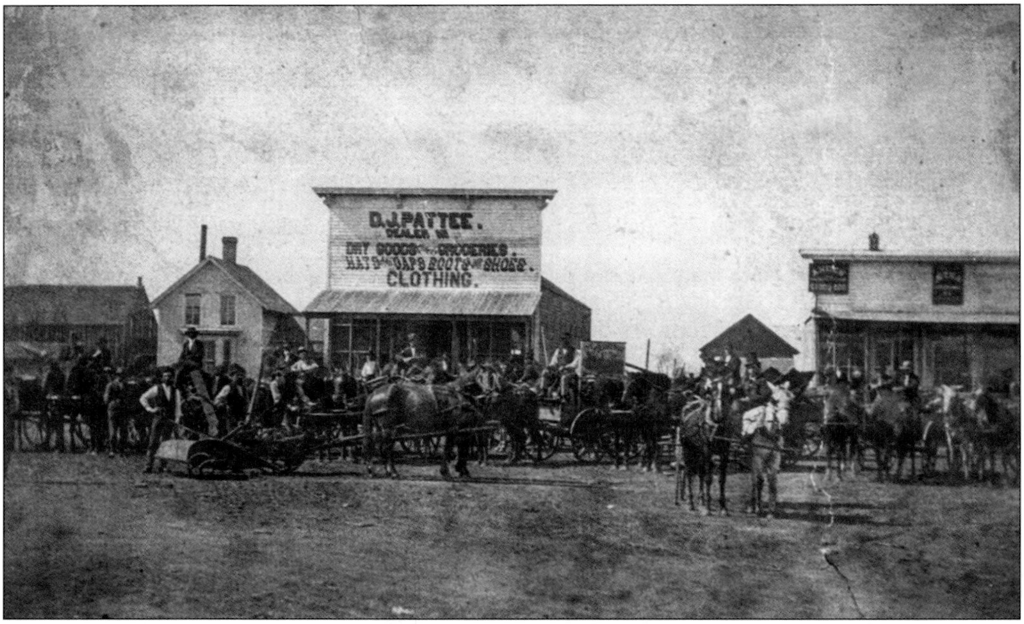

General Store in a Prairie Town. The Pattee Dry Goods and Grocery store in Perry is shown here in 1869. Although merchants made up only about two percent of the workforce in early Dallas County, they provided necessities for farm families and newcomers to settlements on the prairie. Tools, shoes, medicines, fabric, coffee, flour, sugar, and more were traded at their stores. (Courtesy of Dallas County Conservation.)

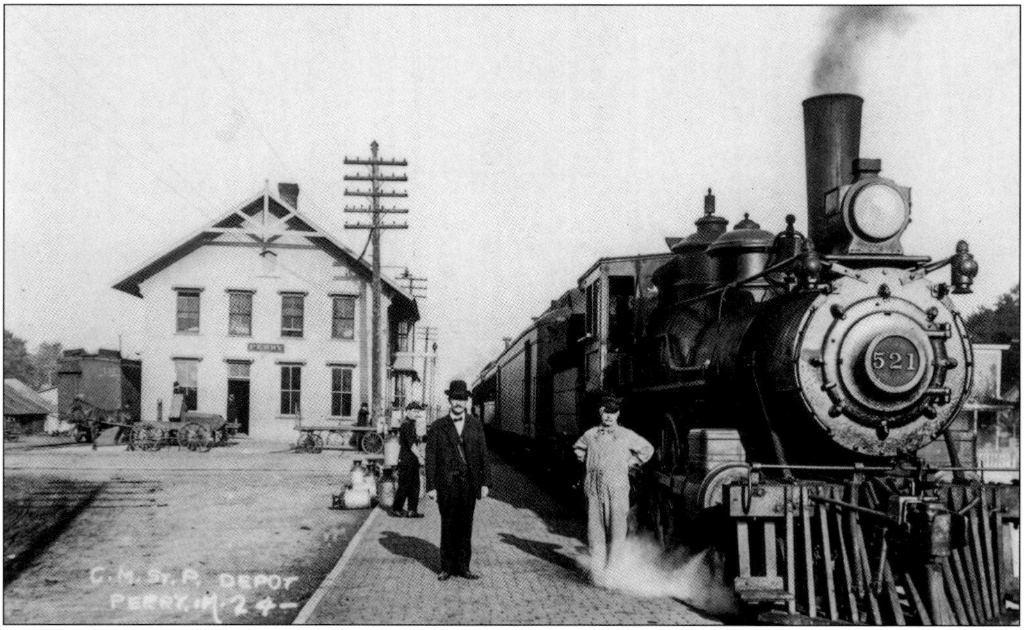

Perry's Railroad History. The first railroad to reach the area that would become Perry was the Des Moines & Fort Dodge Railroad in 1868. The first train arrived in 1869, the year Perry was founded. The first Chicago, Milwaukee & St. Paul Railroad train, running from Chicago to Council Bluffs, came through Perry in 1882. The last train came through Perry on the Milwaukee Road in 1980. The railroad depot (pictured) began operations in 1883. (Courtesy of Brian Eiteman.)

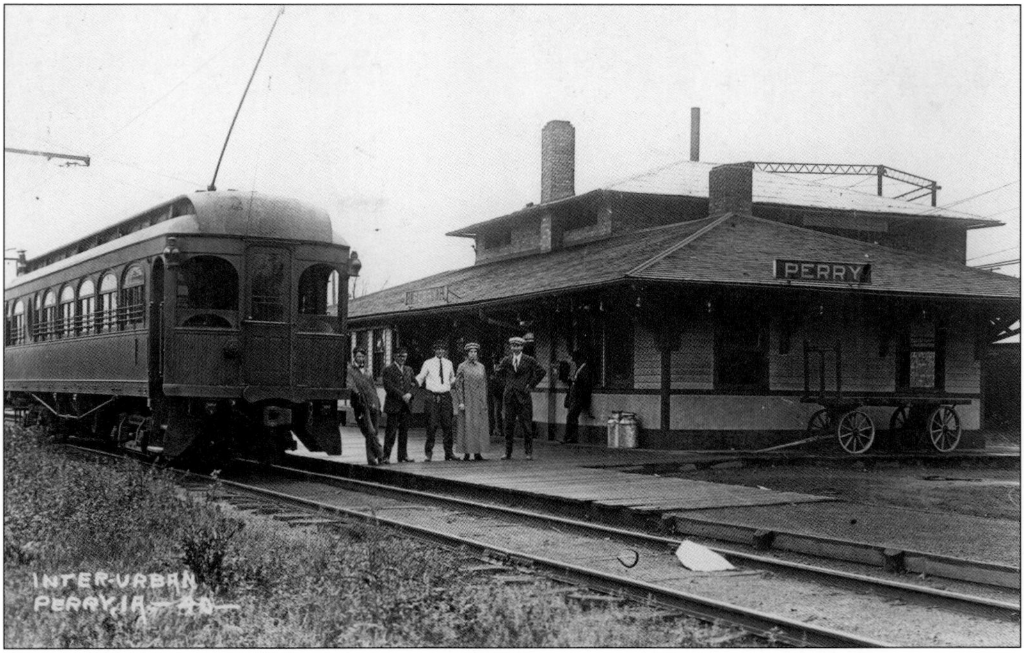

All Aboard the Interurban. An electric rail line operated between Des Moines and Perry from 1906 to 1949. The depot was on the corner of Willis Avenue and West Third Street. The interurban's decline was inevitable, due to more automobiles, trucks, and paved roads. Interurban passenger trains dwindled from 12 round-trips daily to two. While freight service continued through 1953, the rails were removed in 1954. (Courtesy of Brian Eiteman.)

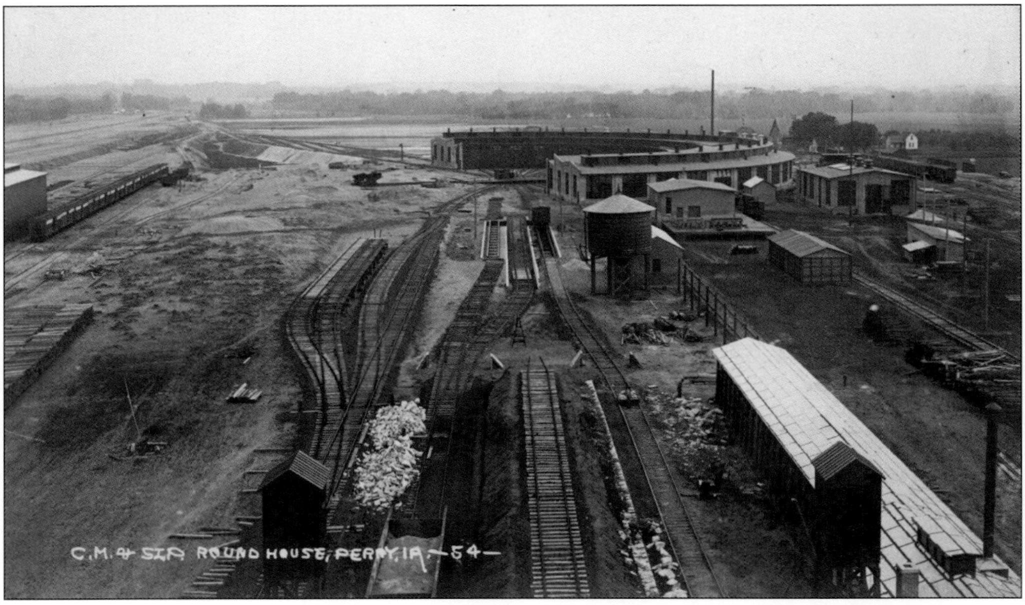

Roundhouse. By 1912, the Chicago, Milwaukee & St. Paul Railroad needed a new roundhouse in Perry. The railroad acquired two farms west of town to build the complex, which included shops, a railyard, and a yard office. Steam locomotives were serviced and stored at the roundhouse, which was named for its semicircular shape and located adjacent to a turntable that helped position locomotives in the right direction. (Courtesy of Brian Eiteman.)

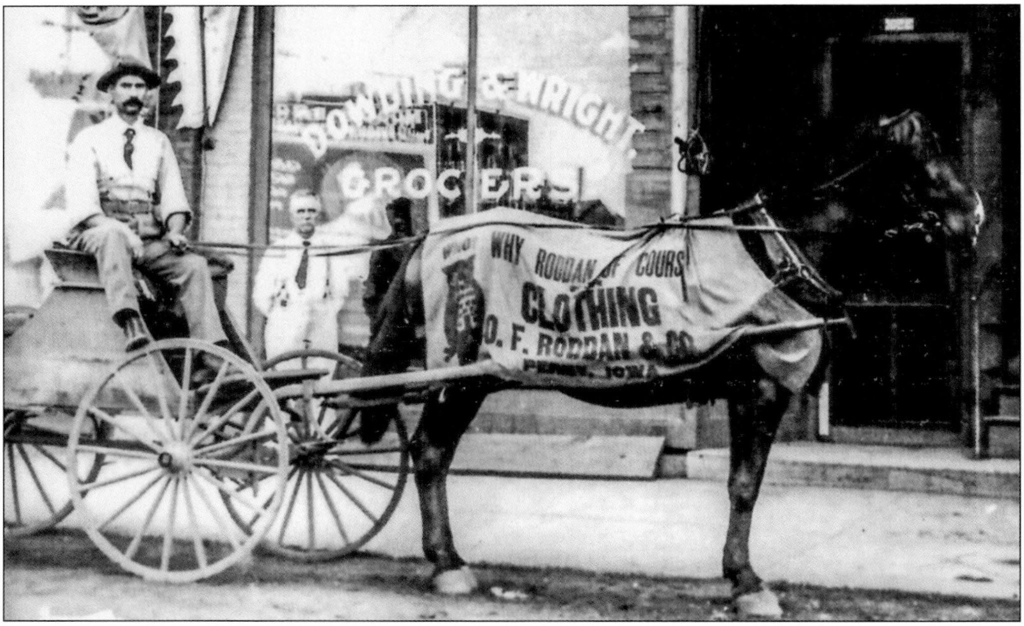

Mobile Advertising. The proprietor of Roddan's Clothing in Perry used a unique way to promote his business in the early 1900s, thanks to this custom-printed banner draped over a horse. The rig is parked outside the Dowling and Wright grocery store. (Courtesy of Jeanette Peddicord.)

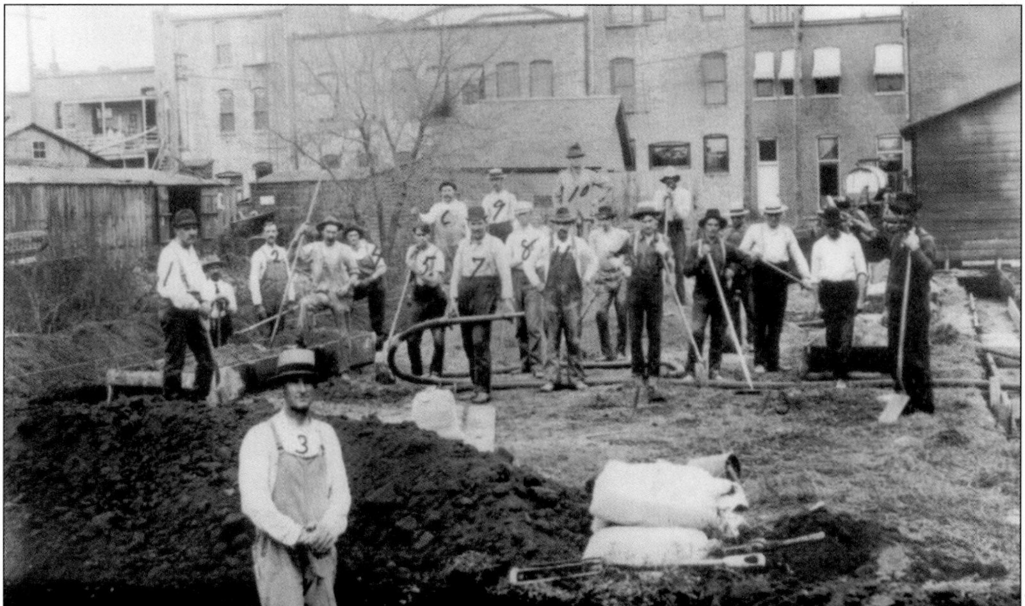

Building a New Fire Station. Perry's firefighters dug the foundation for their new fire station, which was completed in 1905. Chief Fred Knell made it mandatory for all firefighters to spend one day digging. It took them two days to complete the job. Shown here on September 29, 1904, are (1) Chief Knell, (2) Assistant Chief T.R. Phillips, (3) Harry Smith, (4) Loyd Leonard, (5) F.E. Knell, (6) Louis Christ, (7) Reece Orman, (8) R.J. Lysle, (9) Will Miller, (10) Joe Hager, (11) Ed Trouth, (12) Phil Scurey, and (13) Leo Partner. The other men are hired labor or city public works employees. (Courtesy of Brian Eiteman.)

Iconic Architecture. The Perry Fire Station, which opened in the 1200 block of First Street in August 1905, is pictured here around 1934. The station was designed and built by members of the Perry Fire Department starting in 1904. The men worked on the structure during the warmer months. During the winter, they built the windows and doors by hand, and they installed them in the spring. The station was demolished in June 1980 to make way for a parking lot. (Courtesy of Brian Eiteman.)

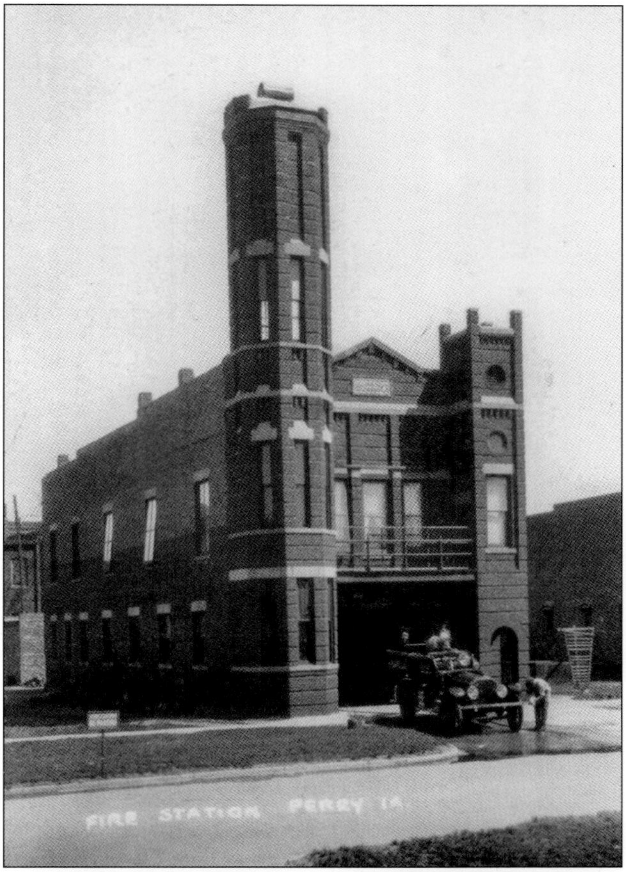

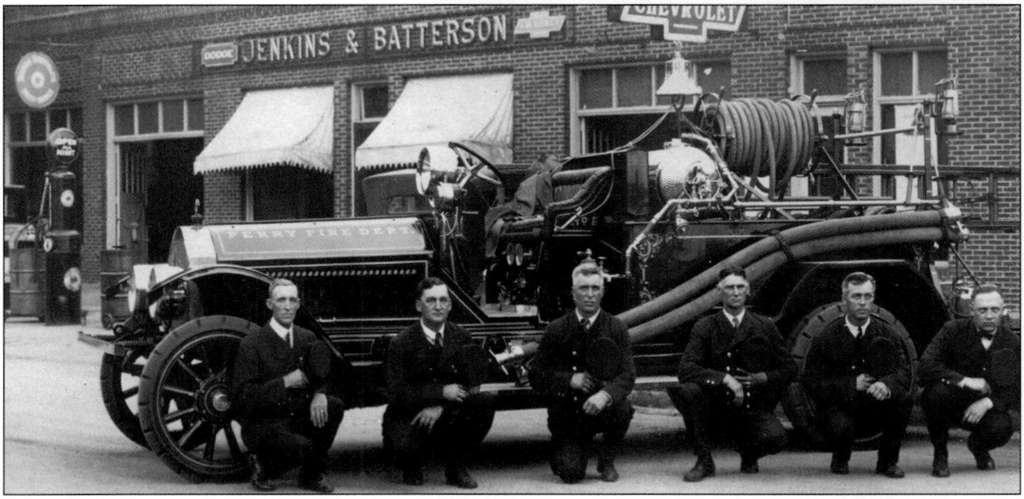

1920s Fire Truck. Perry Fire Department members pose in August 1925 by their 1923 American LaFrance Type 12 pumper, which cost $8,500 when it was delivered on February 28, 1923. This truck was in service until 1972. The firefighters are, from left to right, Chief T.R. "Pard" Phillips, Assistant Chief Harry Timeon, Assistant Chief Frank Reynolds, foreman of Hose 1 Willard Brewer, foreman of Hose 2 Chase Reynolds, and Adrian Brooks Cross (known as "Brooks"). (Courtesy of Brian Eiteman.)

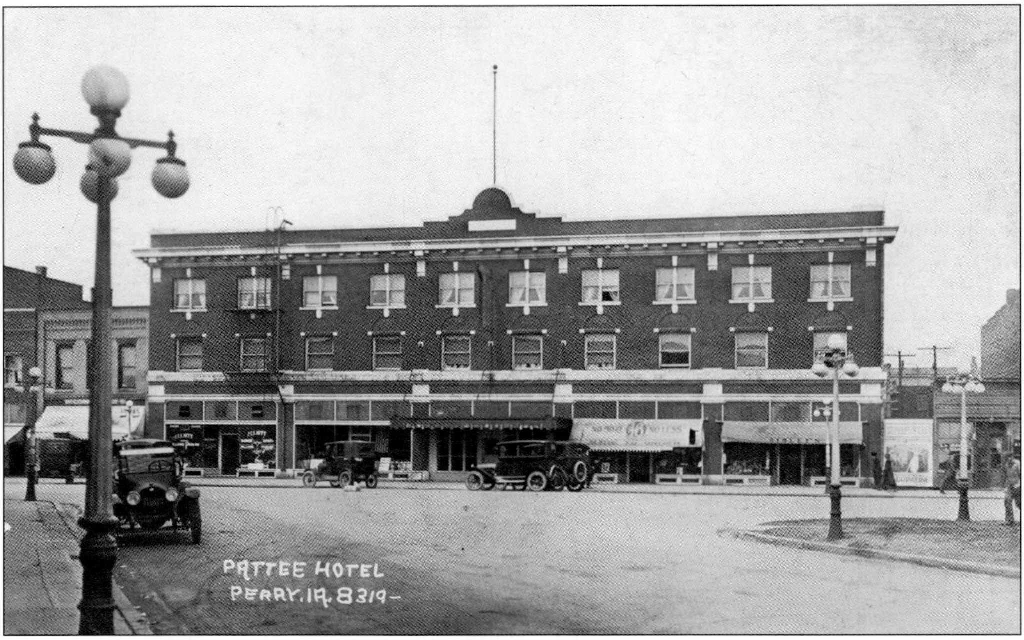

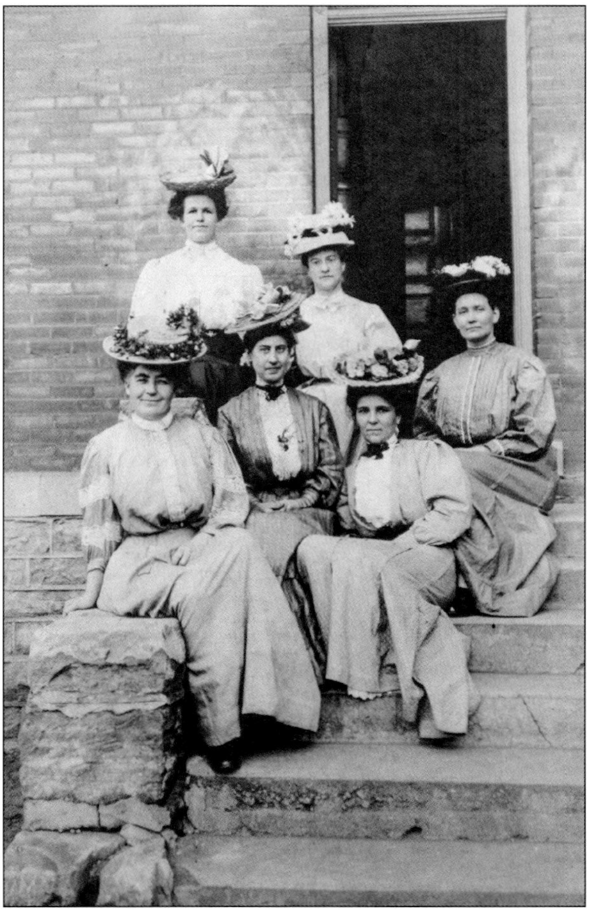

HOTEL PATTEE. The historic Hotel Pattee, which opened on Willis Avenue in 1913 and has been meticulously restored, invites guests to relax in a luxurious setting that celebrates small-town America. With 40 individually decorated and themed guest rooms and suites, a bowling alley, dining options, and more, the award-winning Hotel Pattee honors local history, the immigrant experience, and ethnic pride while paying tribute to noteworthy midwesterners from Perry and beyond. (Courtesy of Brian Eiteman.)

STYLISH LADIES. These women are likely teachers at the Washington School at Second and Pattee Streets in Perry in the early 1900s. From left to right are (first row) Julia Grady, Ethel Kent, and Edith Piatt; (second row) Kate Dana, Lillian Parmenter, and Emma Huffman. Local millinery shops in Dallas County provided the latest fashions in hats, complete with flowers, feathers, ribbons, and more. (Courtesy of Dallas County Conservation.)

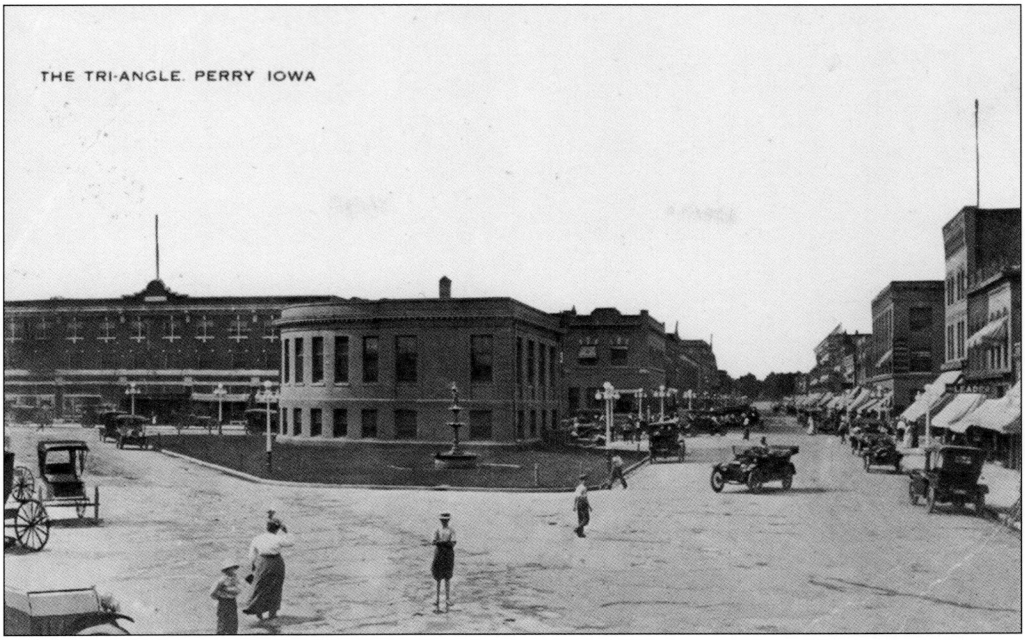

Carnegie Library on the Triangle. Perry's library was built in the downtown triangle area with a $10,000 grant from industrialist and philanthropist Andrew Carnegie. It opened in 1904 with 1,000 titles donated by the Perry community. Its first librarian was Flora Bailey, who served in this role until 1945. After the community built a new public library across the street in 1994, the Carnegie library reopened as the Carnegie Library Museum. (Courtesy of Brian Eiteman.)

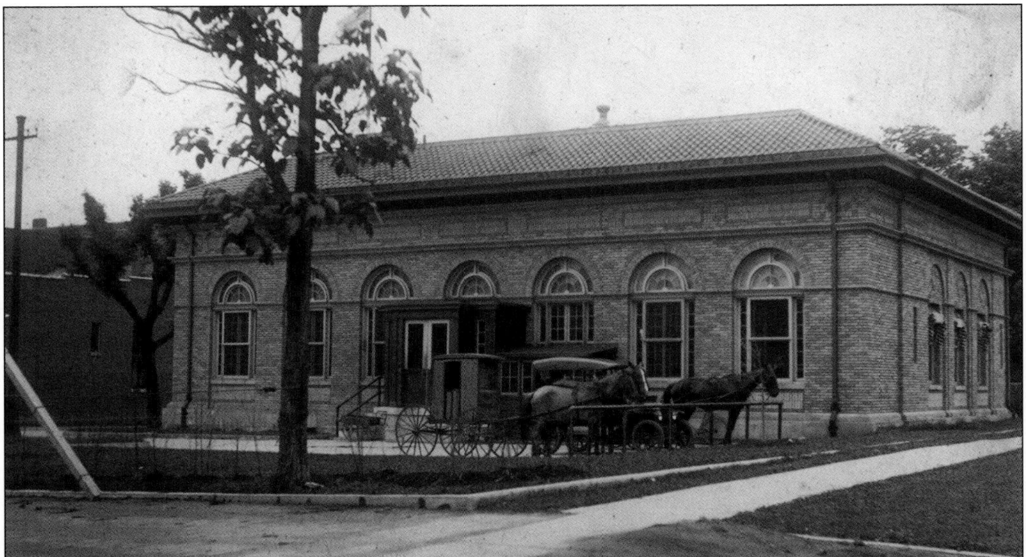

La Poste. When Perry's new post office on Warford Street opened February 15, 1915, three thousand people toured the building, which was constructed of Bedford stone, pressed brick, and tile roofing. The post office cost $63,000 to build, with another $5,000 spent on fixtures. Back then, the Perry Post Office mailed thousands of *Circus Heralds* from the Chief Printing Company that were sent across the United States to advertise various circuses. Today, the building houses La Poste, a social gathering place. (Courtesy of Brian Eiteman.)

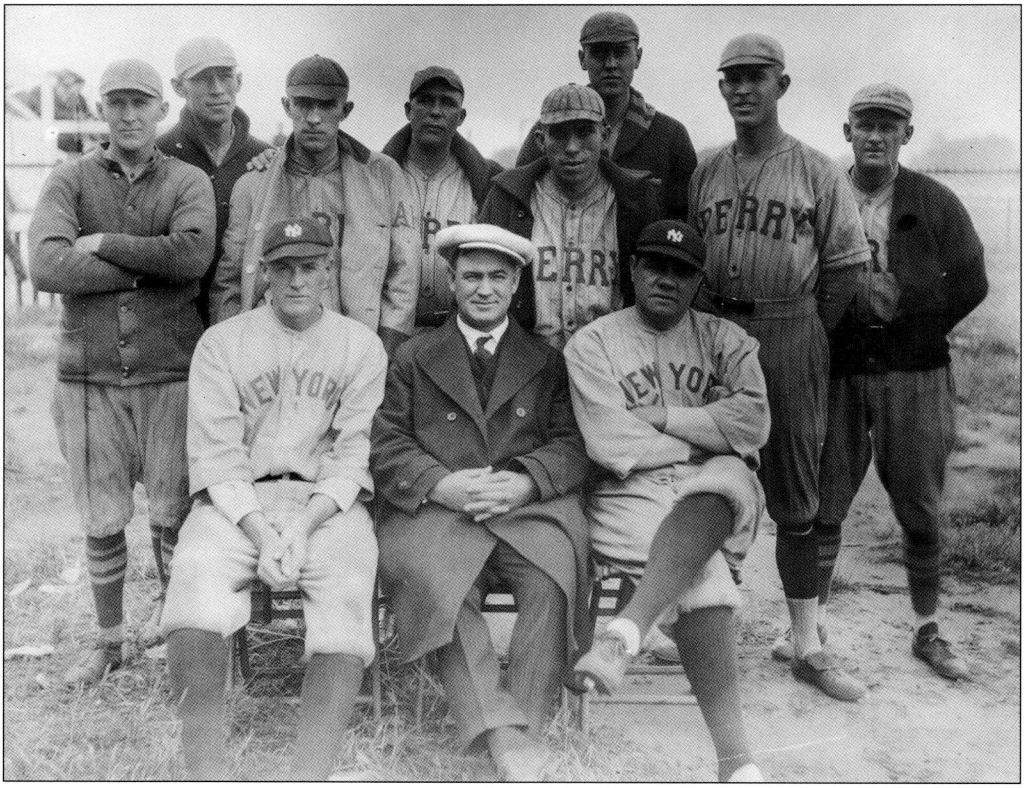

"SULTAN OF SWAT." Perry's American Legion invited New York Yankees stars Babe Ruth (front row, right) and Bob Meusel to Perry to play an exhibition baseball game on Friday, October 13, 1922. "Everyone in town who can get away is going," reported the local newspaper. Fans paid $1 general admission, $1.50 for reserved seats, and $2.50 for box seats to watch Ruth play for Perry and Meusel play for Pella. The baseball legends stayed at the Hotel Pattee. (Courtesy of Dallas County Conservation.)

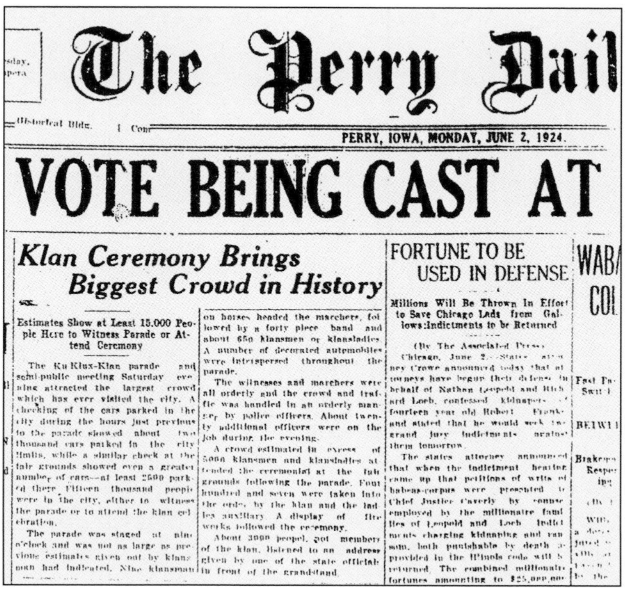

The Perry Dail

PERRY, IOWA, MONDAY, JUNE 2, 1924.

VOTE BEING CAST AT

Klan Ceremony Brings Biggest Crowd in History

Estimates Show at Least 15,000 People Here to Witness Parade or Attend Ceremony

The Ku Klux-Klan parade and semi-public meeting Saturday evening attracted the largest crowd which has ever visited the city. A checking of the cars parked in the city during the hours just previous to the parade showed about two thousand cars parked in the city limits, while a similar check at the fair grounds showed even a greater number of cars—at least 2500 parked there. Fifteen thousand people were in the city, either to witness the parade or to attend the klan celebration.

The parade was staged at nine o'clock and was not as large as previous estimates given out by klansman had indicated. Nine klansman on horses headed the marchers, followed by a forty piece band and about 650 klansmen or klansladies. A number of decorated automobiles were interspersed throughout the parade.

The witnesses and marchers were all orderly and the crowd and traffic was handled in an orderly manner by police officers. About twenty additional officers were on the job during the evening.

A crowd estimated in excess of 5000 klansmen and klansladies attended the ceremonial at the fair grounds following the parade. Four hundred and seven were taken into the order by the klan and the ladies auxiliary. A display of fire works followed the ceremony.

About 3000 peopel, not members of the klan, listened to an address given by one of the state officials in front of the grandstand.

FORTUNE TO BE USED IN DEFENSE

Millions Will Be Thrown In Effort to Save Chicago Lads from Gallows: Indictments to be Returned

(By The Associated Press)

Chicago, June 2.—States attorney Crowe announced today that attorneys have begun their defense in behalf of Nathan Leopold and Richard Loeb, confessed kidnapers of fourteen year old Robert Franks and stated that he would seek grand jury indictments against them tomorrow.

The states attorney announced that when the indictment hearing came up that petitions of writs of habeas-corpus were presented to Chief Justice Caverly by counsel employed by the millionaire families of Leopold and Loeb. Indictments charging kidnaping and ransom, both punishable by death as provided in the Illinois code will be returned. The combined millionaire fortunes amounting to $25,000,000

WAB
COL

KKK CEREMONY BRINGS "BIGGEST CROWD IN HISTORY." The KKK's nationwide revival in the mid-1920s extended to small-town Iowa. In Perry, almost 15,000 people (nearly triple the town's population) witnessed a KKK parade and semi-public meeting on May 31, 1924. The evening rally "attracted the largest crowd which has ever visited the city," reported the local newspaper. In 1925, KKK members in robes and hoods were among the 1,500 mourners who attended a funeral in Perry for Walter Schell, a grand wizard of the KKK. (Courtesy of Larry Vodenik.)

Shall We Dance? She was like nothing Perry had ever seen. With Tahitian headdresses, acrobatics, and props from Chicago, Betty Mae Harris fascinated locals when she moved to Perry with her husband. On October 14, 1927, the former Ziegfeld Follies showgirl from New York opened a dance studio that would impact an entire generation. Harris taught tap, ballet, and more and even made eight trips to Hawaii to perfect her Polynesian dance. She also taught dance at conventions throughout America. (Courtesy of Hotel Pattee.)

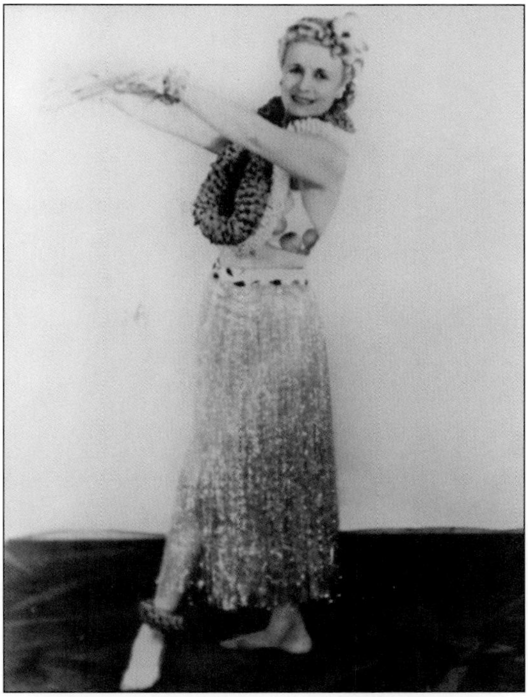

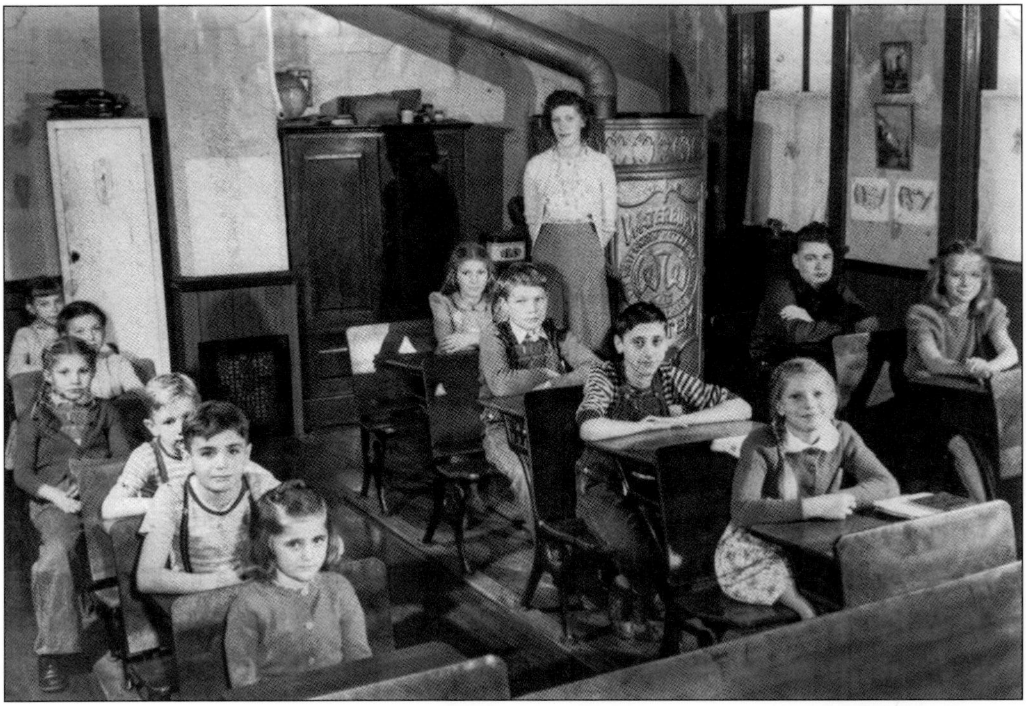

Alton Country School. The Alton country school near Perry served the community from 1867 to 1961. This photograph shows teacher Edna Diddy and her class around 1947–1950. When the school closed, there were only six students registered for classes. In July 1964, the schoolhouse was moved to Forest Park Museum in Perry, where it remains a popular attraction. (Courtesy of Dallas County Conservation.)

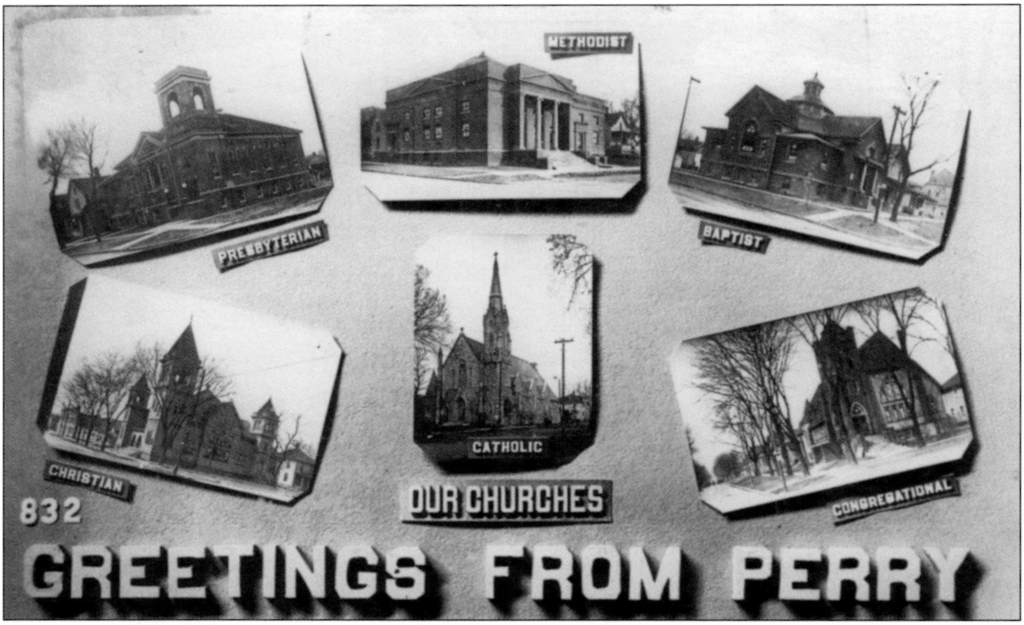

KEEPING THE FAITH. Church congregations were meeting in the Perry area before the city was officially incorporated. At one time, there were more than 16 congregations (including African American congregations) in Perry, whose population varied between 5,000 and 7,000 people. This early-20th-century postcard shows the Presbyterian, Methodist, Baptist, Christian, Catholic, and Congregational churches. Early pastors were often circuit riders who served many congregations. (Author's collection.)

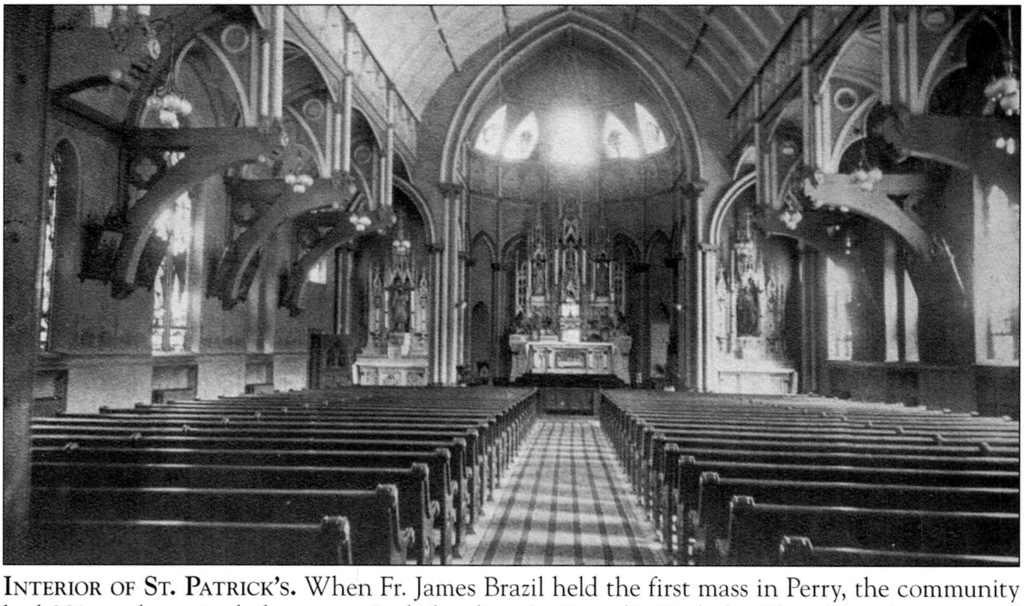

INTERIOR OF ST. PATRICK'S. When Fr. James Brazil held the first mass in Perry, the community had 301 residents, including some Irish families. St. Patrick's Catholic Church, at the corner of Third and Lucinda Streets, was built in 1902 for $25,000. The impressive limestone church, which was the third St. Patrick's Church to be built, still serves the community. Although there have been some remodeling projects through the years, the interior looks much the same as it has for generations. (Courtesy of St. Patrick's.)

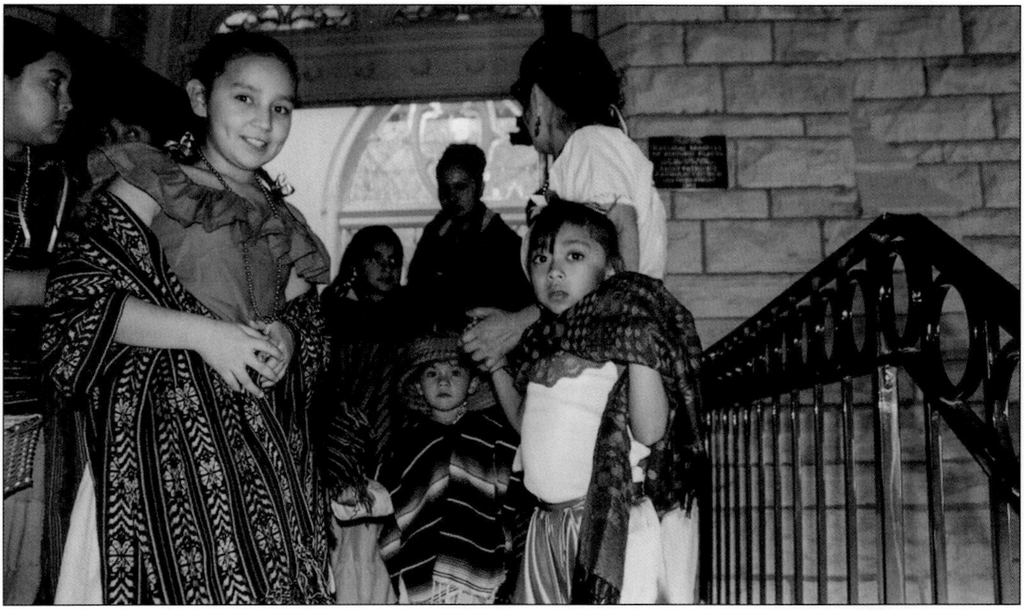

LAS POSADAS. The religious festival of Las Posadas commemorates Joseph and Mary's journey from Nazareth to Bethlehem in search of a safe refuge where Mary could give birth to the baby Jesus. This Hispanic tradition has become a community event in Perry, which has a sizeable Hispanic population, in part due to jobs at the local meatpacking plant. St. Patrick's Catholic Church offers masses in Spanish, and nearly half the students in local schools identify as Hispanic. (Courtesy of St. Patrick's.)

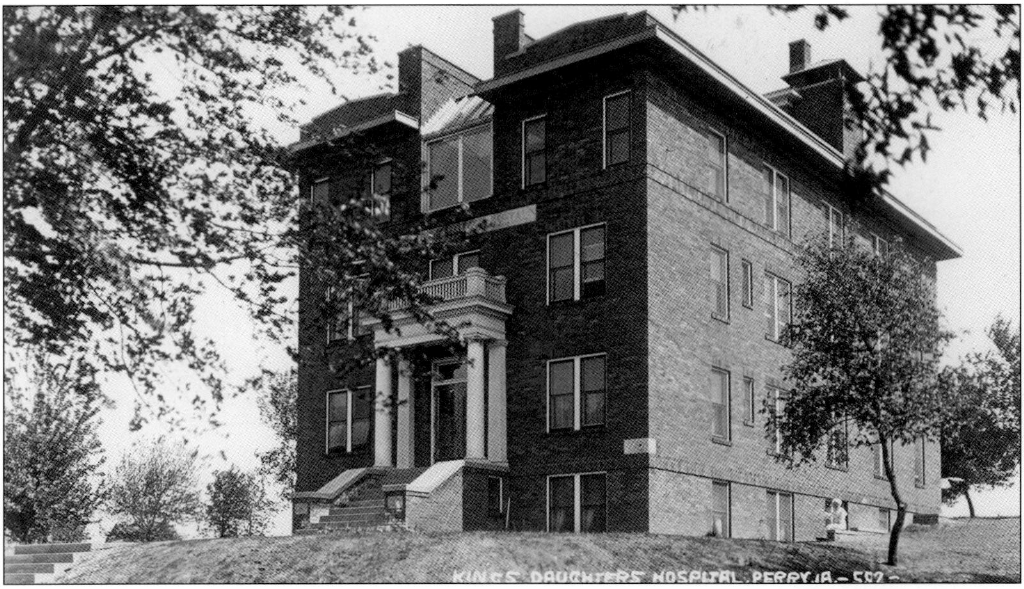

KING'S DAUGHTERS HOSPITAL. Built in 1914, this hospital served the community until the Dallas County Hospital was built in 1956. Perhaps the most famous patient at King's Daughters Hospital was Marvin "Buck" Barrow, Clyde Barrow's older brother, who was shot multiple times during a gunfight with law enforcement at Dexfield Park in southern Dallas County on July 24, 1933. Barrow, 30, died from his wounds five days later, on July 29. The old hospital was demolished in 1978. (Courtesy of Dexter Museum.)

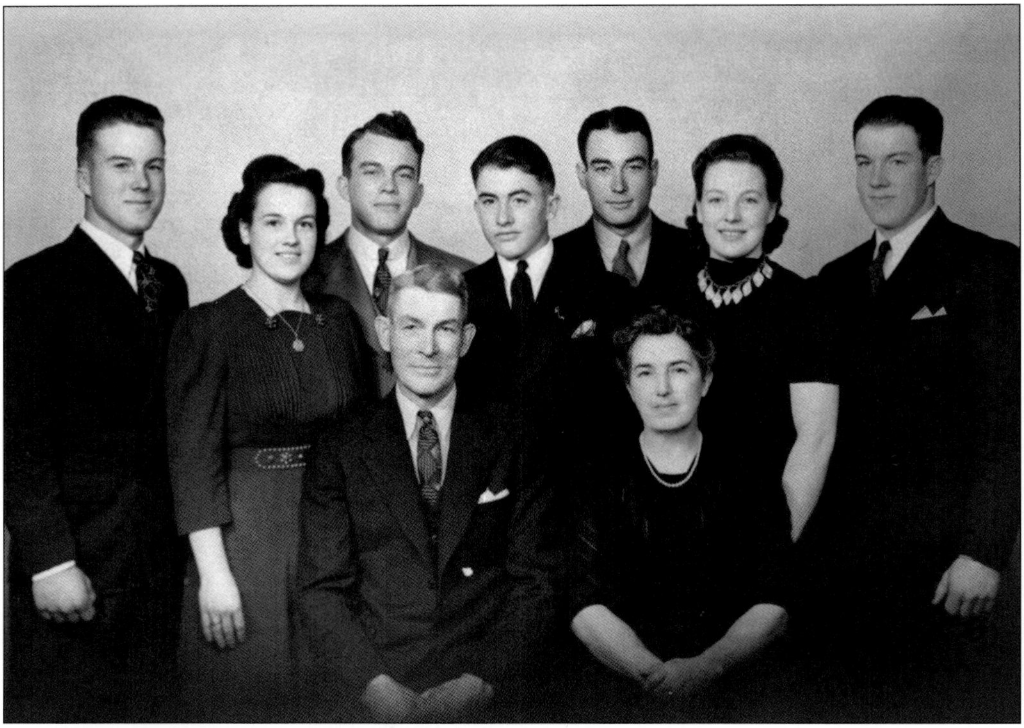

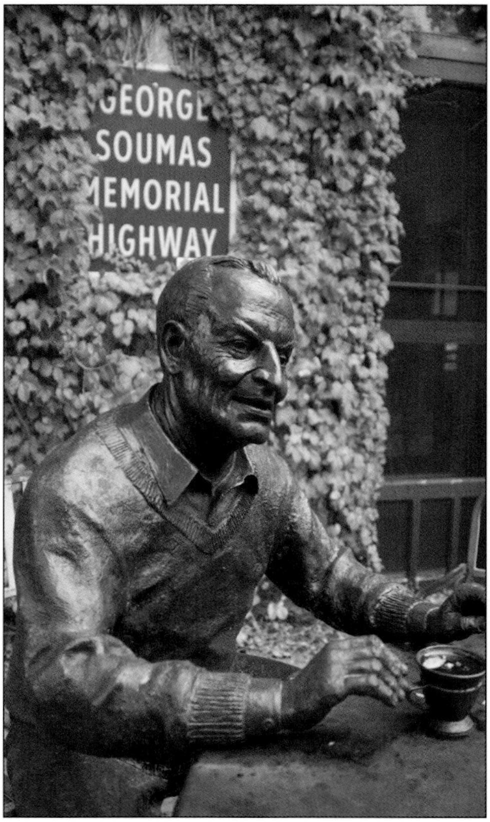

Wilson Family's Sacrifice. Taken in Perry in November 1941, this is the last photograph of Claiborne "Clabe" and Leora Wilson's family. The children include, from left to right in the back row, Daniel "Danny," Darlene Wilson Scar, Donald, "C. Junior," Delbert, Doris, and Dale. Dale, Danny, and C. Junior all died while serving in World War II in the US Army Air Forces. Dale's body was never found, Danny was buried in France, and C. Junior was buried in Perry. (Courtesy of Joy Neal Kidney.)

George Soumas, War Hero. The son of Greek immigrants, George Soumas (1915–1994) was a World War II hero, attorney, and two-time mayor of Perry whose statue graces Soumas Court in Perry and whose story is recounted in the 1969 film *The Bridge at Remagen.* He was serving with the 14th Tank Battalion, 9th Armored Division, on March 7, 1945, when US troops took the Remagen Bridge across the Rhine River, allowing Allied forces to enter Germany. Soumas received the Distinguished Service Cross for extraordinary heroism. In 2013, Highway 141 between Granger and Perry was renamed the George P. Soumas Memorial Highway. (Author's collection.)

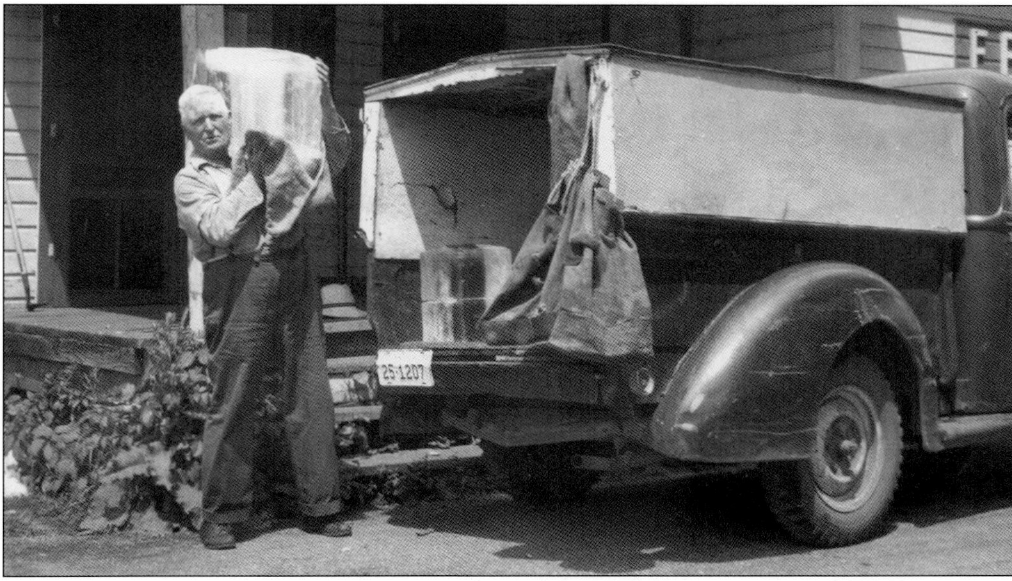

Ice Delivery. Harvesting ice from local rivers was a big business in Dallas County from the 1800s into the early 1900s. Frank Reynolds, shown here in front of the icehouse near the interurban railway depot near Pattee Park, owned and operated the F.E. Reynolds Ice Co. from the 1930s until 1955. Reynolds is preparing to deliver a 100-pound block of ice. He passed away in 1957. (Courtesy of Brian Eiteman.)

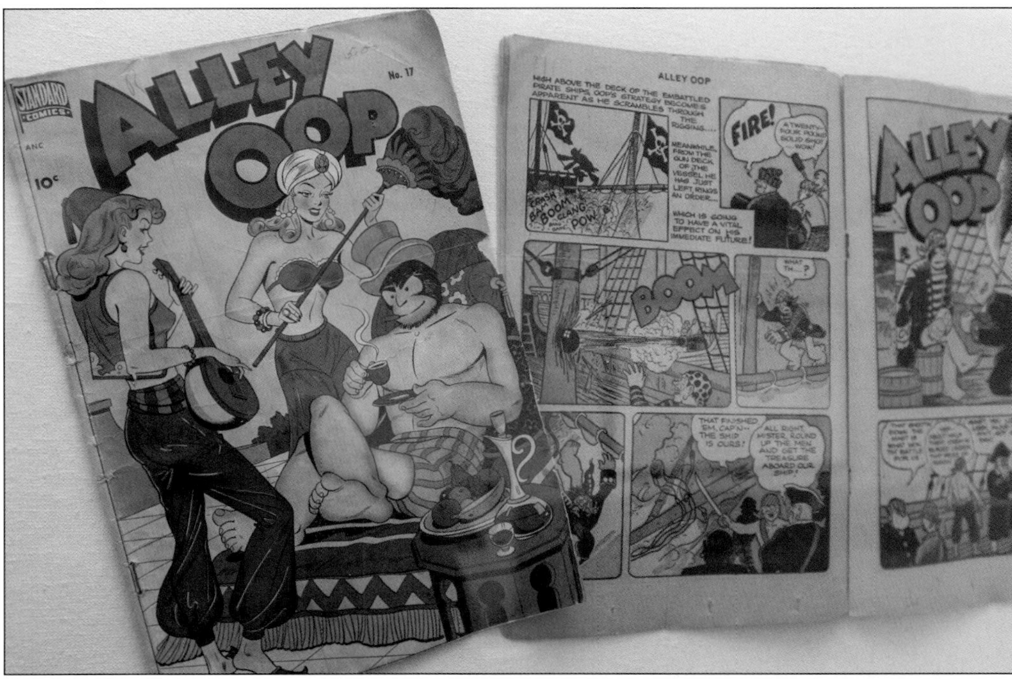

Alley Oop. On August 7, 1933, a caveman named Alley Oop first appeared in America's newspaper comics thanks to Perry native Vincent "Snick" Hamlin. Hamlin (1900–1993), who had once been thrown out of art class, illustrated letters for himself and World War I buddies before becoming a newspaperman in Des Moines and later Texas. Hamlin's Alley Oop and pet dinosaur, Dinny, were always getting into trouble in the prehistoric Land of Moo. (Courtesy of Hotel Pattee.)

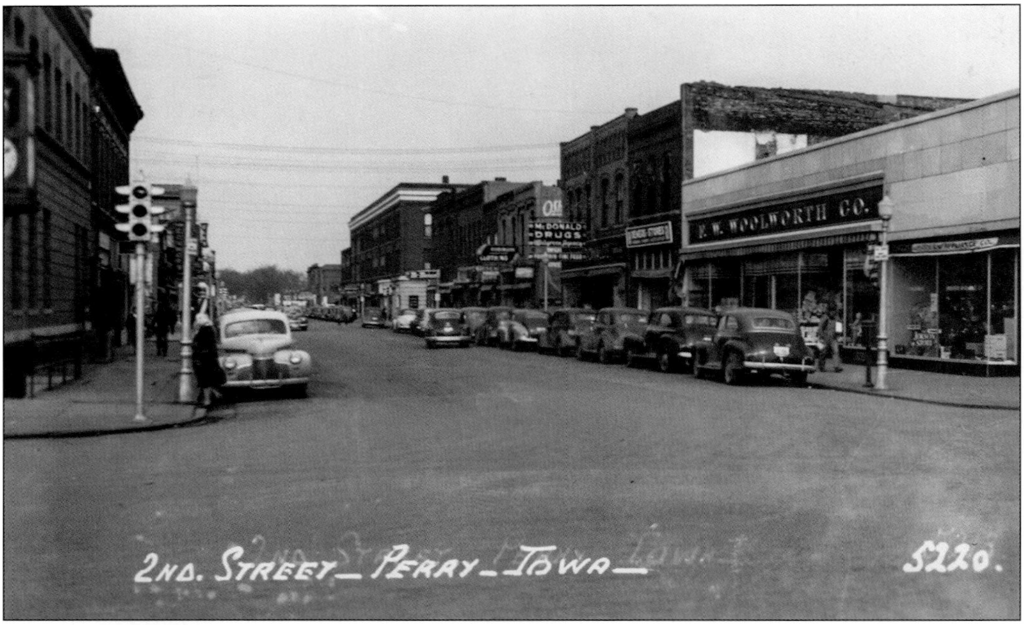

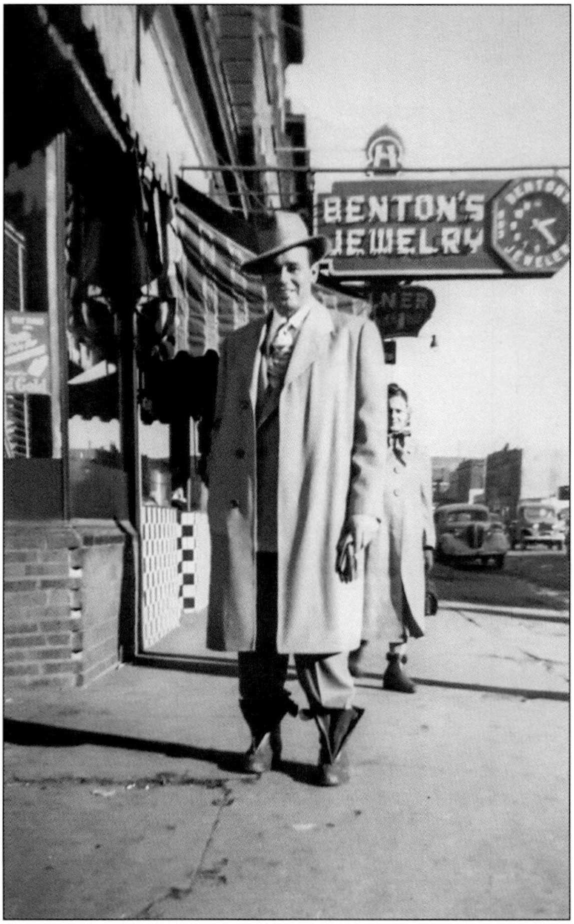

DOWNTOWN PERRY. This view from Second Street shows how downtown Perry boasted a thriving business district by the mid-20th century. The F.W. Woolworth store on the right was part of a nationwide chain that revolutionized retail shopping. In some ways, Woolworth's was the Walmart of its day. Woolworth pioneered the five-and-dime store phenomenon, where customers could select from a wide variety of inexpensive items from towels to toys. (Courtesy of Brian Eiteman.)

PERRY'S GANGSTER MASTERMIND. Tommy Young grew up in the rugged, impoverished Dallas County coal camps near Moran. He is notorious for making the FBI's Ten Most Wanted list during a crime spree in 1951–1952. He spent 10 years as a prisoner on Alcatraz Island in San Francisco Bay. Young was one of the last 27 prisoners to walk out of the infamous prison when it closed in 1963. (Courtesy of the Young family.)

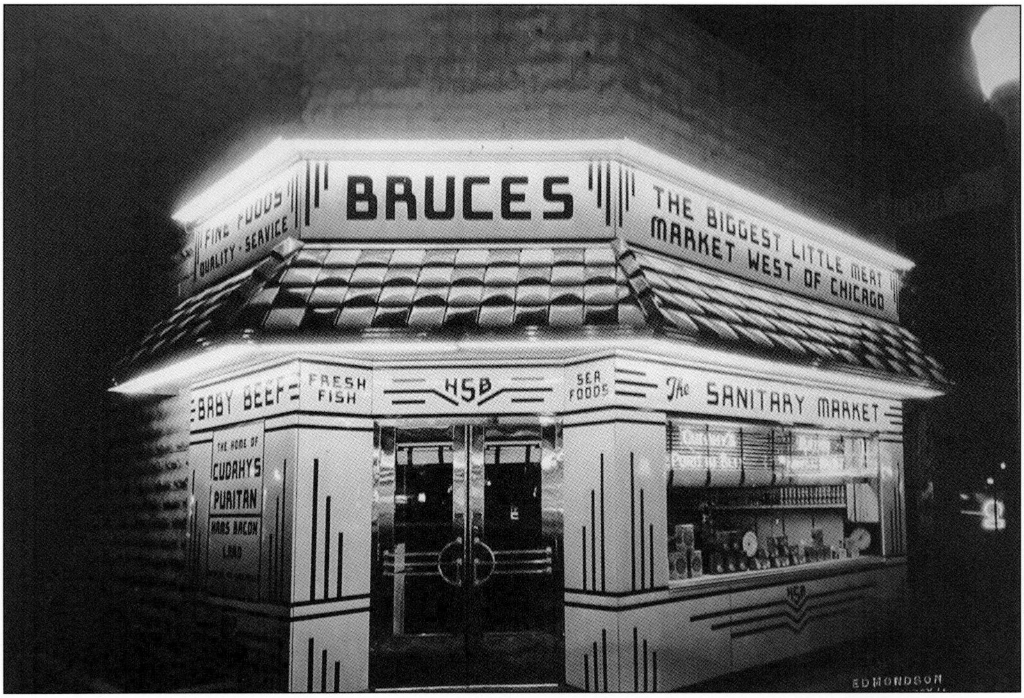

SANITARY MEAT MARKET. Jack Bruce Market/Sanitary Meat Market/Stoner's Market was open continually for business from 1905 through 1999. This specialty store was located on the northwest corner of Second and Lucinda Streets. Harry Bruce was well known for his generosity during the Great Depression. He would offer food to anyone who would sweep the sidewalk in front of the store, no matter how many times a day it had been swept. (Courtesy of Larry Vodenik.)

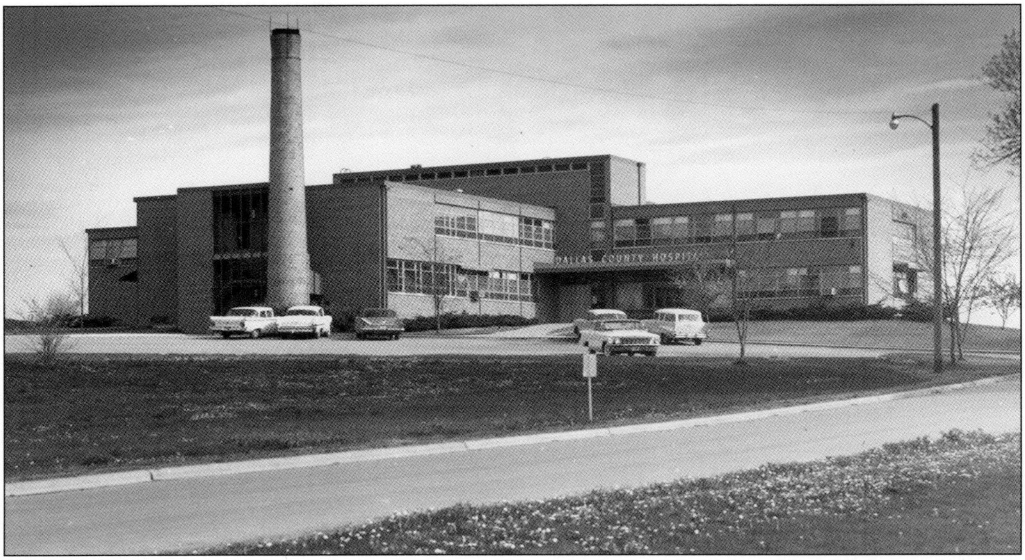

DALLAS COUNTY HOSPITAL. The Dallas County Hospital, which replaced the King's Daughters Hospital, was dedicated in 1956. Today, the 25-bed critical access hospital serves Dallas, Greene, Guthrie, and Boone Counties. The health-care team provides specialized services such as radiology, mammography, chemotherapy, surgery, lab services, and therapy close to home. (Courtesy of Brian Eiteman.)

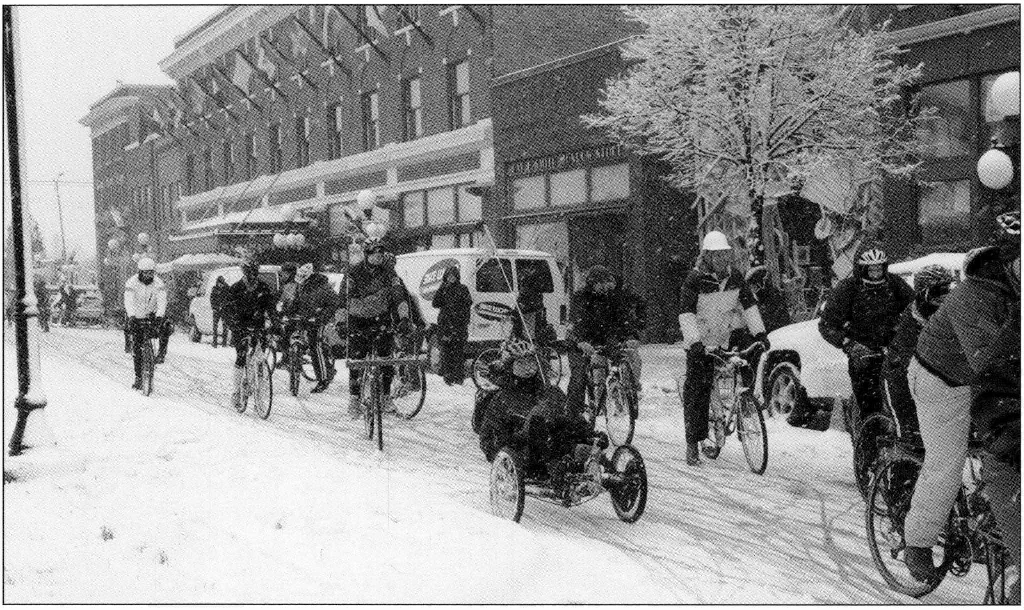

BRR. Perry is home to one of the most unique bicycle rides in the country. Held in February (when the average temperature barely rises above freezing), the Bike Ride to Rippey (BRR) is a 24-mile round-trip ride from Perry to Rippey and back. The ride continues no matter what, even if there is a foot of snow. Founded in 1977, BRR has attracted more than 3,000 riders annually from Iowa and beyond. (Courtesy of Perry Chamber of Commerce.)

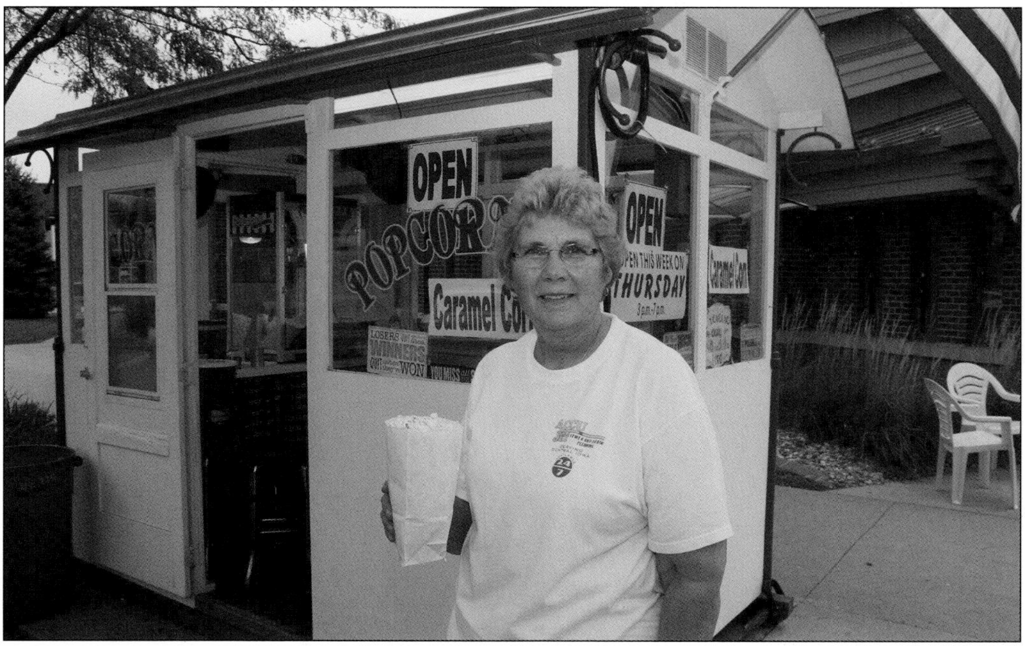

Perry Preserves Classic Popcorn Stand. From spring through the fall, Rhonda Olson carries on a popular Perry tradition each Thursday from 3:00 to 7:00 p.m. She runs a popcorn stand modeled after the one Celeste Council, Perry's "Popcorn Lady," ran for 49 years at the corner of Second Street and Willis Avenue. Olson sells the Tom Thumb Popcorn her family has grown since 1904. (Author's collection.)

Seven

Waukee
The Key to Good Living

Once a sleepy, rural town in southeast Dallas County, Waukee has transformed into a booming suburban community on the western edge of the expanding Des Moines metro area.

While Waukee's founders hoped it would become a bustling town, it is likely even they would be surprised by its transformation. Waukee has become the fastest-growing city in Iowa and is home to one of the fastest-growing school districts in the state.

Waukee traces its roots to 1869, when Gen. Lewis Addison Grant and Maj. William Ragan purchased land around the Des Moines Valley Railroad bed in Walnut Township. The Des Moines Valley Railroad was completed in June 1869, and Waukee was incorporated in 1878. The community soon had 245 residents.

The iconic Triangle Park in the heart of downtown Waukee was formed by the Des Moines Valley Railroad, which was constructed at an angle. The town grew around this hub of the community. Today, the triangle hosts many community events throughout the year.

Agriculture drove the economy in Walnut Township and towns like Waukee for decades. Coal mining also became part of the local economy by the 1920s, starting with the Harris Mine (1920–1928). The Shuler Coal Mine, opened in 1921, employed 500 men and created a whole mining community that impacted a generation of Waukee residents until the mine closed in 1949.

This history is honored throughout Waukee, from Alice's Road (named after restaurant owner Alice Nizzi, one of the most well-known and widely respected community leaders from the coal mining era) to Shuler Elementary. Opened in 2010, the school is named in honor of the Shuler Coal Company.

Waukee embraces its motto, "The Key to Good Living." While Waukee had 500 or fewer residents throughout the first half of the 20th century, the population more than doubled from 687 in 1960 to 1,577 in 1970, according to US Census data. The population hovered in the 2,200–2,500 range throughout much of the 1980s and 1990s, but Waukee boasted 5,126 residents by 2000. Within 10 years, this soared to 13,790. The community will soon have 20,000 residents and continues to grow.

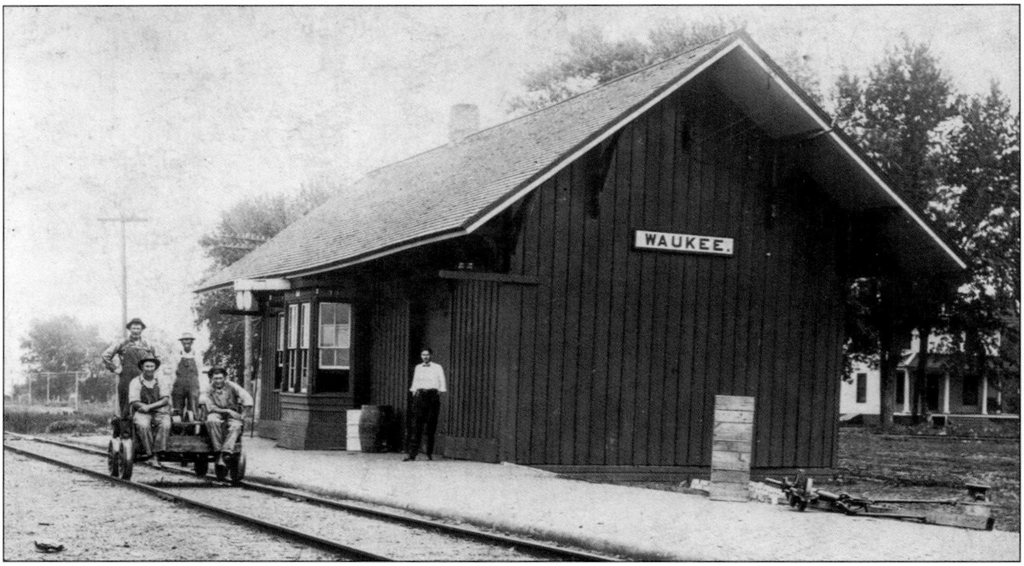

WAUKEE DEPOT. In 1869, the Des Moines Valley Railroad moved west through Walnut Township into the area that would become Waukee. Gen. L.A. Grant and Maj. William Ragan bought land around the railroad bed, and 320 acres were laid out in lots for homes and businesses. When the railroad tracks and depot were completed, farmers could ship their products by rail to Des Moines. (Courtesy of Waukee Area Historical Society.)

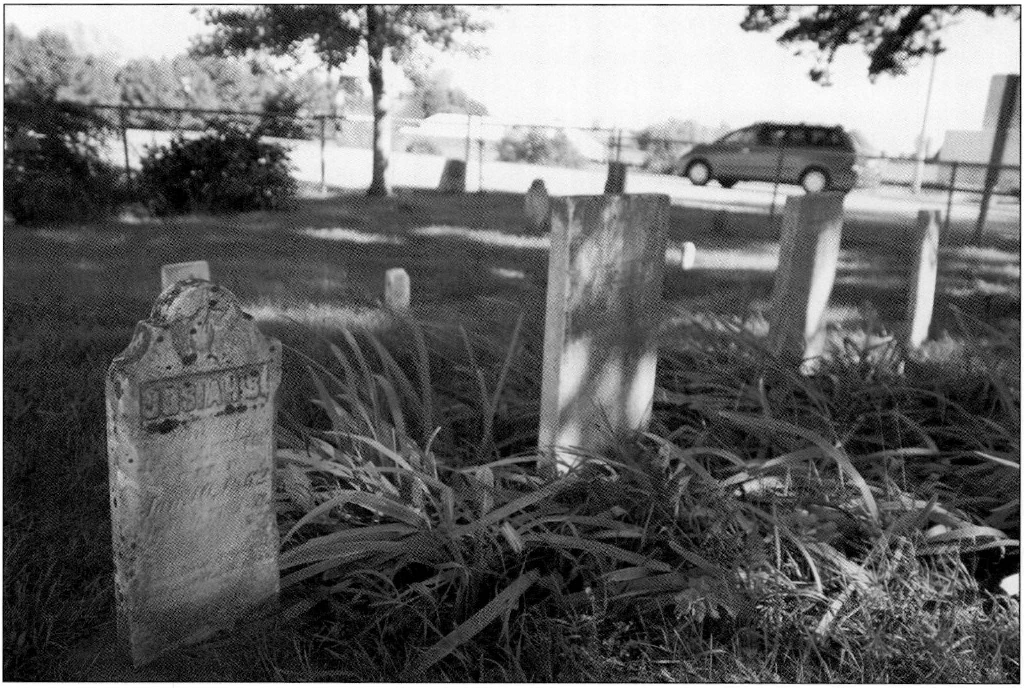

PIONEER CEMETERY. Pioneers began moving into southeast Dallas County long before Waukee was founded. While the Huston Family Cemetery was once located in the country between Waukee and West Des Moines, it has become a roundabout in the middle of a busy intersection. The Huston family settled in Iowa in 1849. The pioneer cemetery has approximately 20 graves, with some markers dating to the 1850s and 1860s. (Author's collection.)

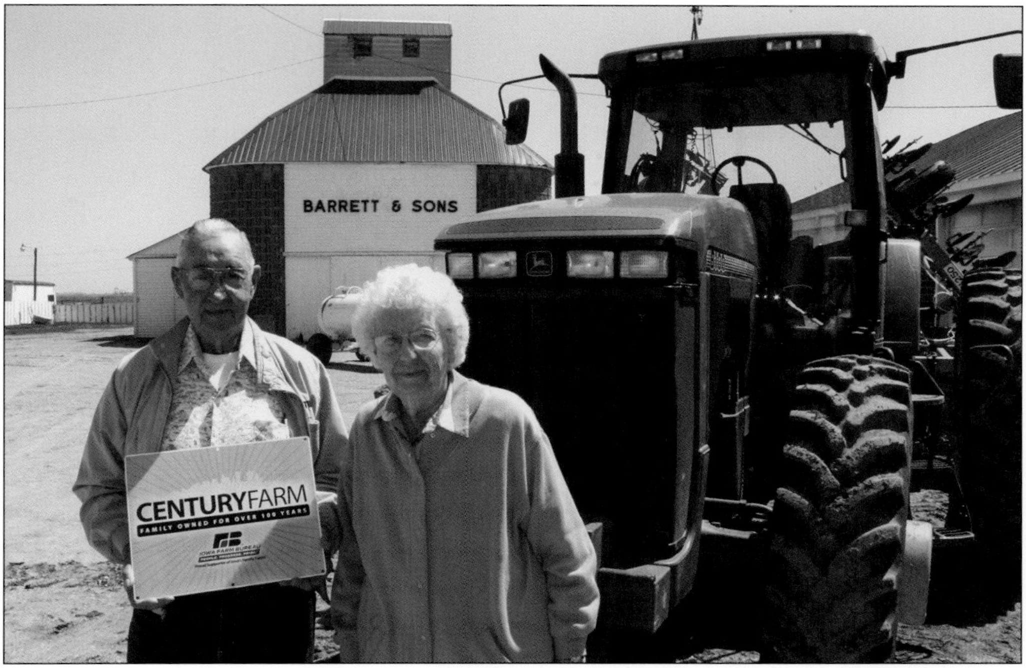

Barrett Century Farm. Harold Barrett's parents paid $7,900 for 160 acres of Dallas County farmland in 1901. Barrett and his wife, Lilla, are shown here in 2008 with their Century Farm award. George W. Bush visited the Barrett farm twice, first when he was campaigning for president in 1999 and again in 2001. Barrett, a 1938 Waukee High School graduate, recalled when a gravel road connected Waukee to Des Moines. (Author's collection.)

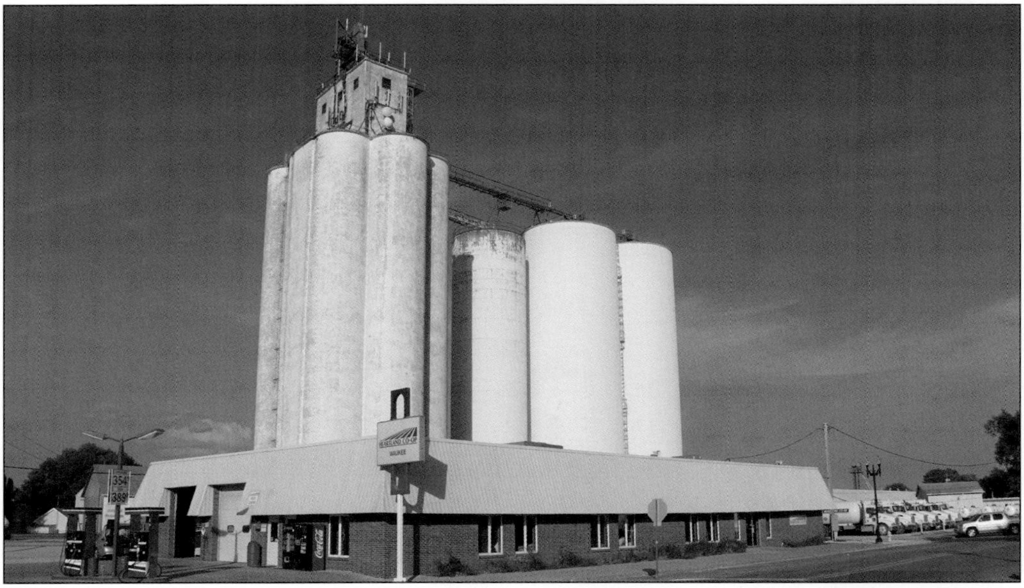

Farmers Cooperative. In 1956, Farmers Cooperative Elevator Company stockholders approved the construction of a new 165-foot-tall concrete elevator near the downtown triangle in Waukee for nearly $200,000. The co-op was sold to Heartland Co-Op in 2000 and continues to offer a place for local farmers to market their grain and purchase agricultural supplies. At Christmas, one bright, decorative star lights up the top of the elevator. (Courtesy of Waukee Area Historical Society.)

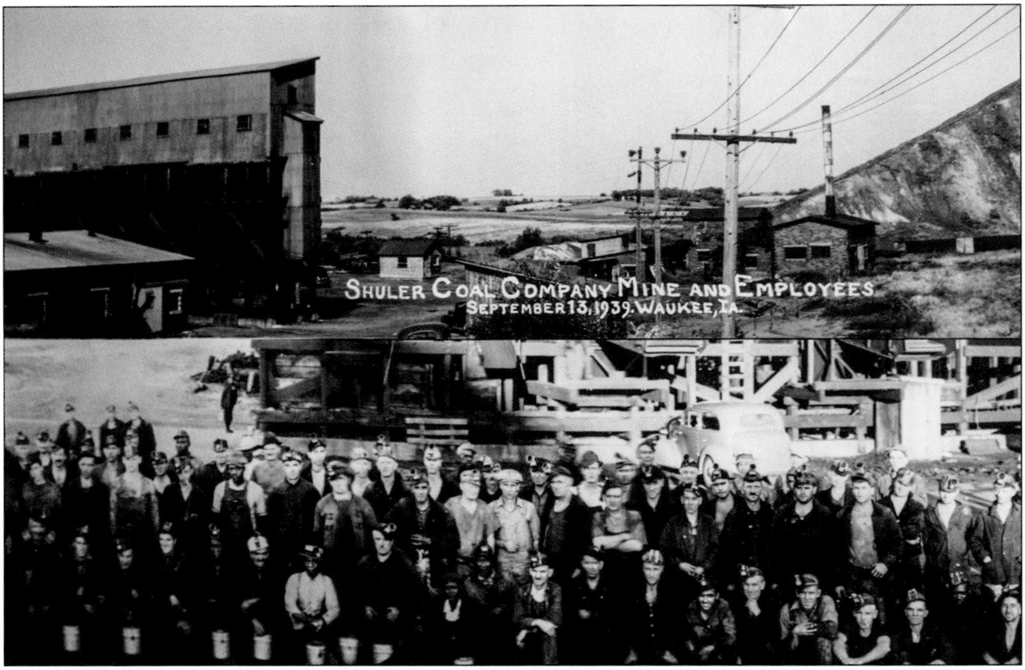

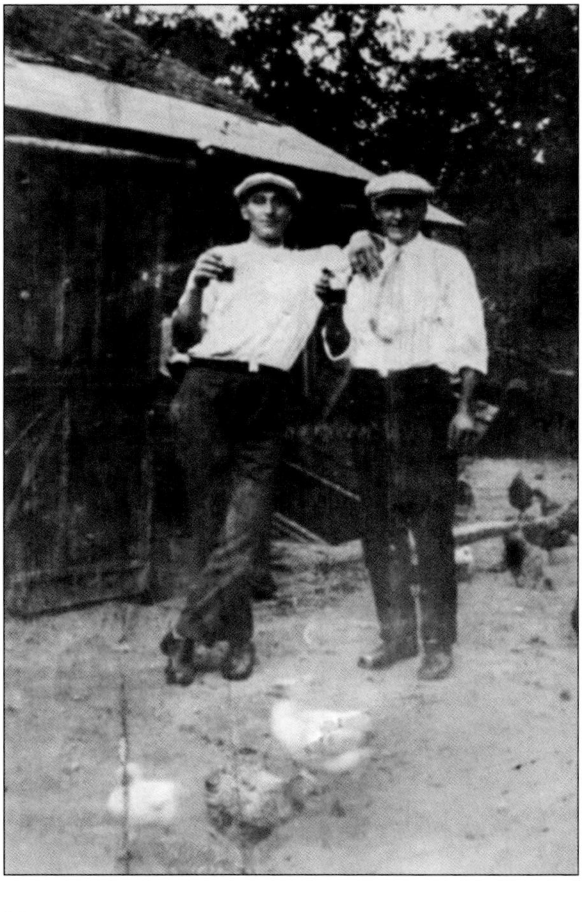

COAL MINING. While agriculture and the railroad drove Waukee's early growth, coal mining spurred economic development starting in the 1920s. The Shuler Mine, shown here in September 1939, provided jobs in the winter for many immigrants from Italy and Central Europe. The Shuler Mine, which operated from 1921 to 1949, had an open mine that reached 387 feet underground. Coal veins extended as far as three miles in all directions. (Courtesy of Waukee Public Library.)

FLAVORS OF THE IMMIGRANT EXPERIENCE. Terzo Fiori (left) and Pete Nizzi enjoy tasting their homemade wine. Excitement spread through Waukee's mining camps when grapes were imported from California and shipped by train in two boxcars so families could make their yearly supply of red wine. Grape distribution was a day of celebration for children. Treats like figs and yams arrived with the grapes and were thrown from the boxcars, much as candy is thrown during parades today. (Courtesy of Waukee Area Historical Society.)

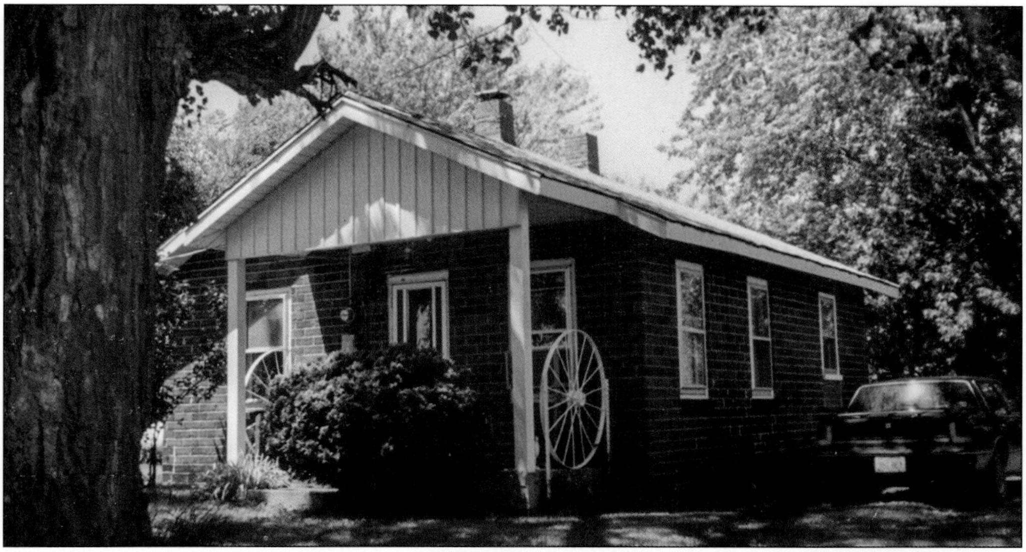

Coal Mining Homes. The small houses in Waukee's close-knit coal camps had no frills, no indoor plumbing, and no carpet. Water obtained from the neighborhood well was heated on a kerosene stove for cleaning and bathing. Outhouses were in the backyards. In cold weather, big coal stoves heated these uninsulated homes. The stoves would typically burn one to one and a half tons of coal per year. (Courtesy of Waukee Area Historical Society.)

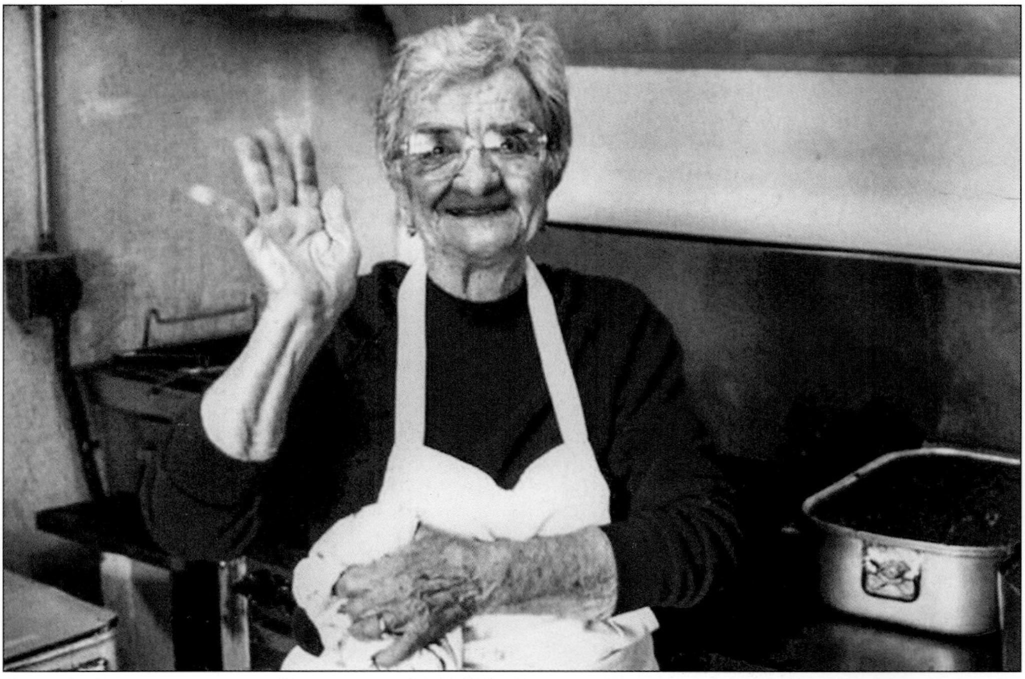

Alice's Spaghettiland. Starting in 1947, Waukee was home to Alice's Spaghettiland, run by Alice Nizzi (1905–1997) in the Shuler mining community just north of Hickman Road. The restaurant's waitresses were required to wear white, starched uniforms. While Alice's closed in 2004, the Waukee Area Historical Society hosted a fundraising dinner in the spring of 2014 featuring Alice's spaghetti and Italian salad. Hundreds of people now attend this annual event. (Courtesy of Waukee Area Historical Society.)

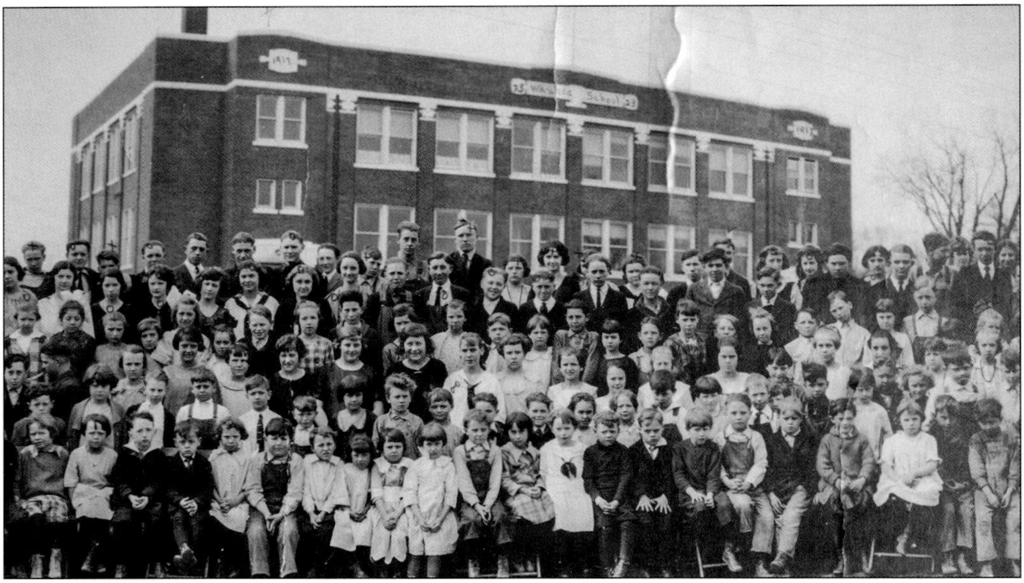

Waukee School in 1920s. The new Waukee School District was created in 1917, and all the one-room schoolhouses in his district were replaced by this new, three-story brick building that opened in January 1918. The first floor included a multipurpose room with a gym and stage for plays. While the school closed in 2010, the building reopened to house the Vince Meyer Learning Center. Some say the structure is haunted. (Courtesy of Waukee Public Library.)

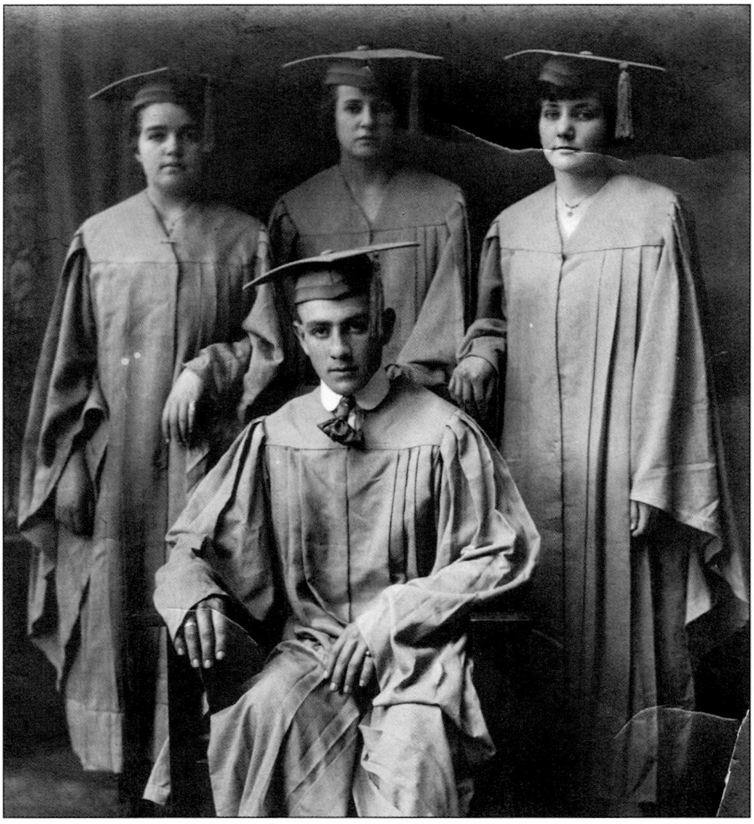

Waukee's First High School Graduates. In 1918, Waukee High School's first graduating class included Hazel Holroy Snyder, Cecile Jones Felt, Sadie Staver Black, and Clint Blake. Classes stayed small for years. In 1938, local farmer Harold Barrett graduated with a class of 26. Things changed dramatically starting in the 1990s, however, as Waukee's population boomed. At the end of the 2015–2016 school year, 549 seniors graduated from Waukee High School. (Courtesy of Waukee Public Library.)

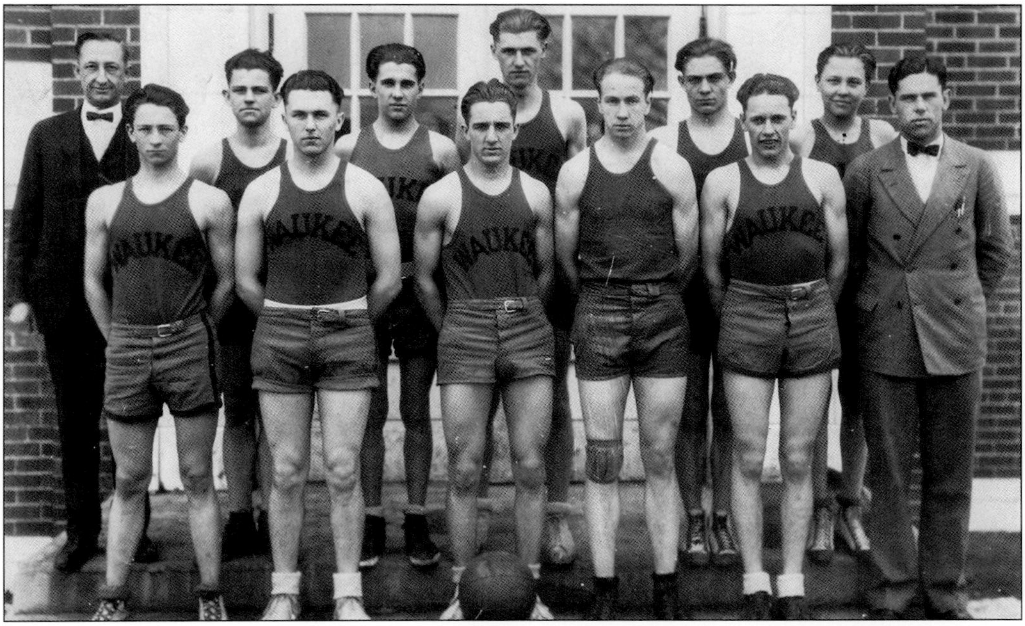

BOYS' BASKETBALL, 1926. Shown in this Waukee High School basketball team photograph on February 22, 1926, are, from left to right, (first row) Frank Howe, George Williams, Danny Boone, Mike Shannan, Ralph Adrich, and Mr. Chrichet; (second row) Superintendent Smiley, Burton Huston, Albert Dallam (who would die in 1927, possibly from a spinal cord abscess), Virgil Highland, Jimmy ?, and Edolen Reynolds. (Courtesy of Adel Historical Museum.)

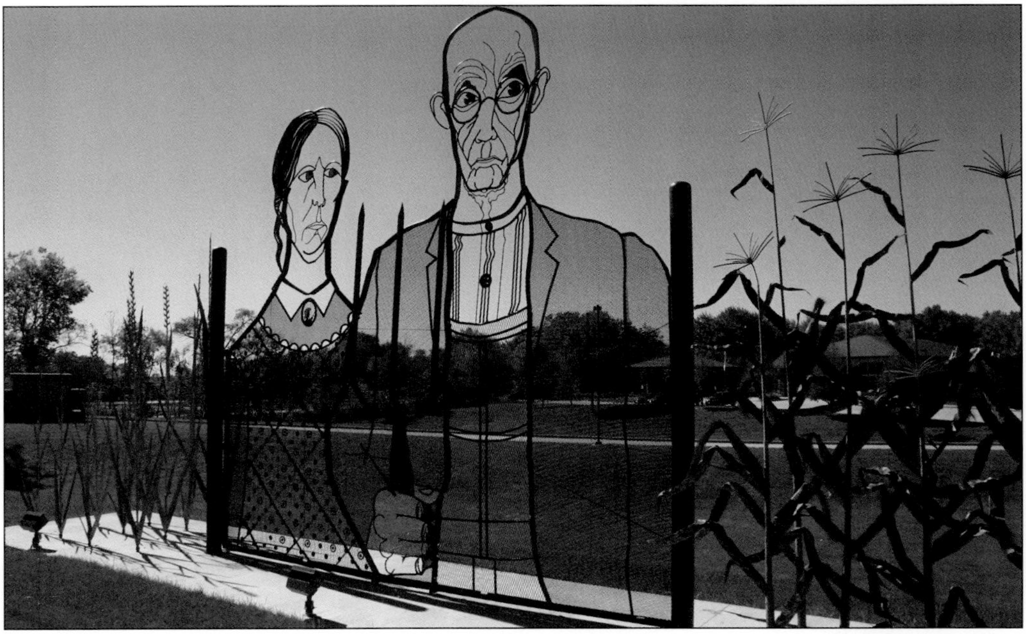

AMERICAN *GOTHIC* INSPIRATION IN WAUKEE. This larger-than-life sculpture accents the Waukee Public Library, across from Waukee Middle School. The metal artwork includes a central section inspired by Grant Wood's iconic 1930 painting *American Gothic*, flanked by prairie grass and cornstalks. Created by John Brommel in 2003 for business executive William Krause, the sculpture was donated to the City of Waukee and was installed in October 2015. (Author's collection.)

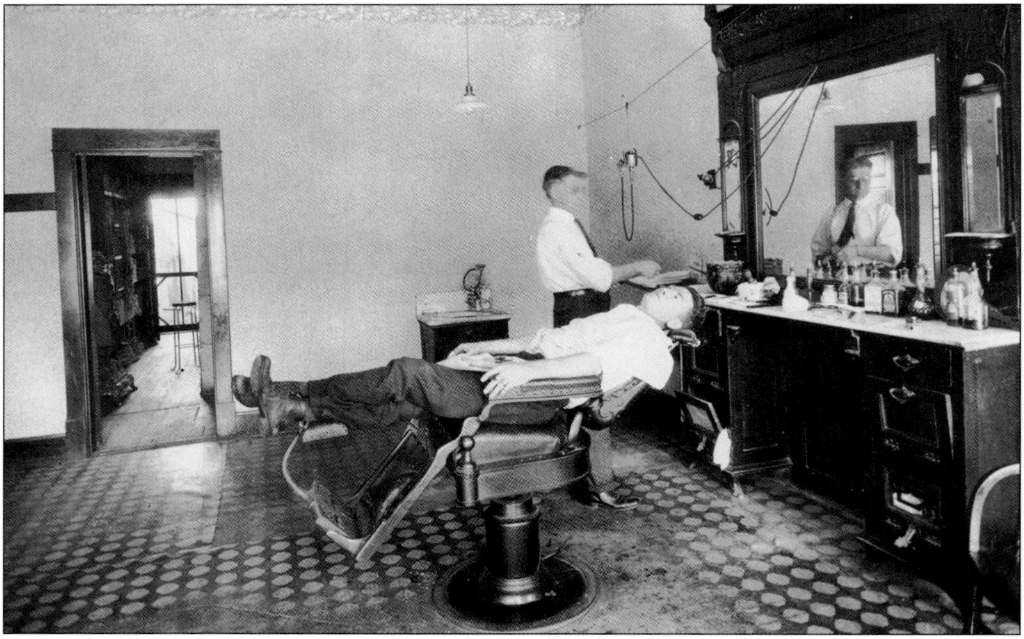

Haircut and a Shave. This 1915 photograph from Waukee shows barber Riley Hughie shaving Hap Williams. This state-of-the-art hydraulic barber chair allowed the back to be dropped easily. The chair, along with the ornate back bar shown in the photograph, are displayed in Jerry's Barber Shop on Sixth Street in Waukee and have been in that building since 1930. (Courtesy of Waukee Area Historical Society.)

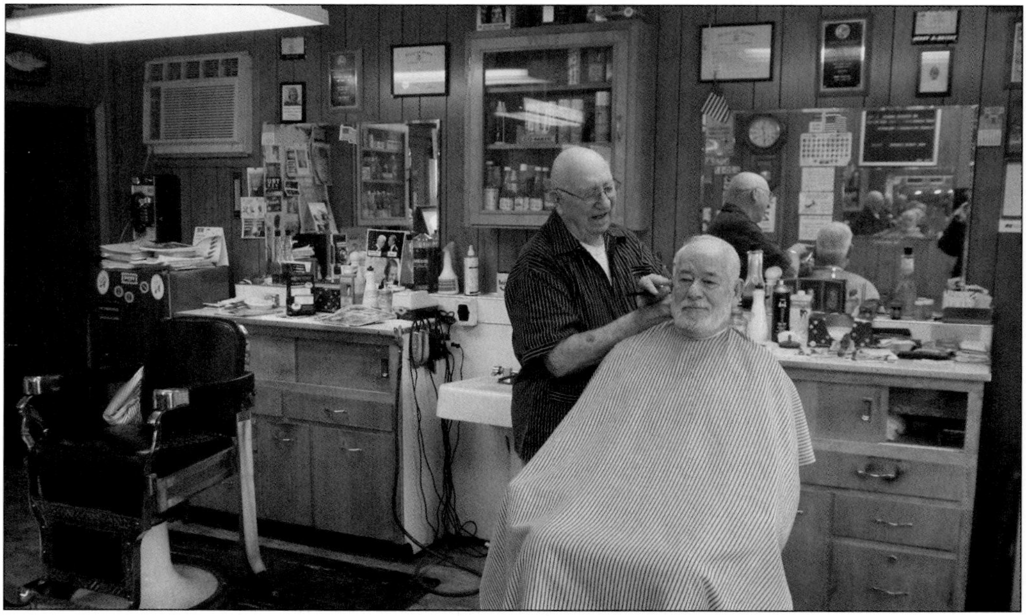

Jerry's Barber Shop. Jerry Wright (shown in 2016) has run a barbershop in Waukee since 1960. Back then, haircuts cost $1.25, flattops were $1.50, and haircuts for children under 12 were $1. The building that houses his shop on Sixth Street was built in 1918. While barbers were once common in most towns, few remain. Wright still cuts flattops and serves customers from Ankeny to Perry to Winterset. (Author's collection.)

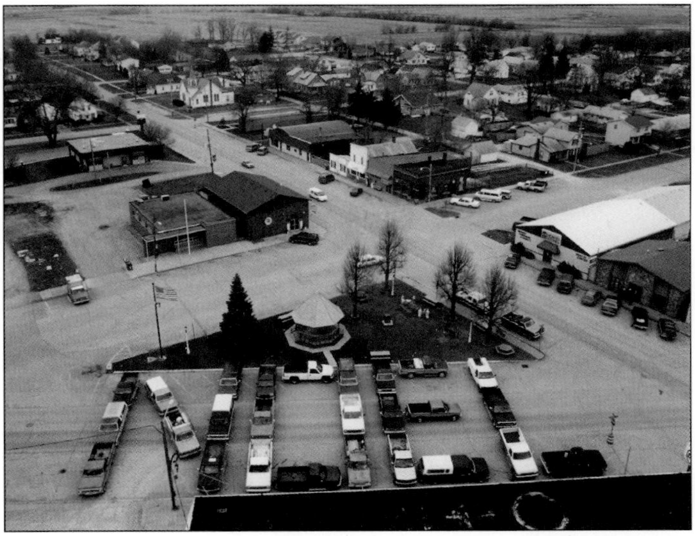

A Unique Look at the Triangle. Waukee native Steve Gerberich, a kinetic sculptor who moved to New York in the 1980s, brought his unique style to Waukee in 1993. He arranged 26 pickup trucks on Ashworth Drive and photographed this *Noel* image. Gerberich's artwork has been displayed internationally and has decorated windows of major department stores, including Bloomingdale's and Macy's. (Courtesy of Waukee Area Historical Society.)

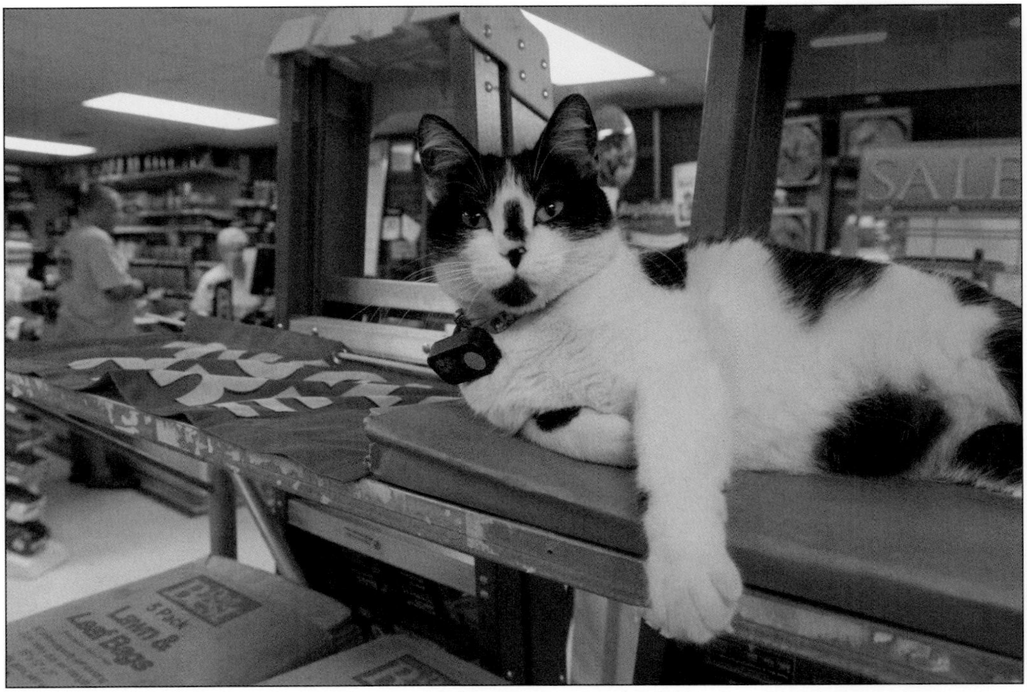

Waukee Hardware Cat. Celebrity cats have distinguished Waukee Hardware, which Geoff Warmouth and his wife, Anne, purchased in 1997. After the 2013 passing of Wesley, a stray cat who became a beloved fixture of Wanukee Hardware during his 22-year life, the store's new cat, Andie (shown here in 2014), had big paw prints to fill. Established in 1889, Waukee Hardware been located downtown on Sixth Street for nearly 60 years. (Author's collection.)

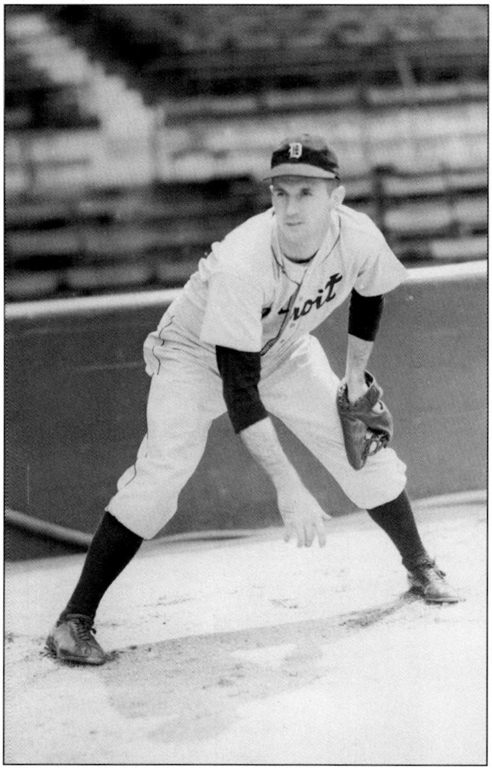

Pro Baseball Player Hal Manders. Harold "Hal" Manders (1917–2010) attended Waukee High School, where he participated in baseball and basketball before graduating in 1935. He attended the University of Iowa before being drafted as a pitcher by the Detroit Tigers. In 1946, he was traded to the Chicago Cubs. Manders later returned to Iowa and spent his career as a farmer near Waukee. His first cousin, Bob Feller of Van Meter, was a pitcher for the Cleveland Indians. (Courtesy of Waukee Public Library.)

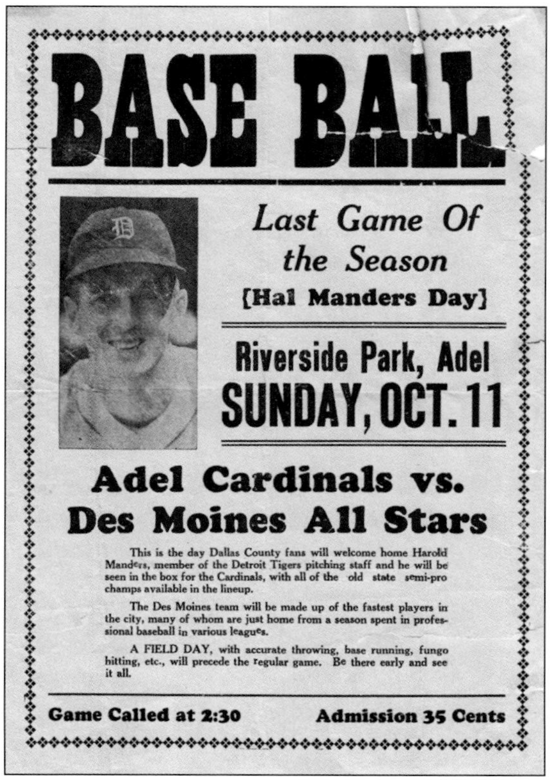

Honoring a Hometown Hero. Dallas County celebrated Hal Manders Day on October 11, 1942, at Adel's Riverside Park. Manders grew up playing baseball on his uncle William Feller's team, which competed on a homemade "field of dreams" that Feller and his son, Bob, built on their Van Meter farm. Before he went pro, Manders pitched for the University of Iowa from 1935 to 1937 and helped recruit Dallas County native and football star Nile Kinnick to the university. (Courtesy of Waukee Public Library.)

Eight

Woodward and Granger
Growing along Highway 141

While towns in southern Dallas County were founded from the 1840s to 1870s, it would take more time before communities were established in northeast Dallas County.

Woodward was born when the Chicago, Milwaukee & St. Paul Railway came through the area. The city was incorporated in August 1883 and grew to 383 people by 1890. In 1885, a new town southeast of Woodward was surveyed, platted, and recorded. Named in honor of railroad man C.T. Granger, the town soon boasted new businesses, including the Geneser and Sons general store. Both Woodward and Granger were eventually connected to Des Moines, Perry, and other communities via the interurban railway.

While agriculture drove the local economy, there was a time in the early 20th century when coal was king in northeastern Dallas County. Coal seams were frequently exposed along the Des Moines River valley. In the early 1900s, coal was discovered in Des Moines Township east of Woodward, leading to the creation of the Scandia and Phildia mining settlements, which have long since faded into history.

After the Phildia mine was abandoned in 1915 and the Scandia mine closed in 1921, miners moved on to the Moran mine, which opened in 1917 west of Woodward. For a time, Dallas County became one of the most important coal-mining counties in Iowa.

Like northeast Dallas County's coal mines, other traces of the past are only memories, such as the Yankee Robinson traveling circus, which spent winters at Granger. Other legacies of local history remain, including the Granger Homesteads and Beneventi Chevrolet in Granger, a growing community where the population soared from 583 in 2000 to 1,244 by 2010, according to US Census data.

In some cases, enterprises like Picket Fence Creamery and Lake Robbins Ballroom, south of Woodward (population 1,024 as of 2010), reveal glimpses of life that were once common in the region, from dairy farming to the great ballrooms that once entertained generations of Iowans. Fortunately, both of these businesses were spared when 12 tornadoes tore through Dallas and Boone Counties (including Woodward) on the afternoon of November 12, 2005, killing one person and causing $18 million in damage.

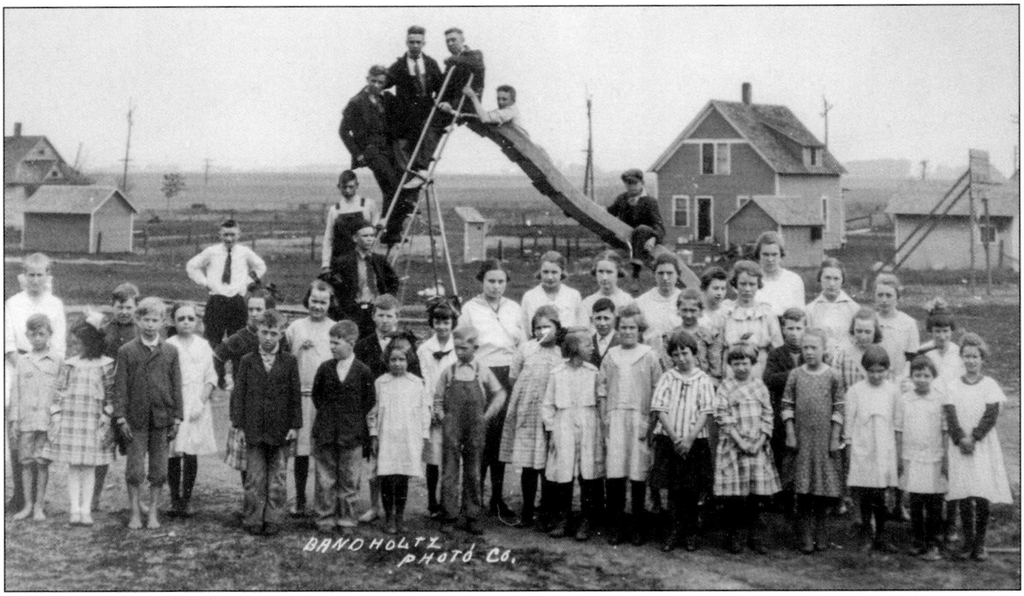

Woodward School Days. The boys on the tall slide outside the Woodward school, which was built in 1907, appear to be having more fun than the other students in this picture, taken on May 19, 1920. The 1983 Woodward centennial book, *Through the Years*, records that Woodward High School's first graduates included "nine lovely girls" who received their diplomas on May 7, 1887. "Each graduate had to give a 10-minute oration that she prepared." (Courtesy of Woodward Public Library.)

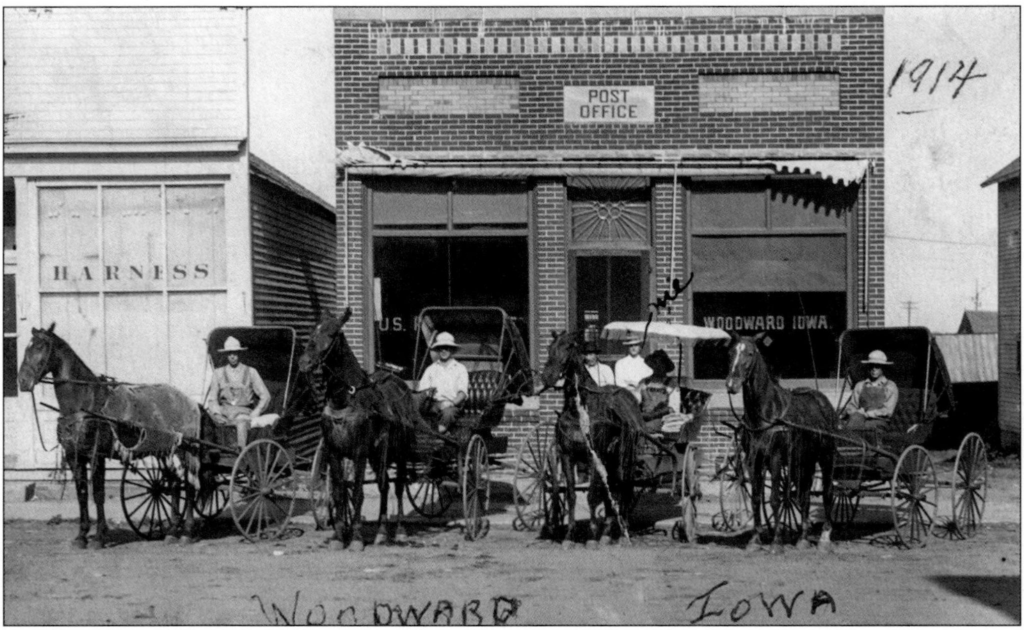

Woodward Post Office. The post office was always a hub of activity in small towns like Woodward. Progress was evident in this era, when these horses and buggies would soon become things of the past. By 1918, paving projects were underway in Woodward, including Main Street. In the early 1920s, hitching posts were ordered off Main Street to allow for automobile parking. (Author's collection.)

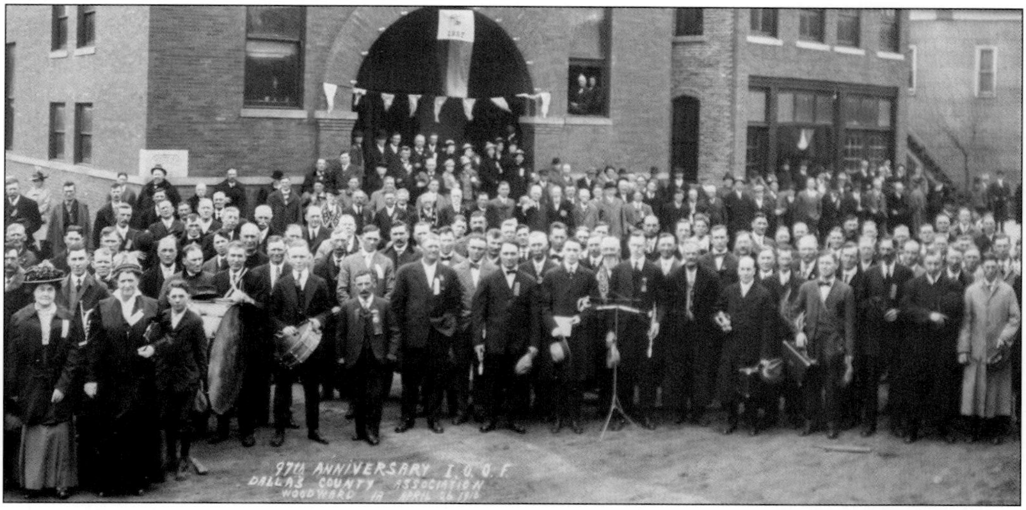

"Odd Bunch of Fellows." The Independent Order of Odd Fellows (IOOF) is a nonpolitical, fraternal order that helps people in need. Members were considered "an odd bunch of fellows" for their selfless actions. On April 26, 1916, Dallas County Association members gathered in Woodward to celebrate the national IOOF's 97th anniversary. Woodward IOOF Lodge No. 460 disbanded around 1960. This three-story building (an IOOF lodge and opera house) was torn down in 1975. (Courtesy of Woodward Public Library.)

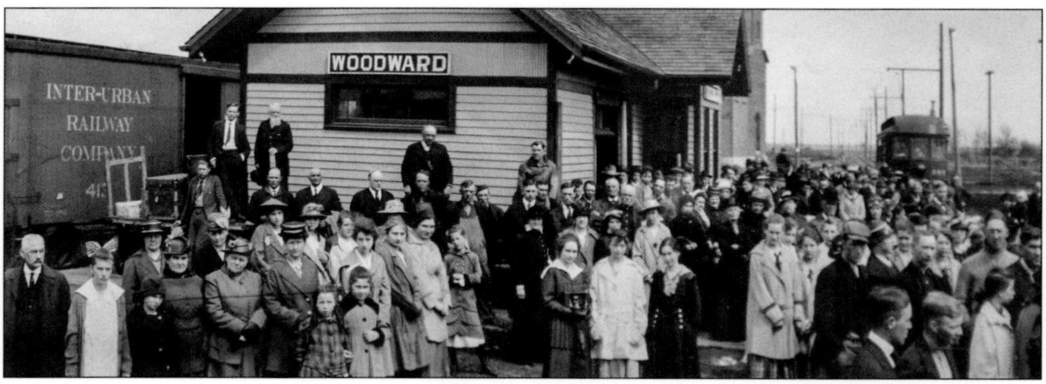

Farewell, Soldiers. A huge crowd of well-wishers gathers at the Woodward depot (notice the interurban on the right) on May 2, 1917, to honor Woodward's first volunteers who are leaving for World War I, including Mervin Robbins, LeRoy Spencer, Arthur Newland, Ralph Murphy, Leonard Anderson, Louis Anderson, Pete Bilney, Roy Bilney, Harry Johnson, George Vickroy, Burt Field, Ralph Grimm, Boyd Wade, Roy Morgan, Lee Sprague, and Paul Beveridge. (Courtesy of Woodward Public Library.)

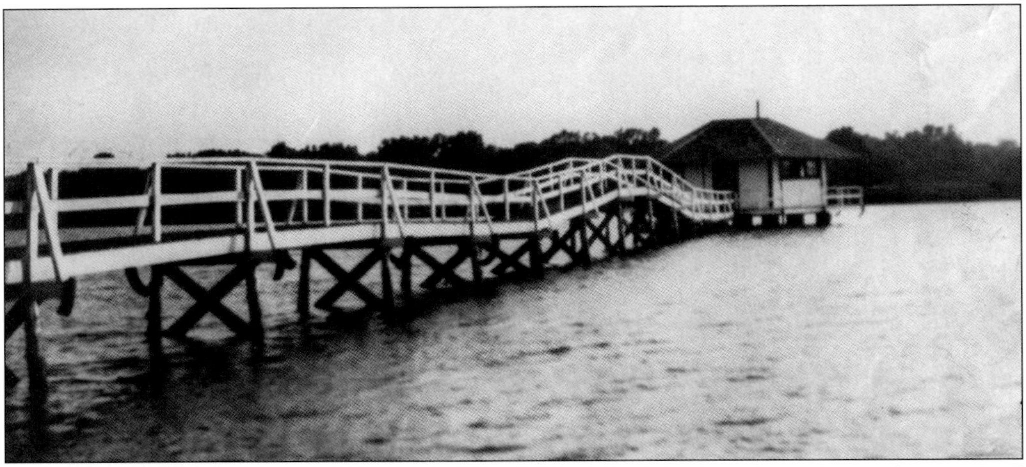

Beginnings of Lake Robbins. Located southwest of Woodward, Lake Robbins started as a natural pond. By the early 1920s, Riley Robbins and his son, Mervin, built a man-made lake dredged out by teams of horses. Robbins built a boardwalk and an eight-sided cabin south of the area that would become the famous Lake Robbins Ballroom. A drought in 1936 decimated the lake, which was not rebuilt. (Courtesy of Lake Robbins Ballroom.)

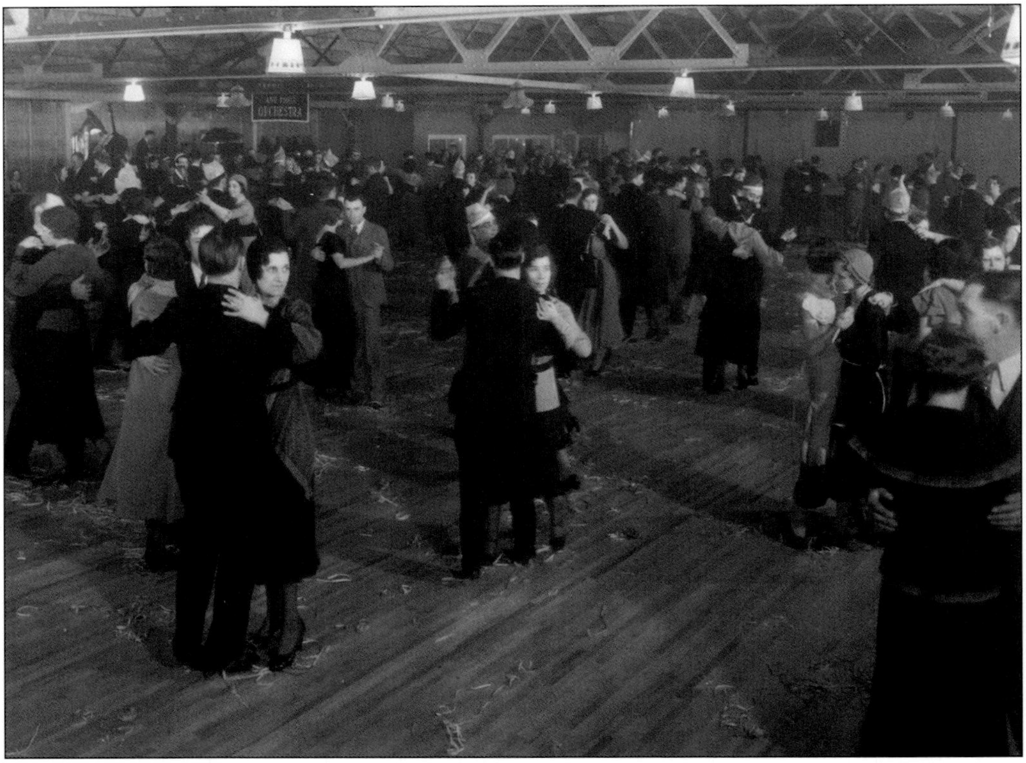

Ringing in the New Year. After construction started in 1929, the legendary Lake Robbins Ballroom opened on November 11, 1931, and became one of the hottest entertainment venues in Dallas County. Advertising its 10,000-square-foot white pine dance floor (with seating, the actual dancing part of the floor is now 4,800 square feet) and music from popular dance bands of the day, the ballroom has been a destination for decades. This photograph was likely taken on New Year's Eve around 1933. (Courtesy of Lake Robbins Ballroom.)

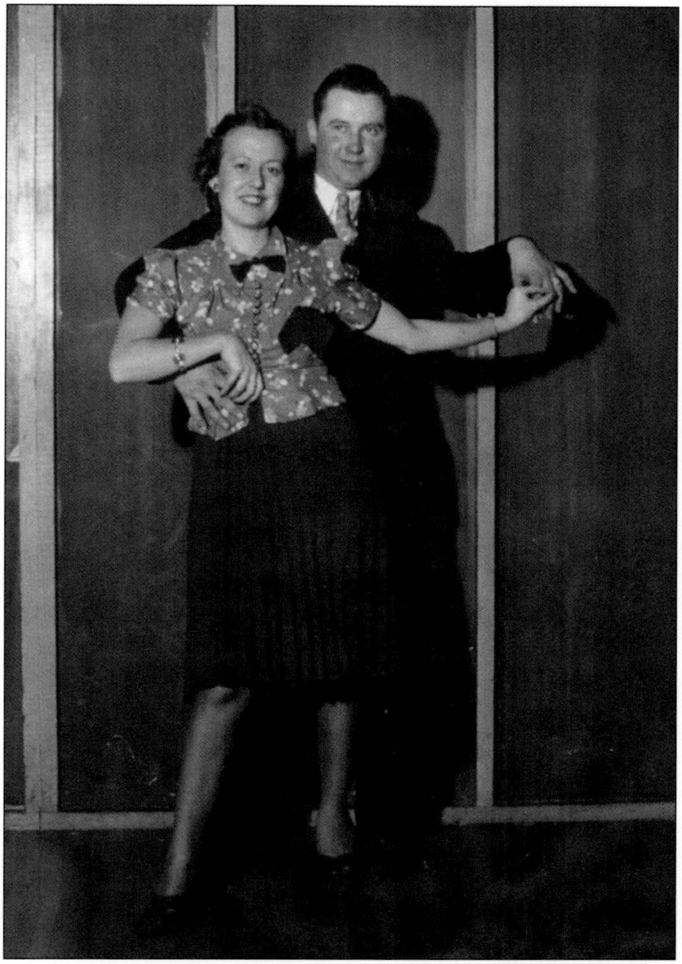

Soon-to-Be-Married Dance Champions. While they were not yet married when this photograph was taken in 1938, Jacob Cushing of Adel and his future bride, Florence, won a dance contest at Lake Robbins Ballroom. The event was sponsored by Chaplin Gas & Oil. This photograph was taken by Edmondson Studio in Perry. (Courtesy of Lake Robbins Ballroom.)

One of Iowa's Last Ballrooms. Lake Robbins has always been in the country, and there is only one way to get there—an unpaved country road. While the ballroom has always had a simple exterior, the magic occurs inside. Through the years, countless married couples first met at Lake Robbins. While many Iowa towns used to have ballrooms, Lake Robbins is one of the few that remains. (Courtesy of Lake Robbins Ballroom.)

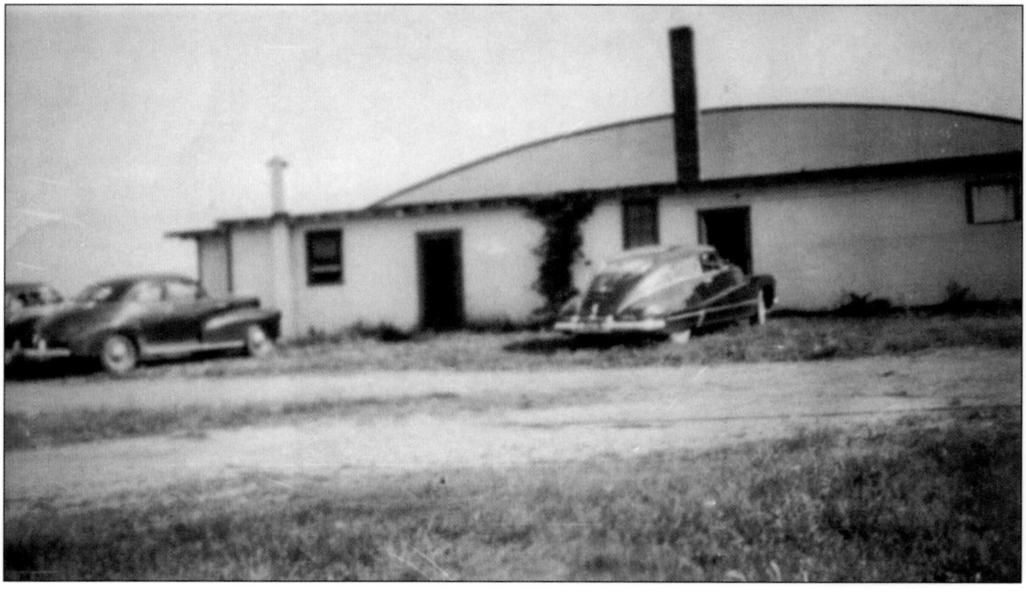

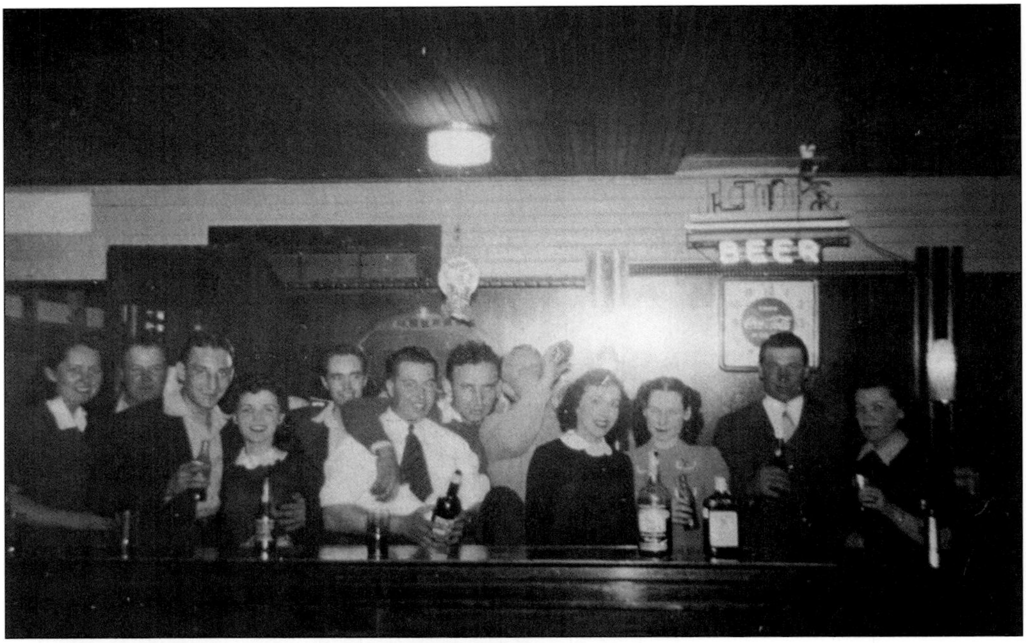

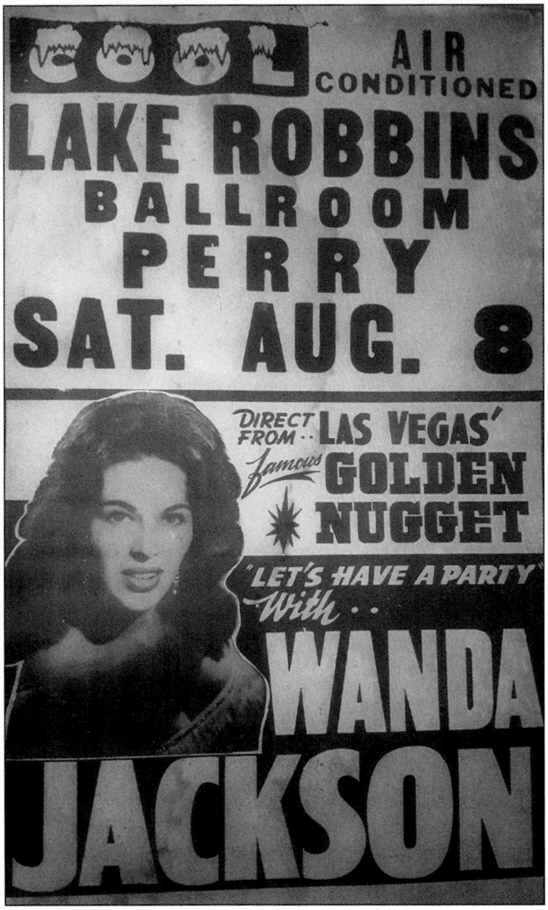

Celebrating the Good Times. Young people from Dallas County and beyond flocked to Lake Robbins Ballroom, one of the few places in the county that had electricity in the early 1930s. Future president Ronald "Dutch" Reagan, who was a WHO Radio broadcaster in Des Moines in the mid-1930s, danced at the ballroom. Lake Robbins was inducted into the Iowa Rock 'n' Roll Hall of Fame in 2007. (Courtesy of Lake Robbins Ballroom.)

Let's Have a Party! While some Lake Robbins performers slipped into obscurity, others became stars. Herbie Kaye's orchestra from Chicago that played opening night in 1931 featured 16-year-old vocalist Dorothy Lamour. By the mid-1930s, Lamour moved to Hollywood and went on to make a series of successful comedies starring Bing Crosby and Bob Hope. Another Lake Robbins singer, Perry Como, performed with Ted Weems from 1936 to 1942 and later had hits like "Magic Moments" and "Catch a Falling Star." (Courtesy of Lake Robbins Ballroom.)

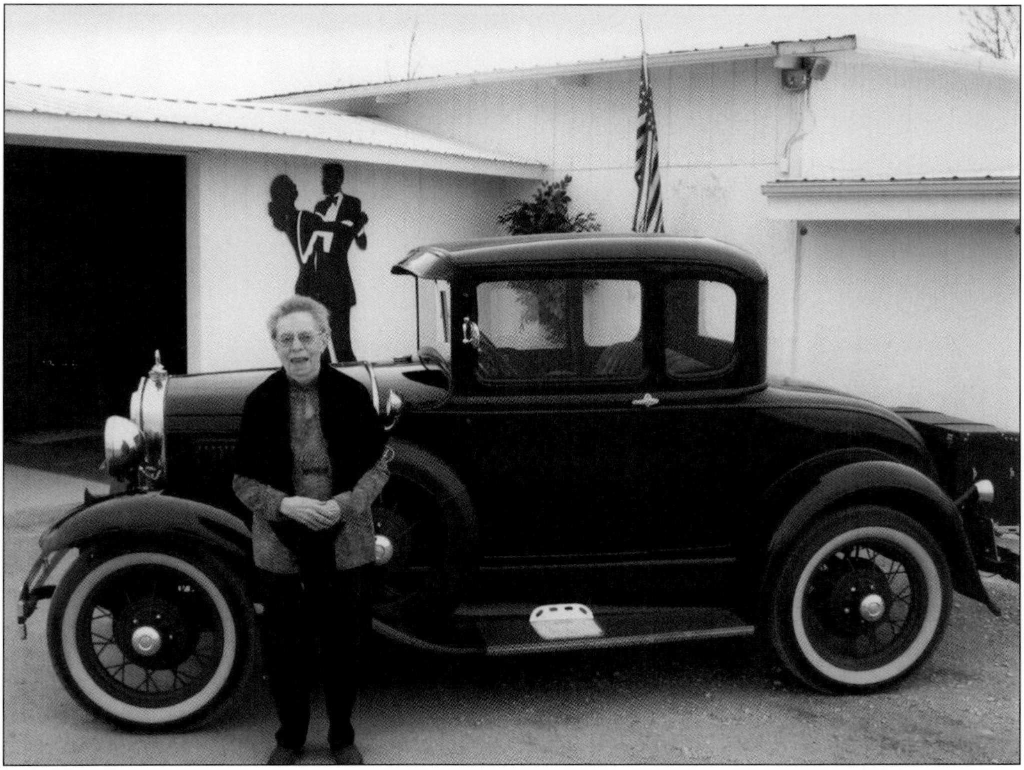

Kip Shannon's 82-Year Career. While she did not work on opening night, 23-year-old Coloma "Kip" Shannon was at the new Lake Robbins Ballroom that Wednesday evening with her family. She got a job selling tickets at Lake Robbins the next night the ballroom was open and handled practically every job at the ballroom during her career, which spanned 82 years at Lake Robbins. Kip died at the age of 105 in 2014. (Courtesy of Lake Robbins Ballroom.)

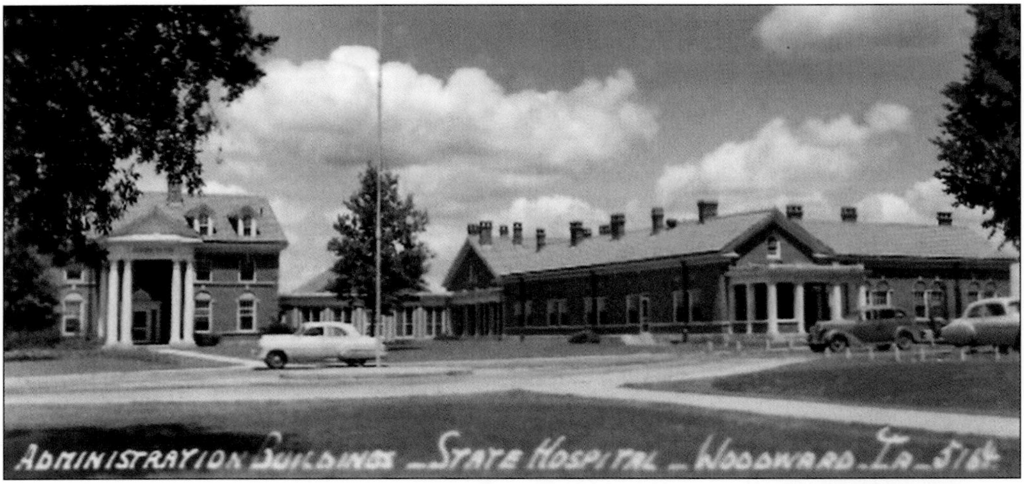

State Hospital. In 1917, the State Hospital for Epileptics and School for the Feeble Minded officially opened half a mile north of Woodward. The spacious campus was praised for its modern, fireproof buildings, attractive landscaping, and many flowerbeds, which reflected the philosophy that color and beauty were helpful to those served by the facility. This image was likely taken in the early 1950s. (Author's collection.)

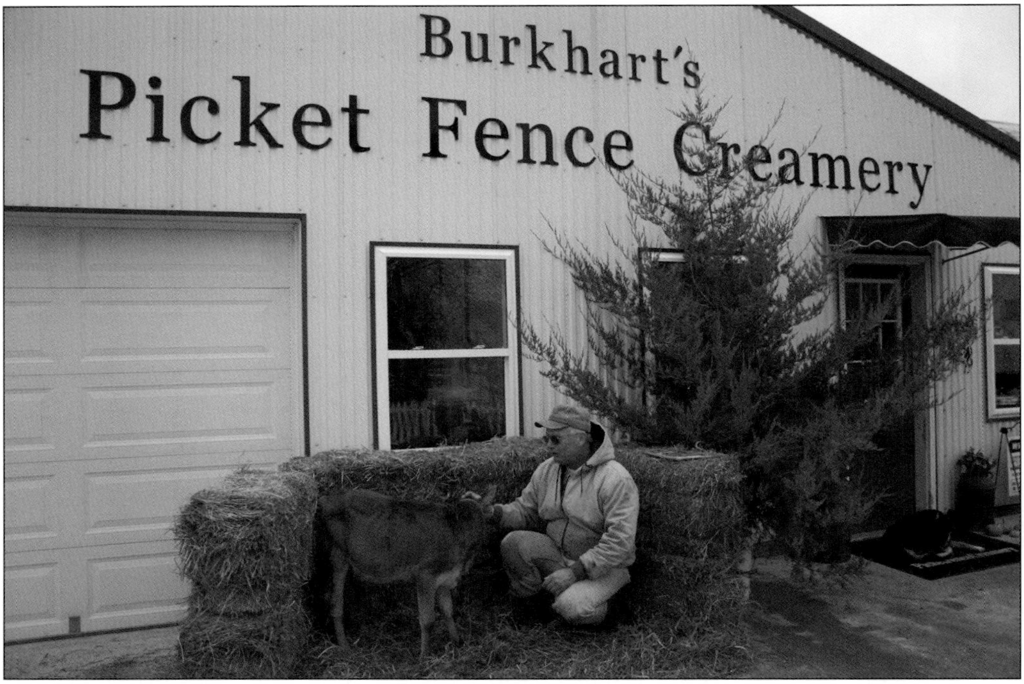

Picket Fence Creamery. While dairy cows were once fairly common on many Dallas County farms, the industry faded away by the 1980s. The Burkhart family (including Jeff [pictured], his wife, Jill, and their children, Jenna and James) still operate a dairy, creamery, and country store south of Woodward. Opened in 2003, Picket Fence Creamery offers many items, including ice cream and non-homogenized milk, in which the cream rises to the top. (Author's collection.)

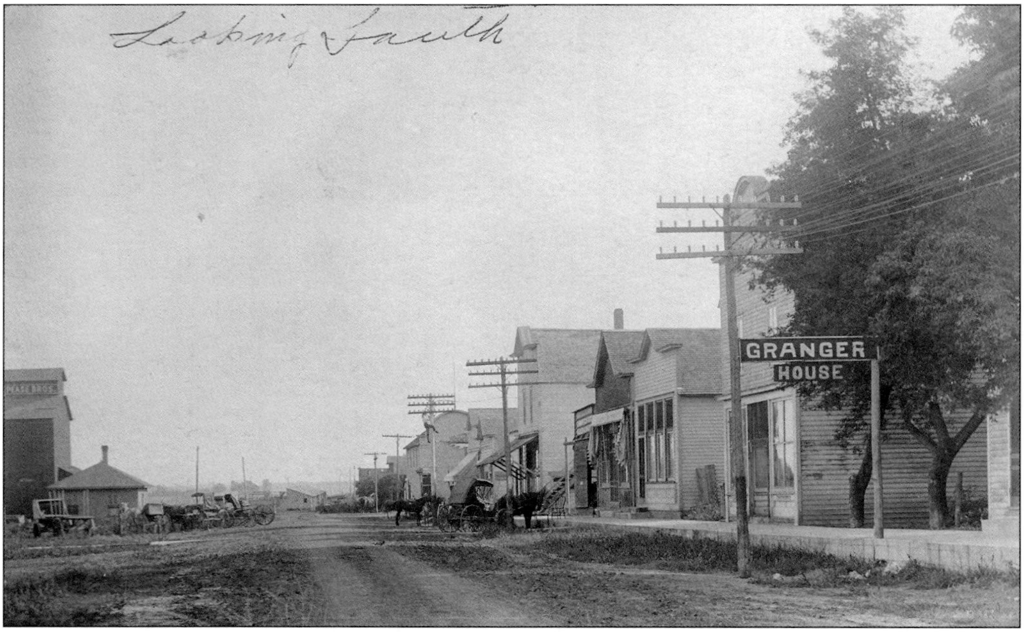

Early Granger. The Granger House and Pease Bros. Elevator can be seen in this early view along Main Street in Granger, where the streets are lined with horse-drawn buggies. These dirt streets turned to mud when it rained. (Courtesy of Granger Public Library.)

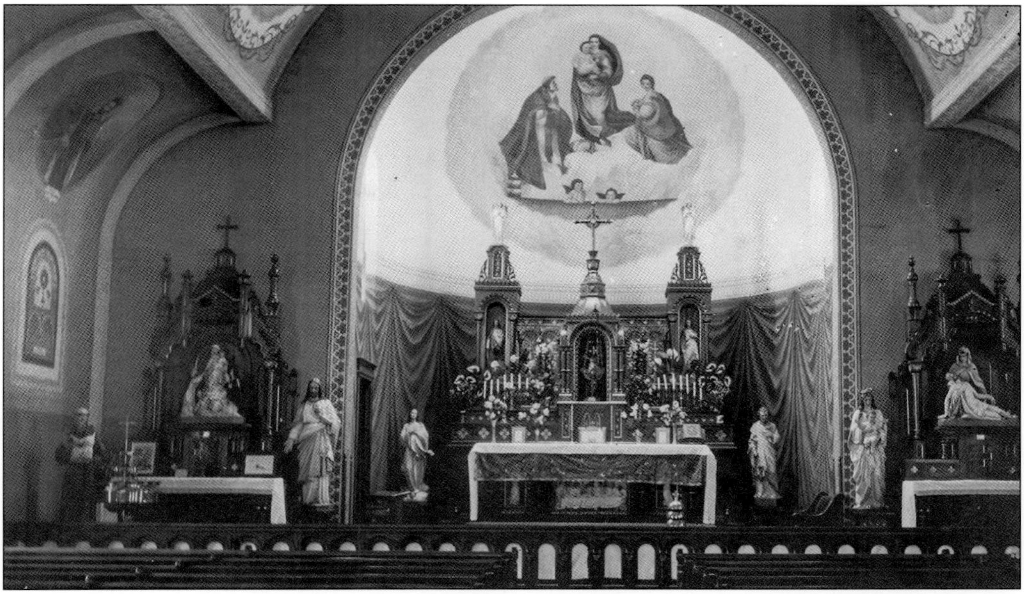

Inside the Catholic Church. The first Catholic church built to serve the Granger area was St. Bridget's Church, which was located about three miles west of town and opened in 1871. Before the current Assumption Catholic Church was completed in Granger in 1992, a stately brick church served Assumption Parish from 1901 to 1988. Here is a view of its altar and ornate interior. (Courtesy of Granger Public Library.)

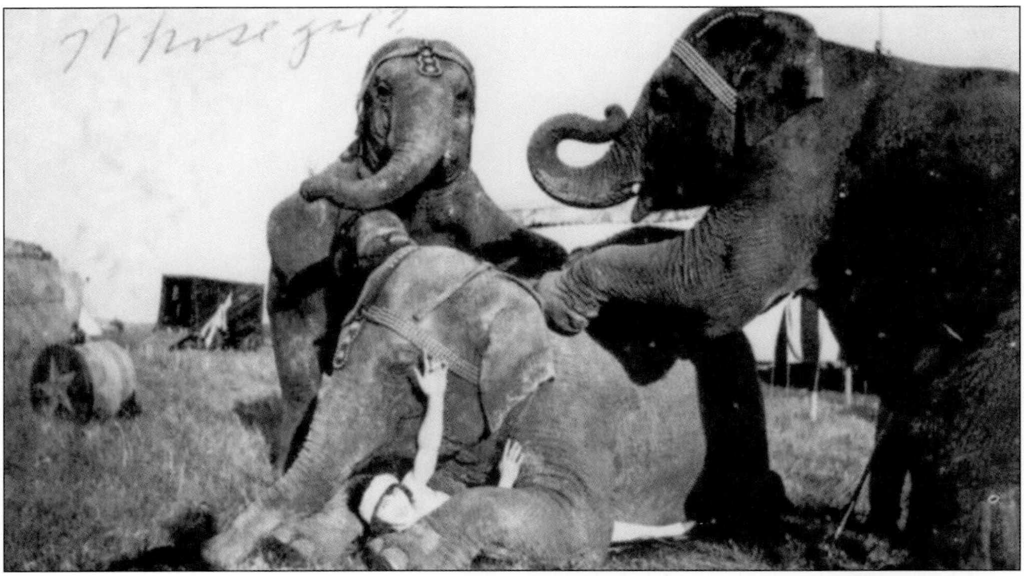

Traveling Circus and the Circle of Life. In 1906, Fred Buchanan established the winter quarters for his Yankee Robinson Show, a midwestern traveling circus, two miles southeast of Granger. The land was along the interurban railroad. By 1926, the site included 20 outbuildings. The spacious area also provided a place to bury deceased circus elephants. Granger may be the only Iowa town to claim an elephant graveyard. (Courtesy of Granger Public Library.)

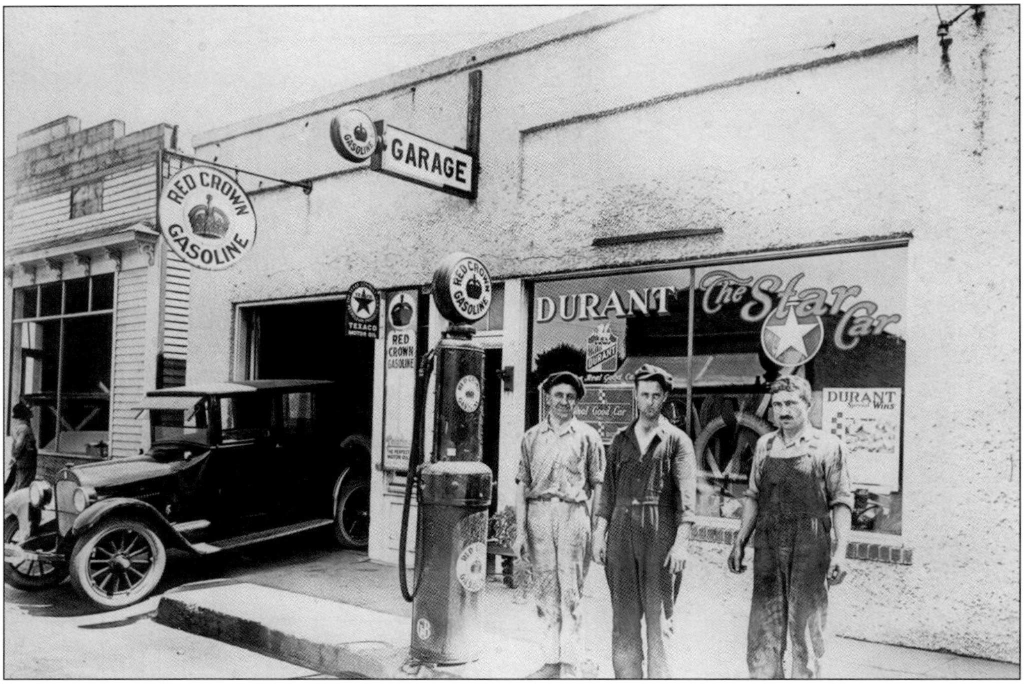

BENEVENTI SOLD DURANTS AND STARS. Settimo "Ben" Beneventi (1893–1977), left, came to Granger around 1915 and opened a car repair shop with a business partner. Beneventi started his own shop around 1923. By 1925, Beneventi (shown here with Sesto Fiori, far right), was also selling Durant and Star cars in downtown Granger. Beneventi began selling Chevrolets in 1932. In 1975, Beneventi Chevrolet moved to its current location along Highway 141 in Granger. (Courtesy of Beneventi Chevrolet.)

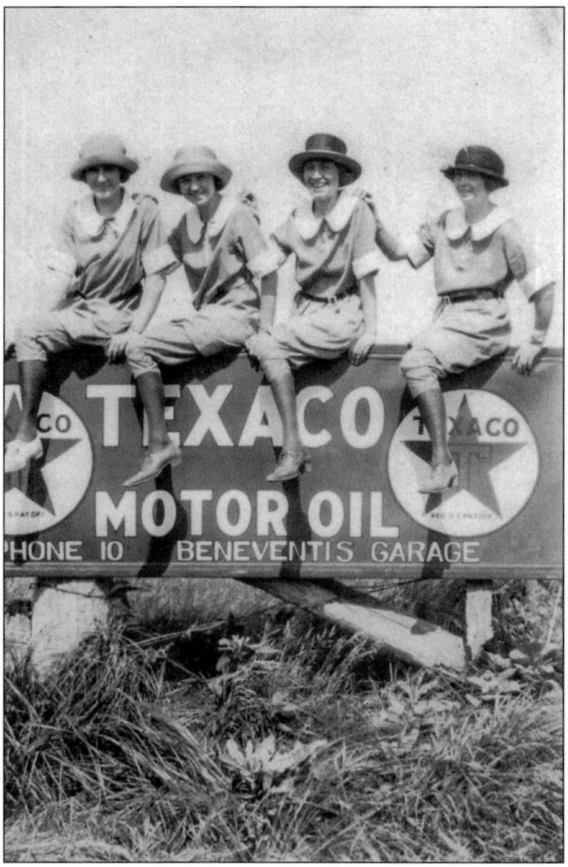

PHONE 10 FOR BENEVENTI'S GARAGE. These vivacious ladies include Elsie Campani (second from right), a niece of Settimo "Ben" Beneventi. After emigrating from Italy at the age of 11, Beneventi worked in a coal mine at LaSalle, Illinois, and took night classes to become a mechanic. After he contracted rheumatic fever, his doctor prescribed fresh country air and fresh milk. Beneventi settled in Granger, home of the Meeks dairy farm, and opened his own garage by the 1920s. (Courtesy of Beneventi Chevrolet.)

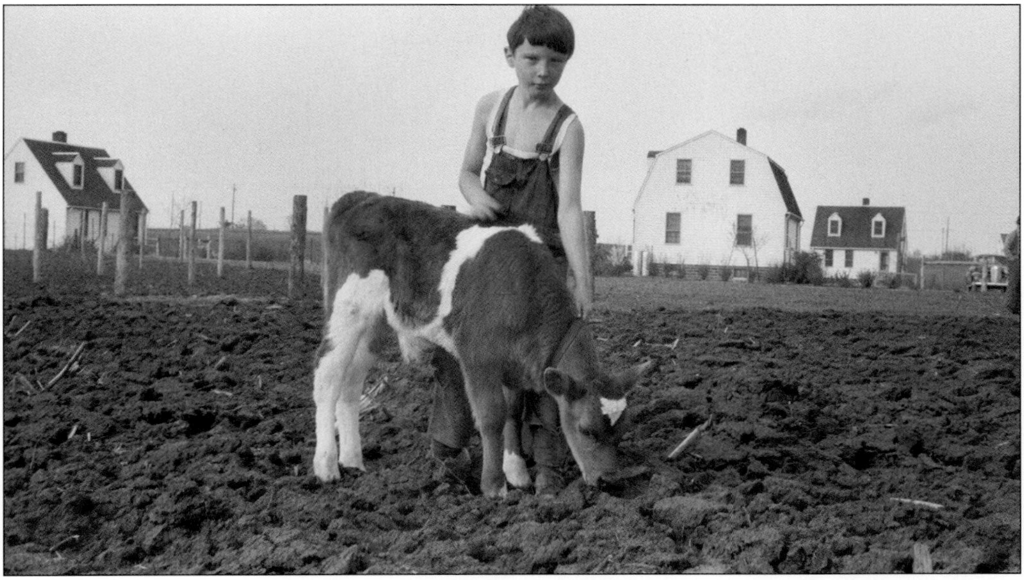

Granger Homesteads. Granger became the focal point of a successful New Deal program inspired by Monsignor Luigi Ligutti, who had served Assumption Church since 1926. Ligutti felt coal camps were an unsuitable environment for children, like this unidentified miner's son. Ligutti looked to the land to address the miners' economic and social challenges. The 225-acre Granger Homesteads, built in 1935, included 50 modern homes like this one, along with approximately four acres each for raising crops and livestock. (Courtesy of Library of Congress.)

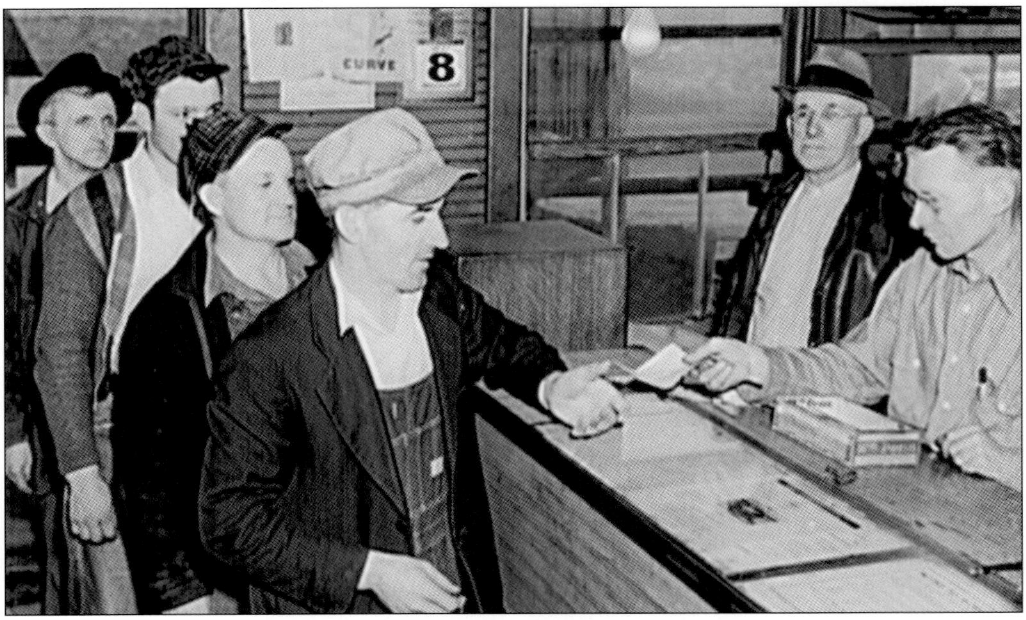

Payday and Hope for the Future. These Granger Homesteads men received their paychecks at the coal mine office. Families supplemented this income by raising crops and livestock. Homesteaders also formed cooperatives to buy farm equipment and sponsor recreational activities. In 1936, First Lady Eleanor Roosevelt visited the Granger Homesteads and praised the success of the project, which cost approximately $200,000. Within 20 years, the homesteaders paid back most of that amount, and none of them defaulted on his loan. (Courtesy of Library of Congress.)

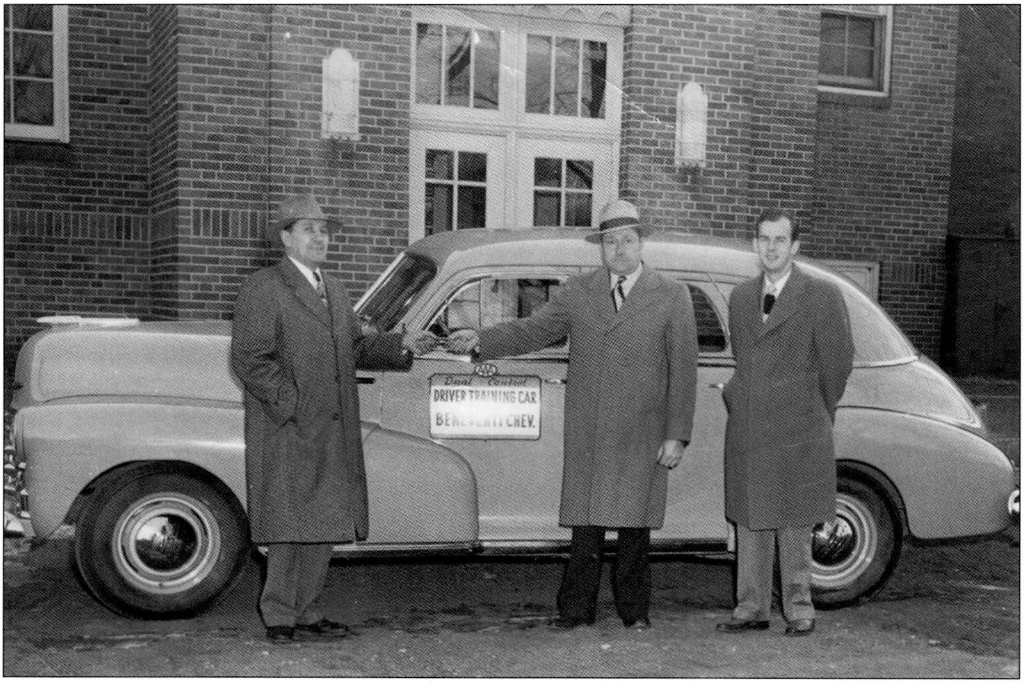

1948 DRIVER'S ED CHEVY. Settimo "Ben" Beneventi (left) delivered this new 1948 Chevrolet dual-control driver's training car to Earl Coulson (center), Granger's superintendent of schools, and an unidentified coach and driver's ed teacher. Don Beneventi recalls how new Chevrolets were shipped four to a railcar in the early 1940s. When they arrived in Granger, five-year-old Don would steer the cars as his father, Ben, unloaded them from the train. (Courtesy of Beneventi Chevrolet.)

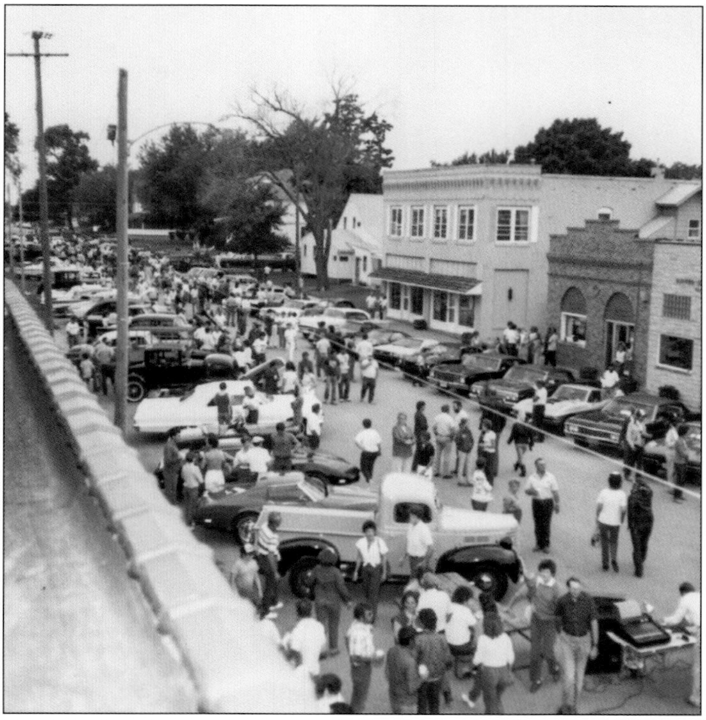

1980S CELEBRATION IN GRANGER. A car show was part of the fun at this summer celebration in Granger, which was likely the town's centennial in 1985. The celebration also included a parade, mud volleyball, and more. (Courtesy of Granger Public Library.)

Nine

Tiny Towns and Ghost Towns

Memories Live On

Some of Dallas County's smallest towns have played some of the most significant roles in the area's history.

Consider Minburn, which is known as a small town with a big heart. Minburn once boasted an opera house (which later showed silent movies) and took entertainment to a whole new level in the 1950s and early 1960s with the Singing Wheels. This group included local roller skaters of all ages who performed three-day extravaganzas at Minburn's outdoor roller-skating rink each summer. Codirector Jackie Snyder said the Singing Wheels could not have happened anywhere but Minburn due to the way the whole community (whose population hovered around 350 people at that time) worked together to make each show a success.

Minburn was also the site of one of Dallas County's great tragedies. Around 3:30 a.m. on July 23, 1931, the telephone switchboard operator notified city marshal Virgil Untied, 33, that robbers were ransacking a grocery store in Minburn. The robbers ambushed the marshal. At least 10 shots were fired during the gun battle, with five shotgun slugs striking Untied, including one that shot out his right eye and lodged in his brain. Untied, a husband and father of three young girls, died on July 27, 1931, at King's Daughters Hospital in Perry. The robbers escaped, and no one was ever charged with the crime.

Just as the thieves vanished long ago, so have some of Dallas County's smallest settlements. Ortonville, once located between Adel and Waukee, was the winter headquarters for the famous Orton Bros. Circus. Coal mining communities like Moran, which sprang up west of Woodward when a mine opened in the area in 1917, faded away once the mines closed. Other places, like Panther, were more crossroads trading centers than towns, but they, too, disappeared as times changed.

Much of the history of Dallas County's tiny towns, as well as some of its larger communities, is preserved in restored railroad depots and historical markers along the 89-mile Raccoon River Valley Trail, which connects Linden (once known for the Linden Merchants semipro baseball team), Minburn, Dawson, Perry, Redfield, Dallas Center, Adel, and Waukee.

Founded in 1946, the Linden Merchants baseball team made history in 1948, when Linden became one of the first small towns in Iowa to have its own lighted baseball field. The Merchants played teams from Davenport to Creston to Fort Dodge. The Linden Merchants also played many traveling teams—including those composed of only African Americans, from Kansas City, Louisiana, and North Carolina. In 1956, the Merchants played the All-American Girls team, which defeated Linden 2-1 before a crowd of 500 spectators. The Linden Merchants played until 1959 or 1960. One player, Dick Bertell, made it to the major leagues, where he played for the Chicago Cubs in the early 1960s.

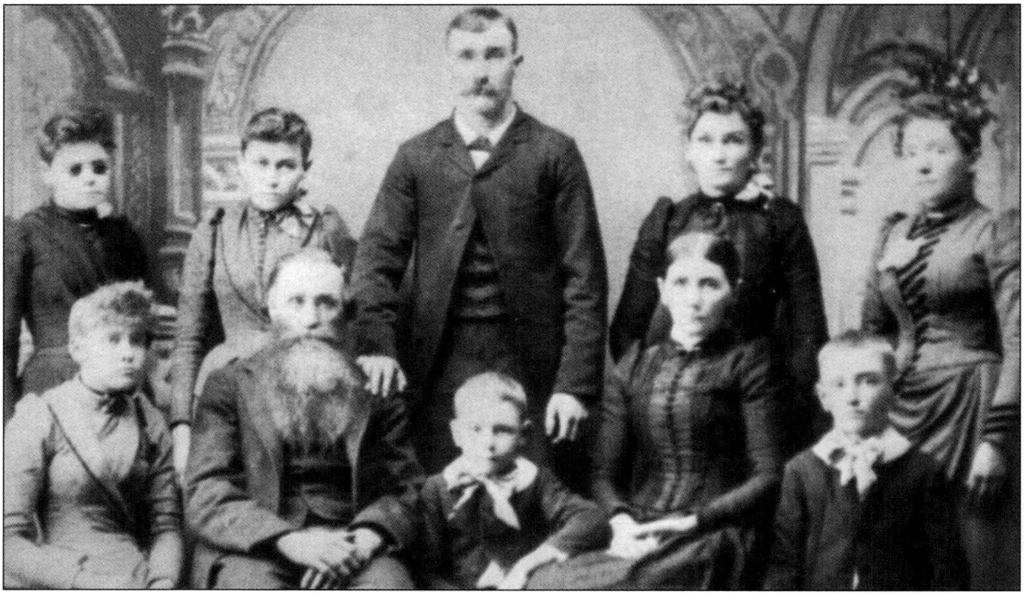

Seth Dayton Family. The Dayton Stagecoach Inn, south of Bouton, was built in 1868 by Seth Dayton (front row, second from left), the first registered settler in Beaver Township in northern Dallas County. Portions of the stagecoach route that once passed near the inn, which is located south of Highway 141, were later incorporated into the interurban railroad line, a light-rail service that ran between Perry and Des Moines from 1909 to the early 1950s. Today, the inn has been restored as a historic site for tours, programs, and overnight rentals. The rustic setting is surrounded by 150-year-old oak trees. (Courtesy of Dallas County Conservation.)

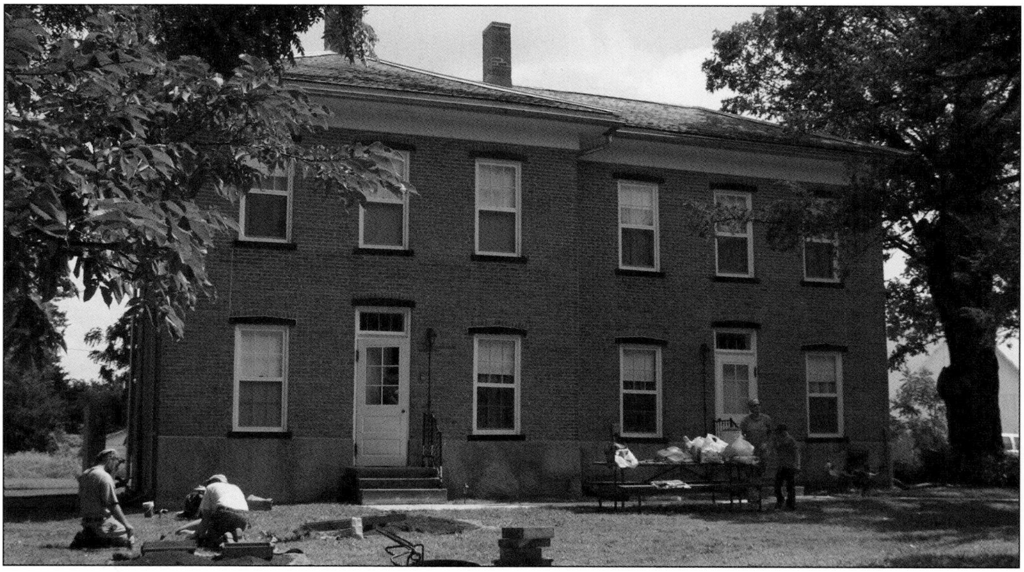

Dayton Stagecoach Inn. Seth Dayton's two-story brick inn and tavern along the old Des Moines–to–Fort Dodge stagecoach route was only used as a stagecoach stop for a few years before train travel transformed transportation in this part of Iowa. The inn offered dancing, drinking, and horse racing. By some accounts, Dayton lost the property in the mid-1880s on a bet. Dallas County Conservation staff and volunteers conducted an archaeological dig on the property in the summer of 2016. (Author's collection.)

DAWSON DEPOT. In 1882, the Milwaukee Railroad reached Dawson; the depot there was a busy hub from the 1880s to the 1950s. In addition to passenger service, freight of all kinds was shipped by rail—from produce crates and barrels shipped to local general stores to household items like furniture and pianos. Farm implements, windmill equipment, and other tools were also shipped by rail. (Courtesy of Dallas County Conservation.)

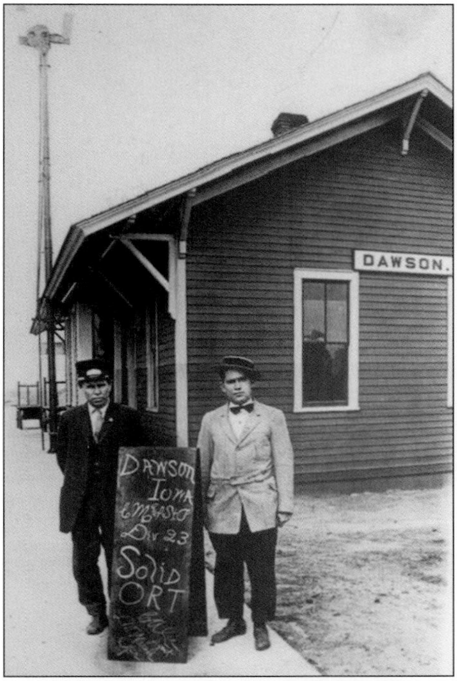

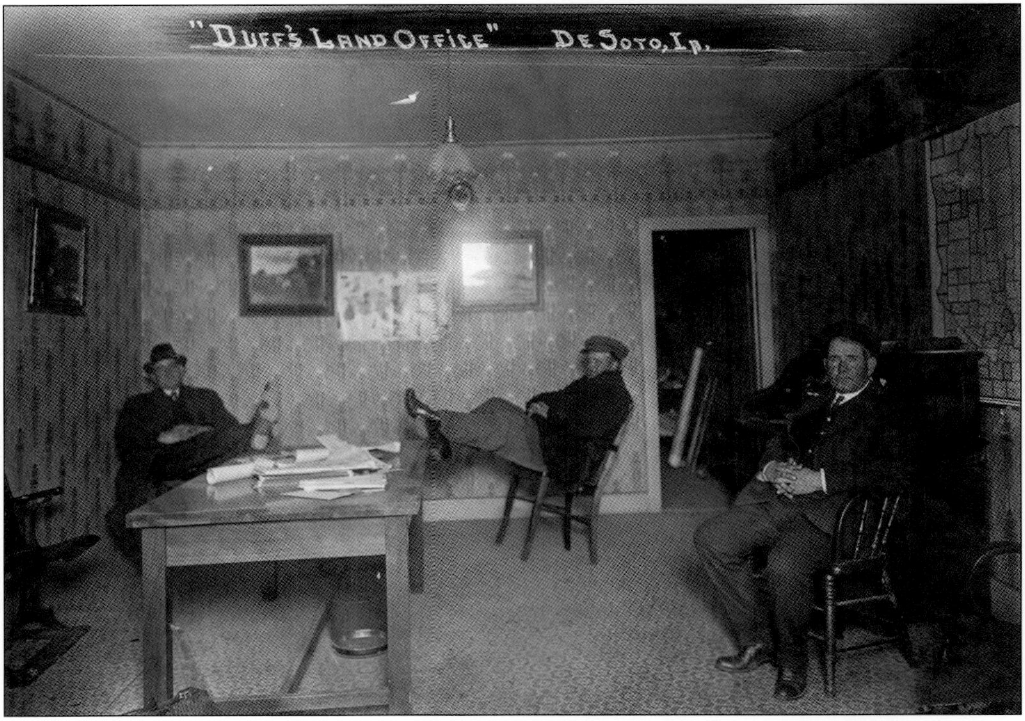

DE SOTO LAND OFFICE. Dallas County settlers could purchase land through local land offices like this. After land in Iowa was surveyed, it was laid out in townships, which measure six miles by six miles. Land in these townships could be purchased from the government or the railroads. The government granted land to railroads to encourage their expansion across Iowa, and railroad companies sold some of this land to settlers. (Courtesy of Van Meter Public Library.)

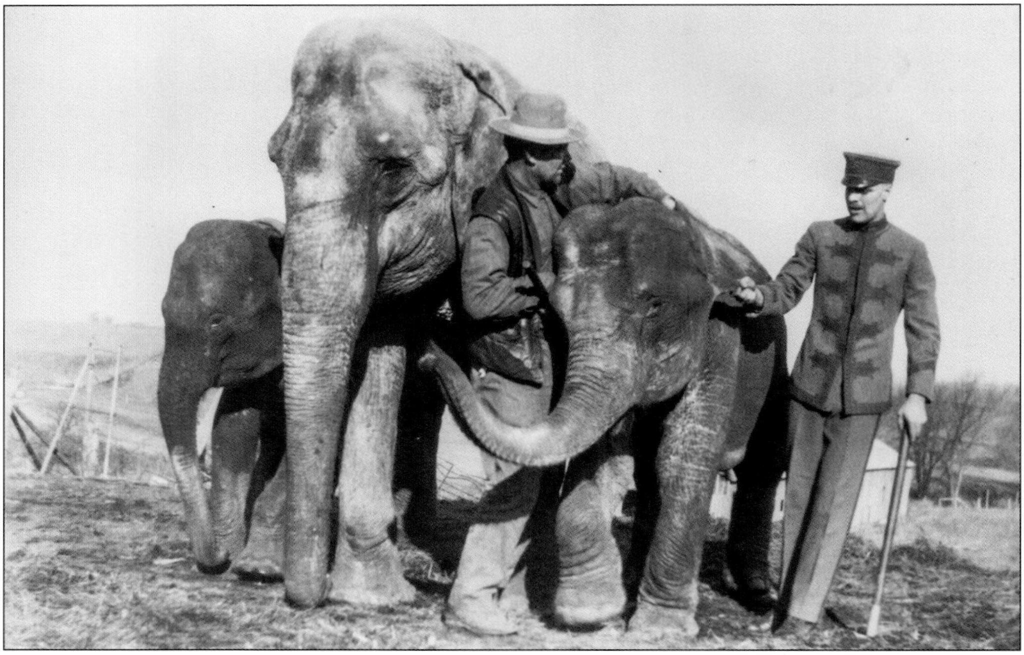

ELEPHANTS AT ORTONVILLE. After Hiram Orton and his family organized their first circus in the early 1850s in Portage, Wisconsin, it became a must-see midwestern event, complete with elephants. The one-ring circus performed many shows in Iowa, including one in Adel. Orton liked Dallas County so much that in the early 1860s, he started making his winter quarters each year west of Waukee and about three miles east of Adel near Highway 6. This was about half a mile north of where the future town of Ortonville would be located. (Courtesy of Dallas County Conservation.)

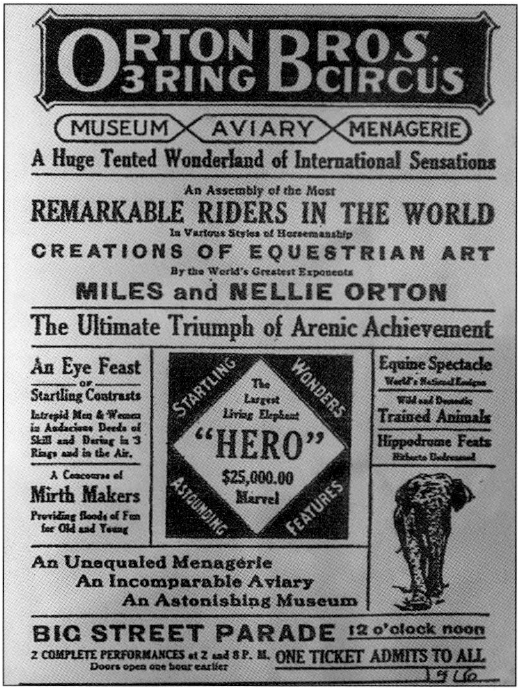

THREE-RING CIRCUS. This Orton Bros. Three-Ring Circus poster from 1916 promotes a "huge tented wonderland of international sensations," including Hero, the largest living elephant (dubbed a $25,000 marvel); a big street parade; an incomparable aviary; wild and domestic trained animals; intrepid men and women in "audacious deeds of skill;" and a "concourse of mirth makers providing floods of fun for old and young." (Courtesy of Adel Historical Museum.)

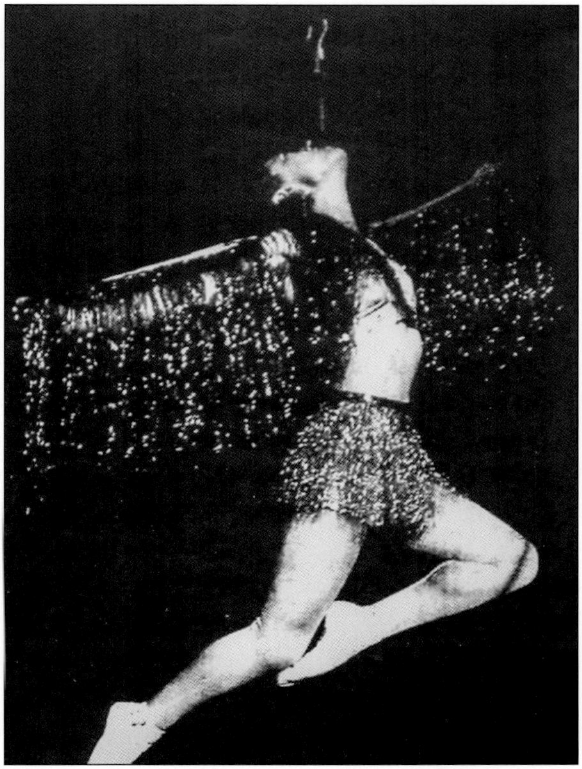

The Sensational Ortons. Five generations of the Orton family, including Gracie Orton, thrilled audiences for years. In her most famous act, Gracie would hang by her teeth using an "iron jaw" and slide down a 300-foot cable stretched from the top of a 50-foot pole. She also used the iron jaw to spin around while being held by her husband, Vernon Leidke, 110 feet in the air. Gracie and Vernon (whom she later divorced) never used a net. He was killed in Texas while practicing a sway bar act. (Courtesy of Adel Historical Museum.)

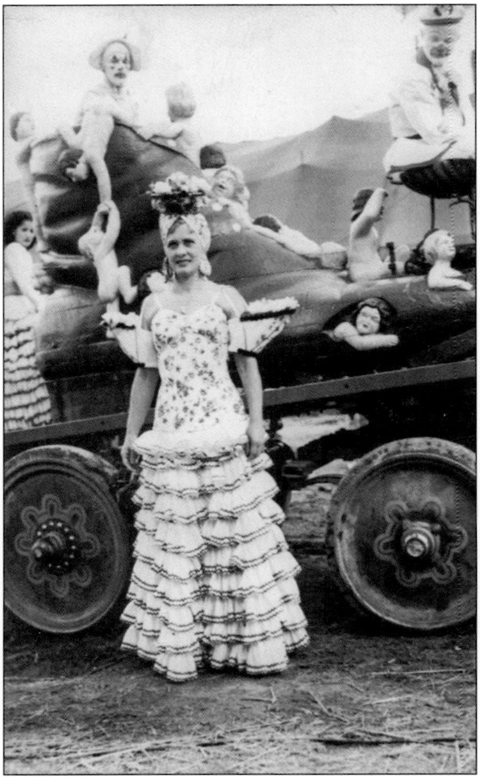

It's Showtime. Along with monkeys, horses, elephants, and other animals, Orton Bros. Circus entertainment included a band, trapeze artists, acrobats, and other performers, like mambo dancer Sadie "Babe" Orton Woodcock, shown here with clowns in the background. In the early years, the circus traveled by wagon from town to town on unpaved roads. For a short time, the circus traveled by train, and later it traveled by trucks and trailers. (Courtesy of Adel Historical Museum.)

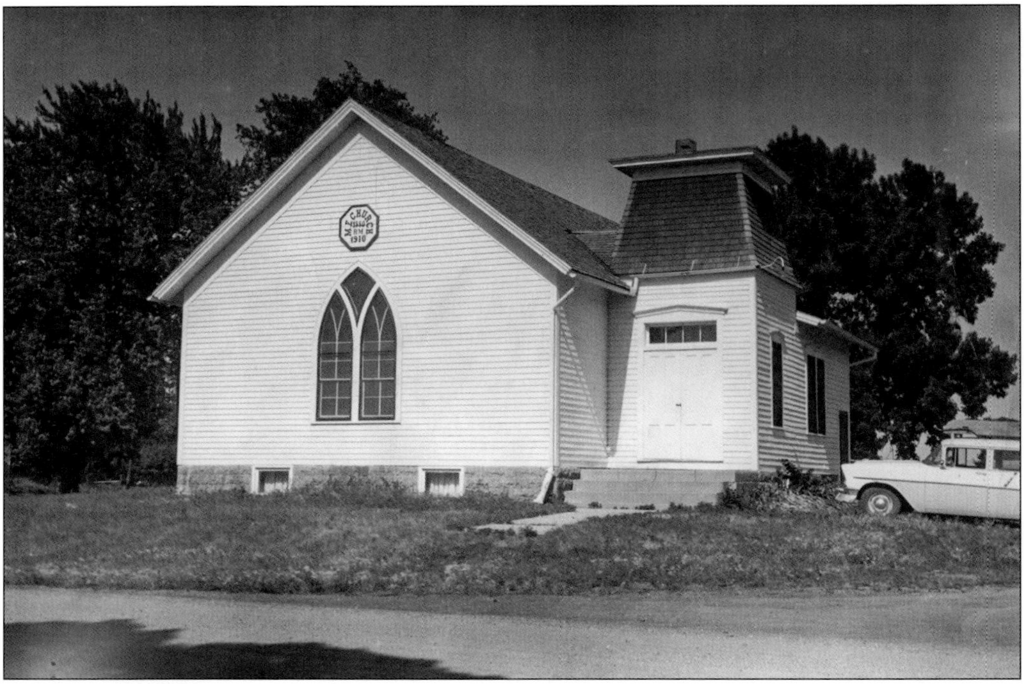

Country Church. Prairie Center Church was founded in Lincoln Township in 1866. The church served pioneer farm families in the area as well as nearby towns like Linden, Yale, Panora, and Jamaica. Services are still held at the church once a month. This tiny pocket of Iowa's heritage, which is situated in an exclusively rural township in a tranquil setting surrounded by cedar trees, has endured for more than 150 years. (Courtesy of Prairie Center Church.)

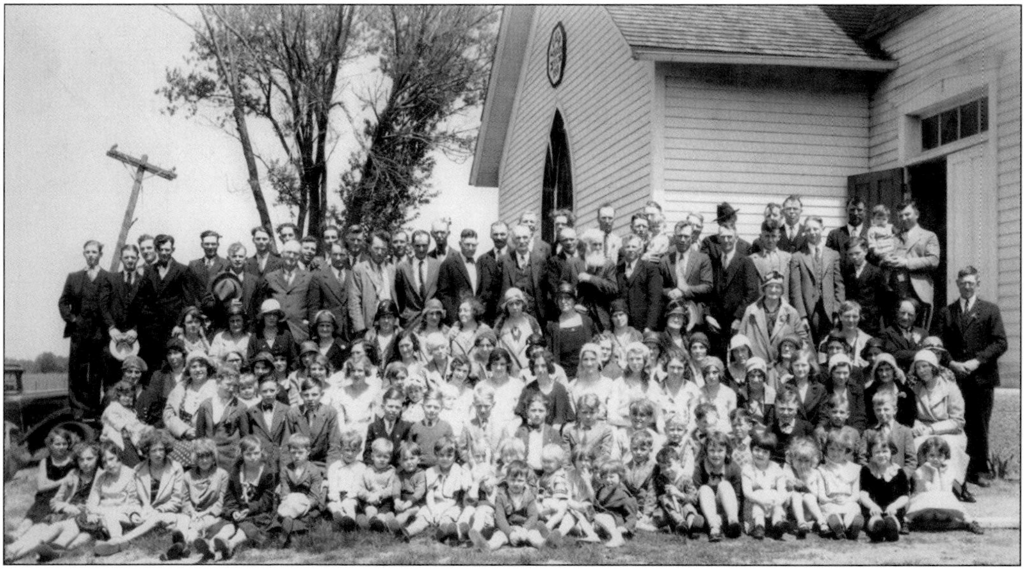

Dressed in Their Sunday Best. The congregation of the Prairie Center country church is shown here around 1928. The church, which was built in 1880, was listed in the National Register of Historic Places in 2004. While Prairie Center Church was a Methodist church for decades, today it is a nondenominational Christian church. It includes the Pleasant Hill Cemetery to the west of the church. (Courtesy of Prairie Center Church.)

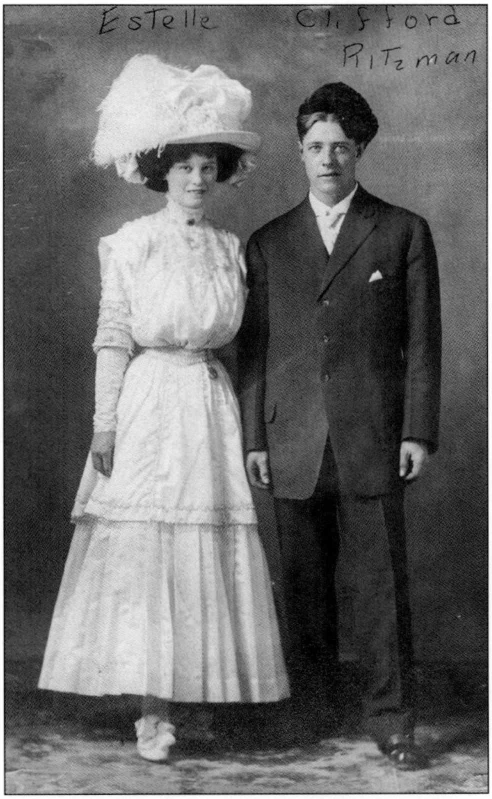

A Life Cut Short. Estelle and Clifford Ritzman were married at Minburn on Wednesday, January 4, 1911, at 7:00 p.m. Just two days after Estelle, 25, gave birth to the couple's son, Dean, on January 18, 1919, she died at home from Spanish influenza, a global pandemic that killed millions of people in 1918–1919. Many family members and friends attended Estelle's funeral, which was held in the Ritzmans' farm home west of Minburn on January 22, 1919. (Courtesy of Paul and Carolyn Snyder.)

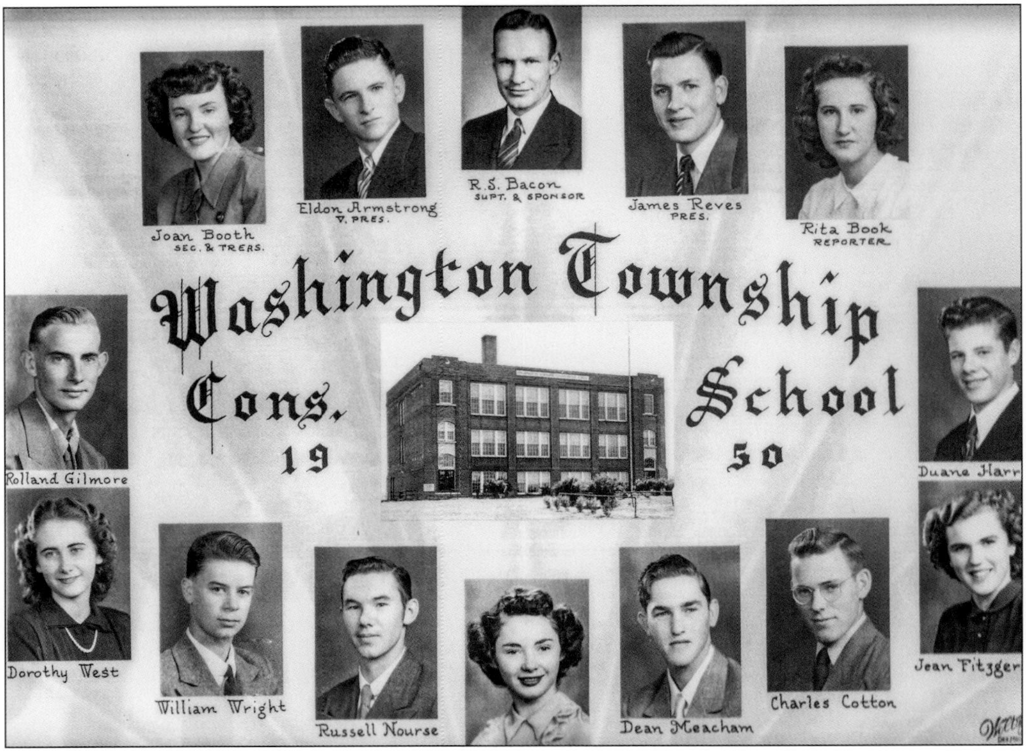

Washington Township School. Located west of Minburn and south of Perry, Washington Township School was built in 1921 for $90,000 after nine one-room country schools were consolidated. Unlike most rural locations at the time, the school had electricity, thanks to a Delco plant consisting of two engines and 56 batteries. The last senior class graduated in 1958. The school closed permanently in 1982 and is now a museum. (Courtesy of Washington Township School.)

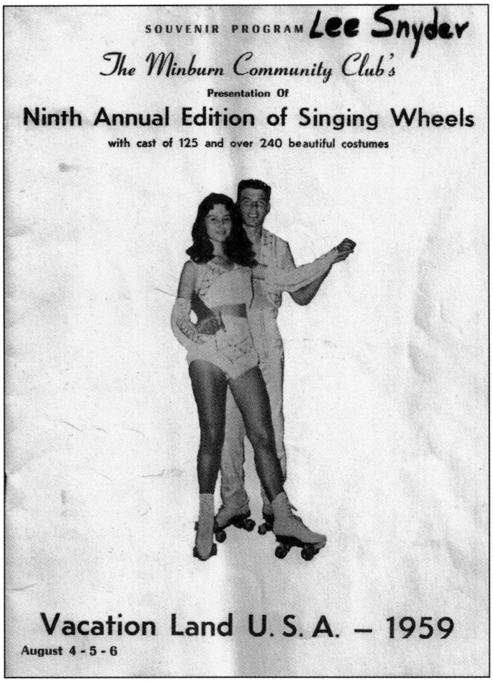

MINBURN'S SINGING WHEELS. Minburn's legendary Singing Wheels debuted in 1950. Music teacher John Sanders produced the first show, featuring high school students from the Minburn Roller Club. The Singing Wheels' performances were held in Minburn each summer throughout the 1950s and into the early 1960s and showcased a different theme each year. Susan Susich and Bobby Rittgers are featured on the 1959 program cover. (Courtesy of Paul and Carolyn Snyder.)

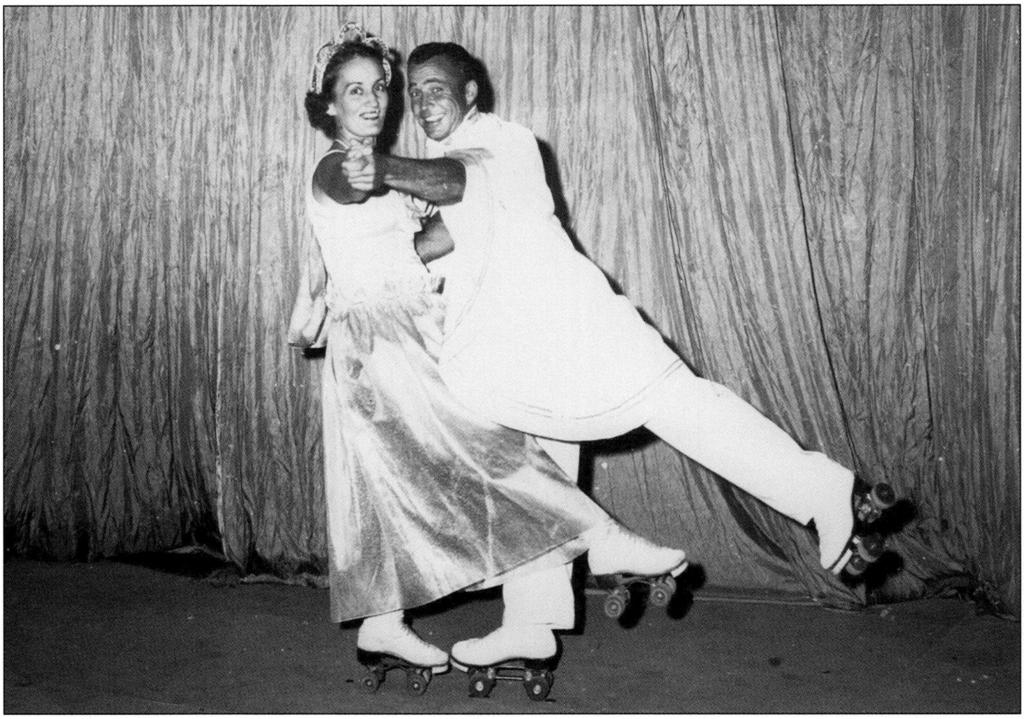

JACKIE AND DEE. Jackie Snyder (left), a New York City native who married Minburn-area farmer Harold Snyder, began producing the Singing Wheels' shows in 1956. Dee Thompson (right) served as a codirector for many years and skated duets with Snyder in the shows. The pair recruited locals of all ages, from grade-school kids to adults, to skate in the shows, which featured elaborate, homemade costumes, music, and more. (Courtesy of Paul and Carolyn Snyder.)

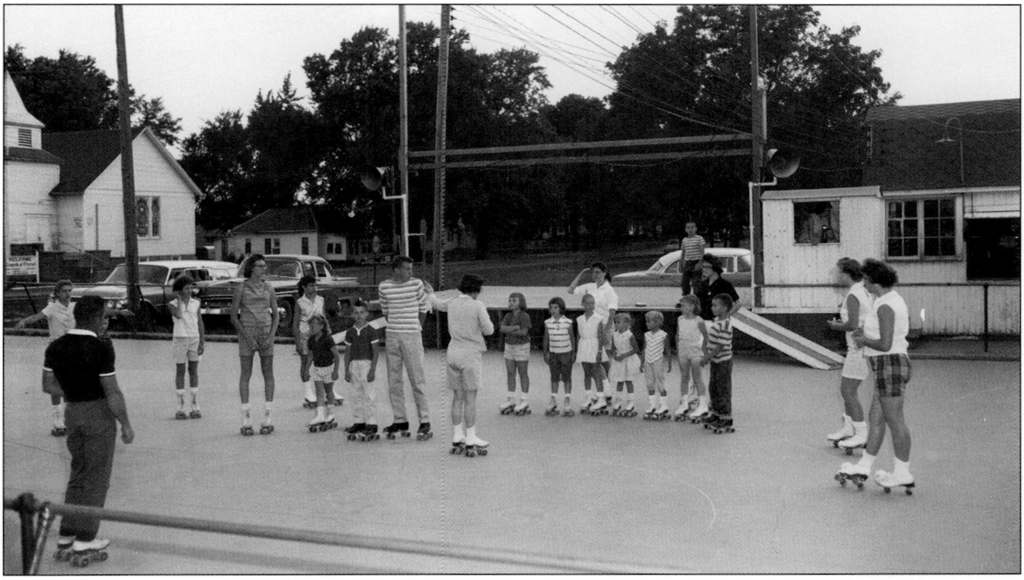

Practice at the Rink. Minburn's roller-skating rink was built around 1946 and was known for being one of the smoothest concrete slab rinks in central Iowa. Singing Wheels performers practiced several evenings each week, starting in May after school ended. Up to 150 people would perform in the Singing Wheels' shows, which became three-day extravaganzas held around early August. The rink is still located in downtown Minburn. (Author's collection.)

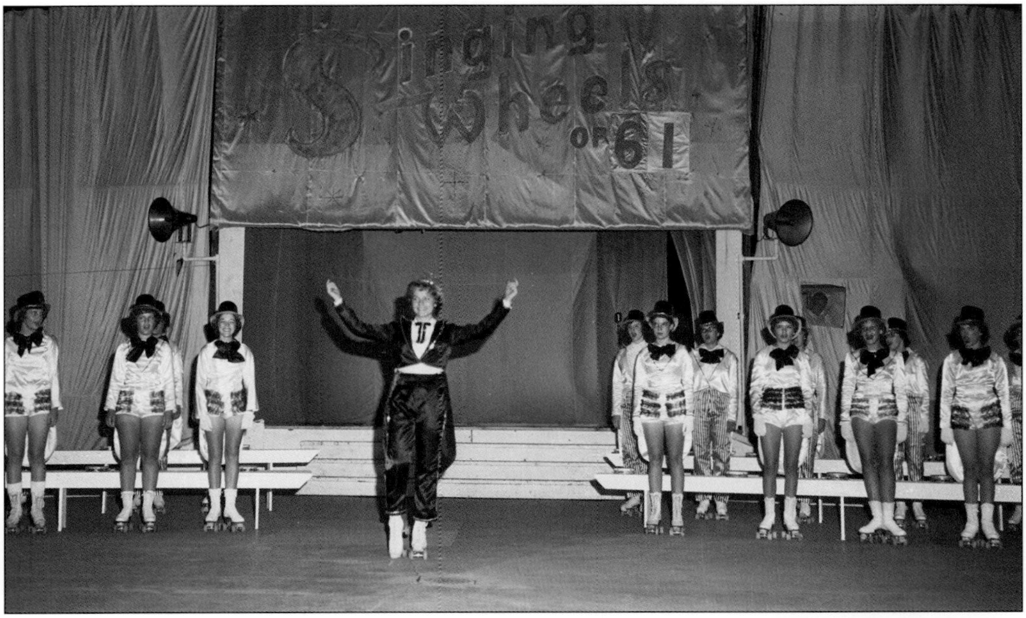

Planning a Production. Each January, the Singing Wheels' codirectors began brainstorming a theme for the upcoming year's program, and they selected music in February. Costume and prop design started in March. Themes included 1957's "Around the World" and 1958's "Salute to Music." Each show concluded with a military tribute consisting of 16 boys (the Cadets) and 16 girls (the Starrettes) skating in an interlocking pinwheel formation. (Courtesy of Paul and Carolyn Snyder.)

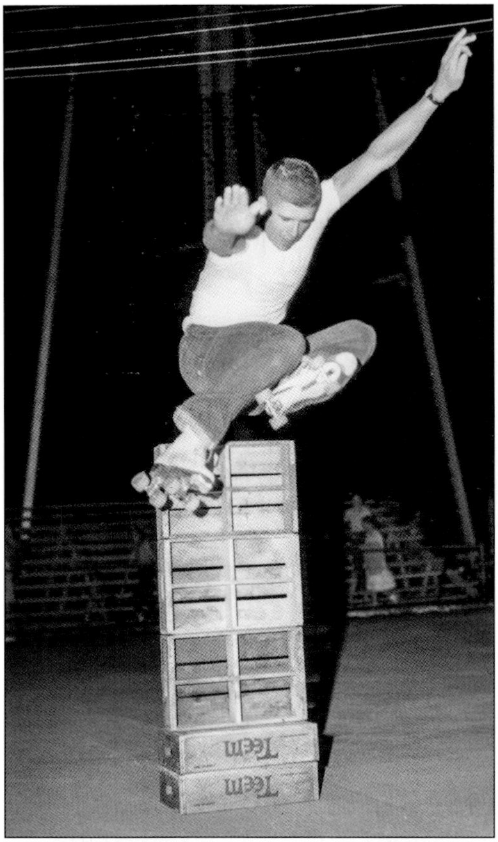

STUNTS GALORE. There was not much that some of Minburn's most talented roller skaters, like Tim Hinchcliff, could not do, including jumping stacks of wooden crates. Stunts like this were always popular at the Singing Wheels' shows, which attracted thousands of spectators each summer. People would start saving their seats at 2:00 p.m. for the 8:00 p.m. show. There was no admission fee, although audience members were encouraged to make donations at intermission. (Courtesy of Paul and Carolyn Snyder.)

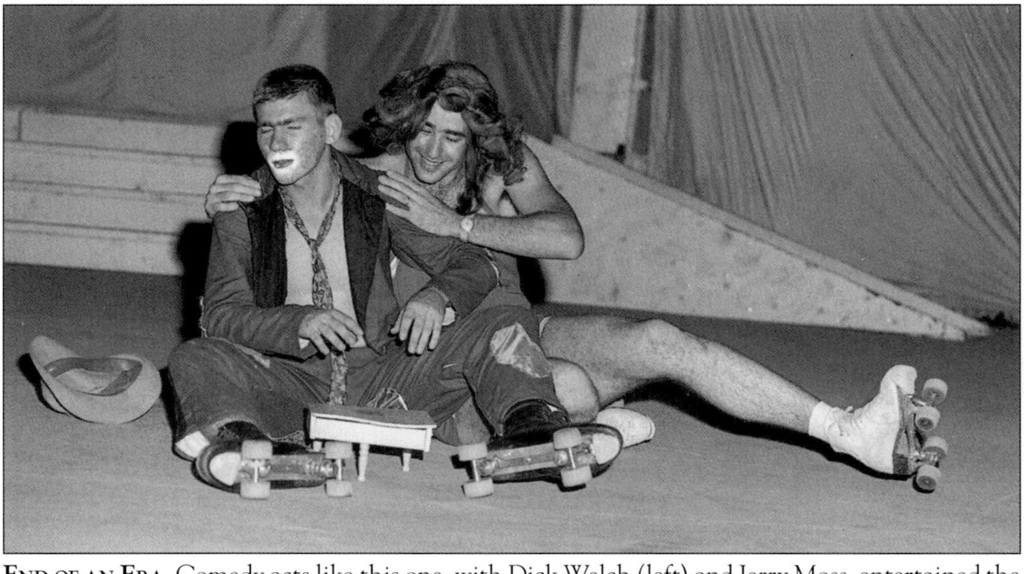

END OF AN ERA. Comedy acts like this one, with Dick Welch (left) and Jerry Moss, entertained the crowds during stage changes at the Singing Wheels' shows. The era of the Singing Wheels came to a close by the early 1960s. As kids became busier with other activities, the codirectors decided to end the Singing Wheels on a high note. The final performances were held July 30–August 1, 1963. (Courtesy of Paul and Carolyn Snyder.)

Ten

A Posse to a President
How Harry Truman, Bonnie and Clyde, and Dallas County Changed American History

In the early morning of July 24, 1933, a troop of Girl Scouts camping at the old pavilion in Dexfield Park north of Dexter took an early-morning hike. Without knowing it, the girls and their leader, Della Gowdey, walked right into the Barrow Gang's campsite.

Maxine Schell Hadley, a member of this troop from Dexter, recalled how the men and women in the camp acted quite surprised. Hadley had no idea who these people were, although they smiled and returned the welcome when the Girl Scouts said good morning. None of the troop thought any more about it until hours later, when word spread of a big shoot-out at Dexfield Park that led to the capture of Buck Barrow and his wife, Blanche, while other Barrow Gang members escaped, including Bonnie and Clyde.

More than 15 years later, the attention of the nation would focus once again on Dallas County when Pres. Harry Truman delivered a fiery speech to 100,000 farmers on a sweltering September day at the National Soil Conservation Field Days and Plowing Matches north of Dexter, not far from the old Dexfield Park. This rural venue sparked the "Give 'em hell, Harry" slogan and helped propel Harry Truman to an unlikely victory in the 1948 presidential campaign.

These remarkable stories are literally set in stone on two markers along Dexfield Road north of Dexter, preserving the memories of those unforgettable days when Dallas County changed the course of American history.

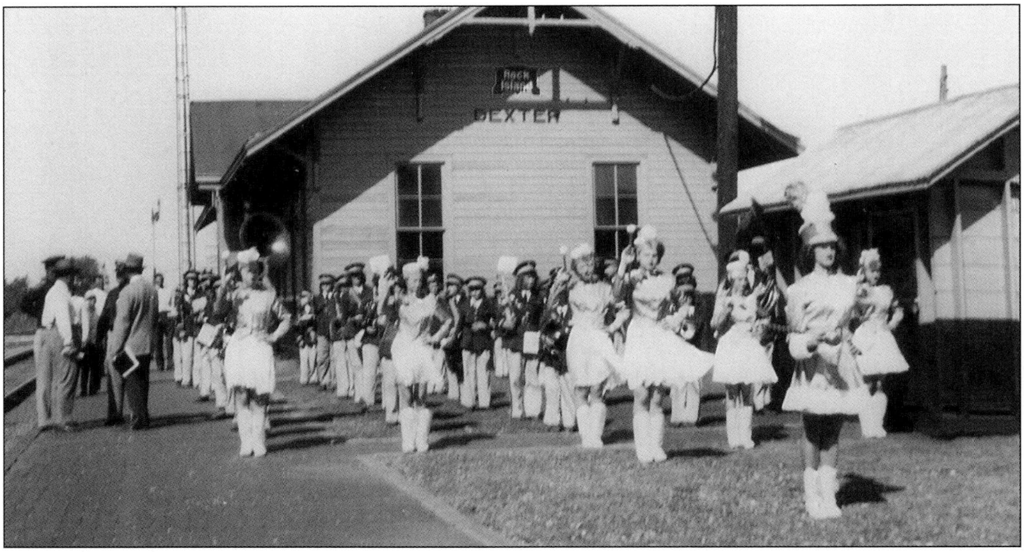

Welcoming the President. In September 1948, all roads led to Dexter and the National Soil Conservation Field Days and Plowing Matches, the nation's largest farm event. When Pres. Harry Truman's train arrived at the depot, a crowd welcomed him, his wife, Bess, and their daughter, Margaret, in grand style with the Dexter school band, a parade, and a queen and her court. Truman rode in his convertible to the farm site north of town. (Courtesy of Dexter Museum.)

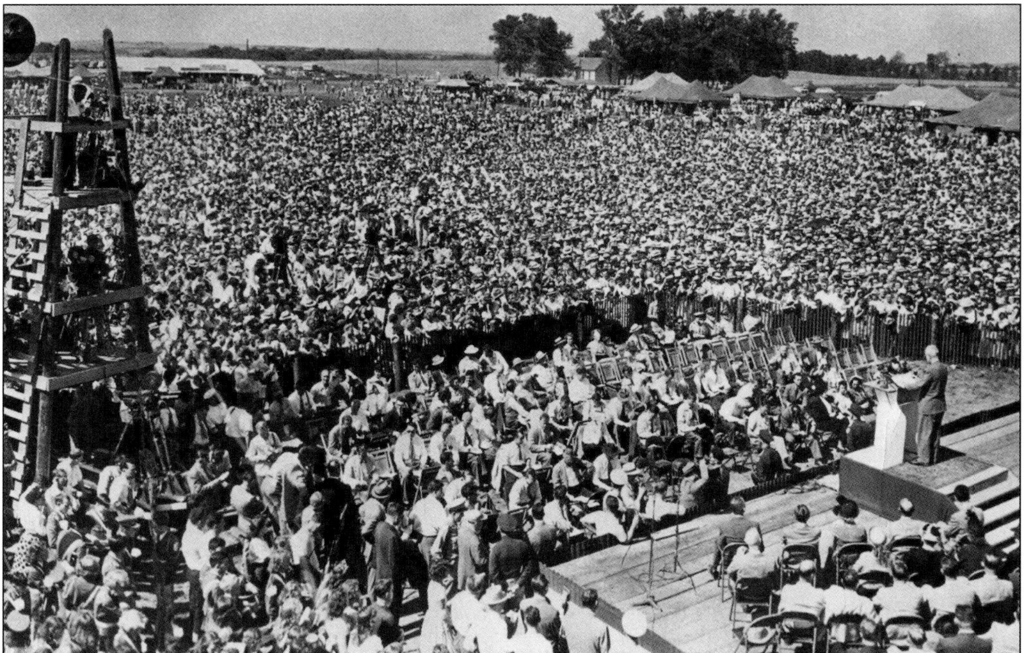

Truman Was a Farmer at Heart. As the mercury soared on September 18, 1948, bumper-to-bumper traffic clogged the roads to the plowing match. When President Truman came to Dexter as part of his whistle-stop presidential campaign, he was a 50-to-1 underdog against New York governor Thomas Dewey. Truman connected with common people, however. "Truman was a farmer, not a politician, at heart," said Bob Larson, who met Truman at the event. (Courtesy of Dexter Museum.)

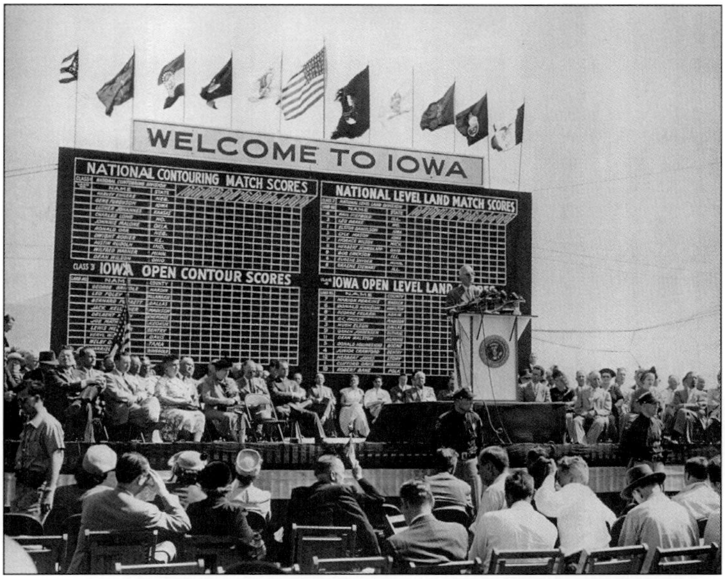

GIVE 'EM HELL. During Harry Truman's 29-minute farm policy speech to a crowd of 100,000 people, the loudest cheers came when he referred to the 80th Congress as the "do nothing Congress." This was the first speech that was referred to as "Give 'em hell, Harry," a slogan that stuck with Truman throughout the campaign and helped propel him to victory in the 1948 presidential election. (Courtesy of Dexter Museum.)

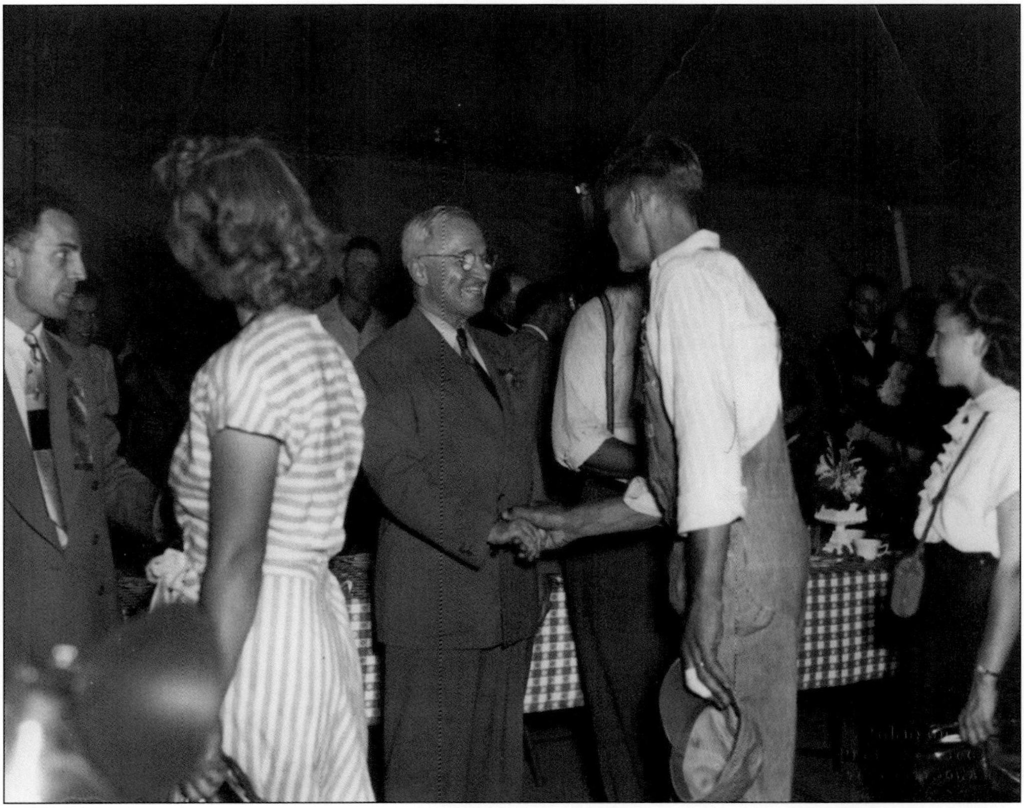

CONNECTING WITH THE VOTERS. After his speech at the National Soil Conservation Field Days and Plowing Matches, Truman and his entourage dined on fried chicken and greeted people before heading to the demonstration sites to see terraces, ponds, and other conservation practices. Truman took off his suit jacket, rolled up his sleeves, and asked questions as he rode on Bob Larson's bulldozer while the Secret Service looked on. (Courtesy of Dexter Museum.)

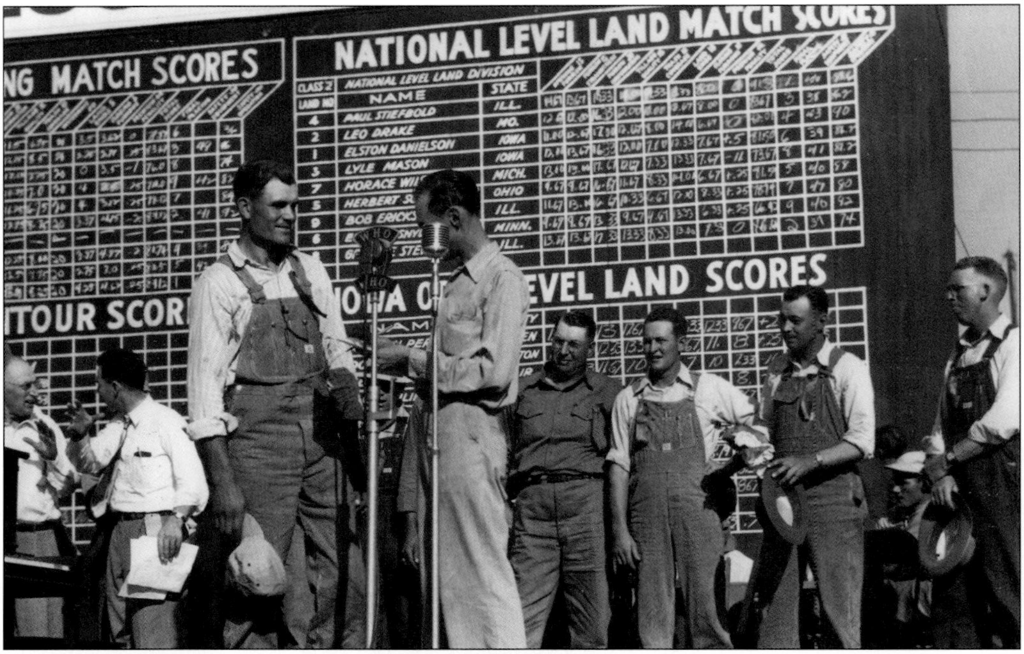

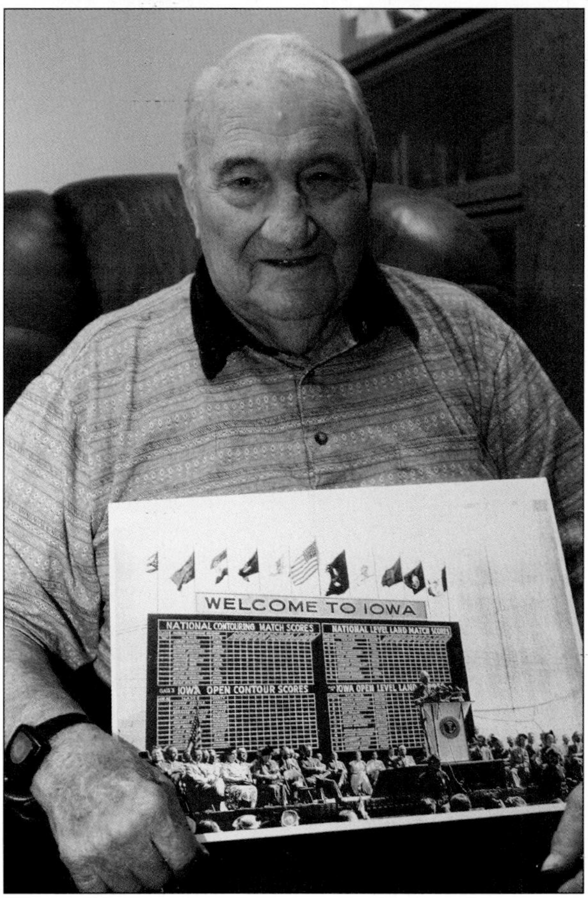

Top Honors at the Plowing Match. Donald Hanson (left of the radio microphone), a farmer from Roland, Iowa, and competitor at the 1948 National Plowing Match near Dexter, was interviewed on WHO Radio during the event. Hanson is the grandfather of Eric Hanson, a television reporter and anchor on KCCI in Des Moines. (Courtesy of Dexter Museum.)

Remembering Truman. Bob Larson of Perry was an 18-year-old farm boy from Casey when he met Harry Truman on September 18, 1948, at the National Soil Conservation Field Days and Plowing Matches. Construction crews had been told to shut down their machines when Truman was in the conservation demonstration area. Truman told Larson, "Get your dozer started and get back to work. I want to watch you." Truman rode with Larson on his bulldozer for about 10 minutes. (Author's collection.)

Bonnie and Clyde. After a shoot-out with police in Platte City, Missouri, the Barrow Gang was on the run and hid out on a wooded hilltop north of Dexter, overlooking the abandoned Dexfield Amusement Park. Gang members included Bonnie Parker, Clyde Barrow, Buck Barrow (Clyde's older brother), Blanche Barrow (Buck's wife), and W.D. Jones. They spent four to five days in area, recuperating from their wounds. Part of Buck's skull had been shot off, and Blanche had glass in her left eye. (Courtesy of Dexter Museum.)

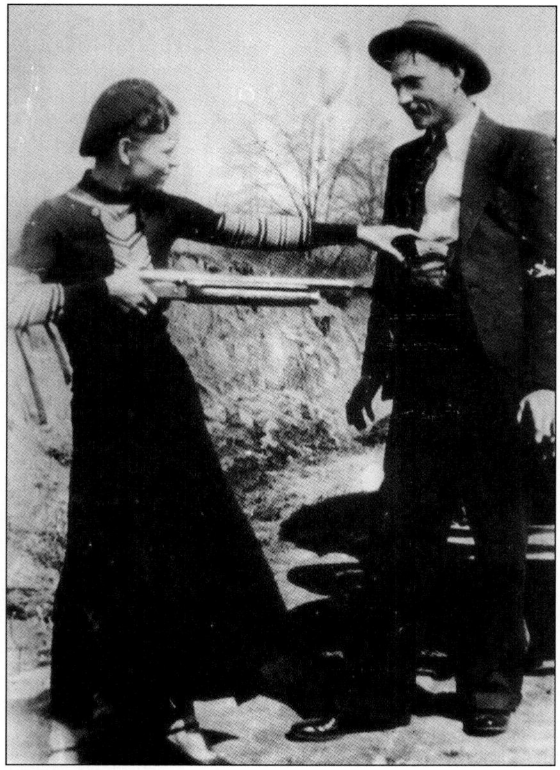

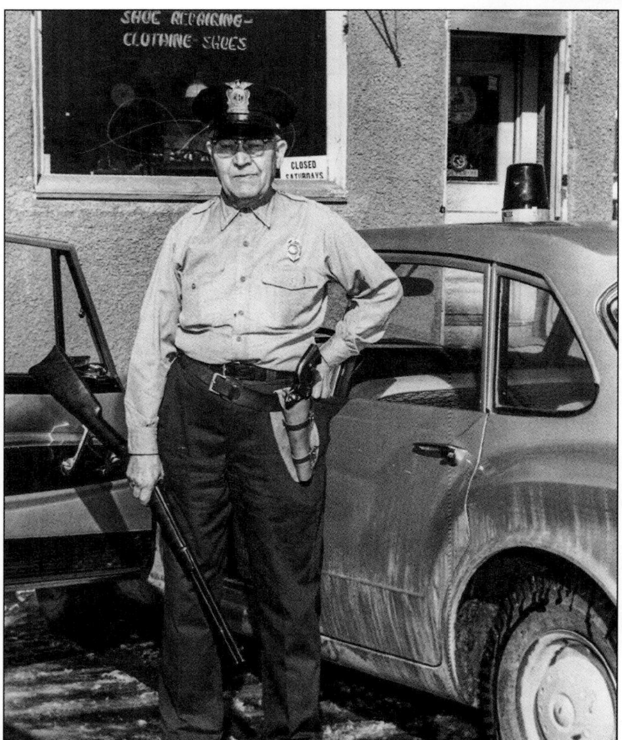

Officer John Love. After a local man, Henry Nye, noticed suspicious activity near Dexfield Park, he alerted John Love, a Dexter police officer. Love contacted Dallas County sheriff Clint Knee, who had heard reports of the Barrow Gang in the area. Sheriff Knee quickly organized a posse of about 50 men, including Des Moines police officers and detectives; a Des Moines dentist, Dr. Hershel Keller, who brought his own submachine gun; and many locals. (Courtesy of Dexter Museum.)

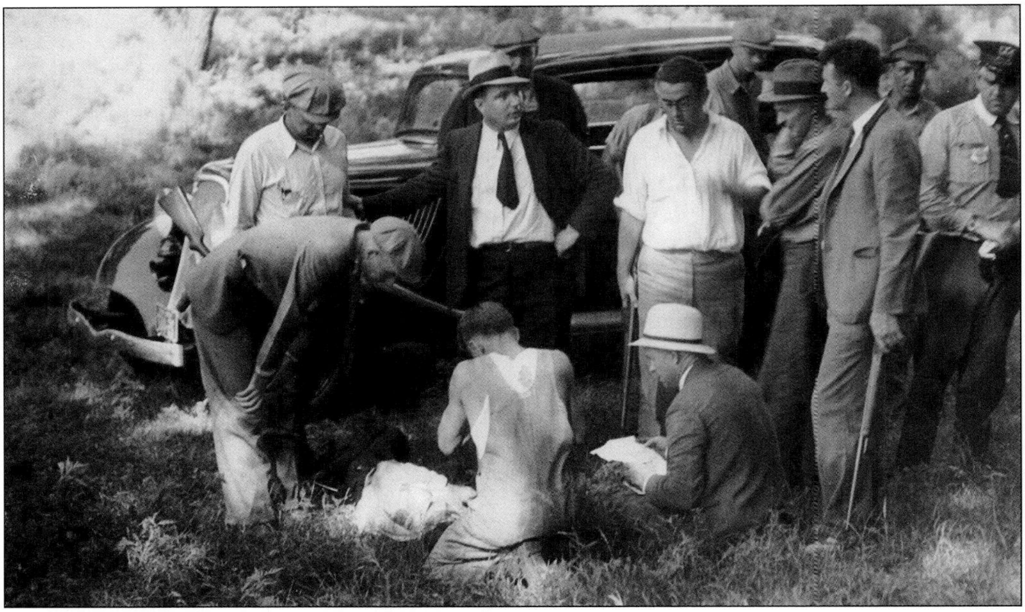

Posse Captures Buck Barrow. The posse opened fire after converging on the Barrow Gang's campsite around 5:30 or 6:00 a.m. on July 24, 1933. The gang returned fire with Browning Automatic Rifles stolen from National Guard armories. The posse retreated under heavy fire, giving the gang time to attempt an escape. While the gang members were wounded and bleeding, Bonnie, Clyde, and W.D. Jones ran off, leaving Blanche and a severely injured Buck (shown here lying on the ground), who were taken into custody. (Courtesy of Dexter Museum.)

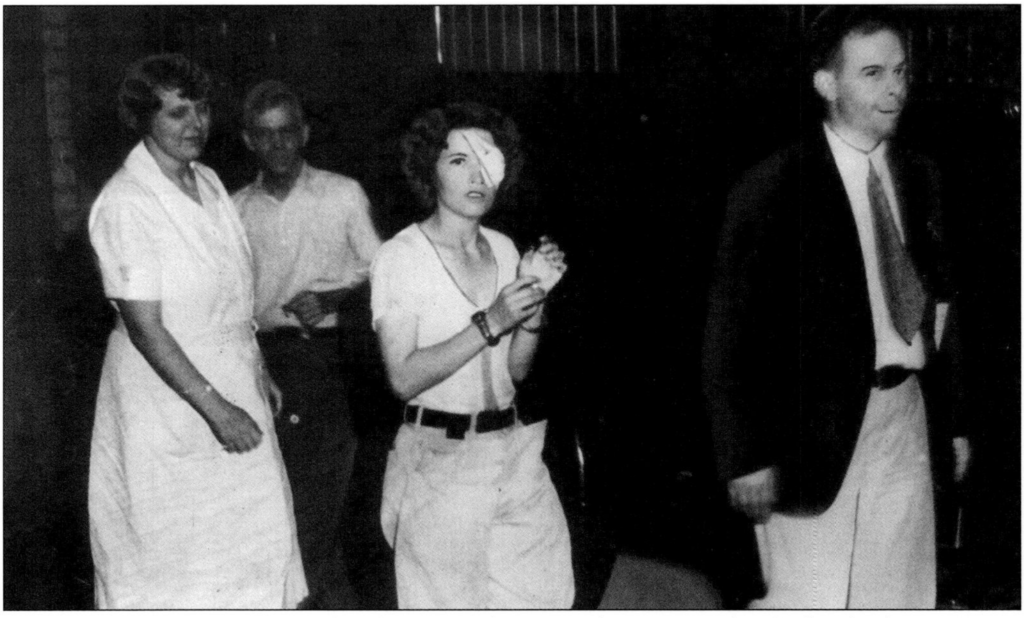

Blanche Barrow Arrested. Blanche Barrow (1911–1988) was arrested and taken back to Missouri, where she was tried for her part in the Platte City shoot-out. She was convicted and sentenced to 10 years in prison and served nearly six years before being released on good behavior. Barrow wrote her memoirs between 1933 and 1939 while serving time at the Missouri State Penitentiary. She later remarried and led a crime-free life. (Courtesy of Dexter Museum.)

Marvelle Feller Survived Bonnie and Clyde. In the early morning of July 24, 1933, nineteen-year-old Marvelle Feller (1913–2010), his father, Vallie, and their hired man were getting ready to milk the cows. The Fellers' police dog, Rex, alerted them to Clyde Barrow, who was armed and covered with blood. Clyde asked for help carrying Bonnie to the Fellers' 1929 Plymouth. Marvelle had to show Clyde how to shift, since all Clyde drove were Fords. Before speeding off, Clyde said, "You'll be well repaid for this." (Author's collection.)

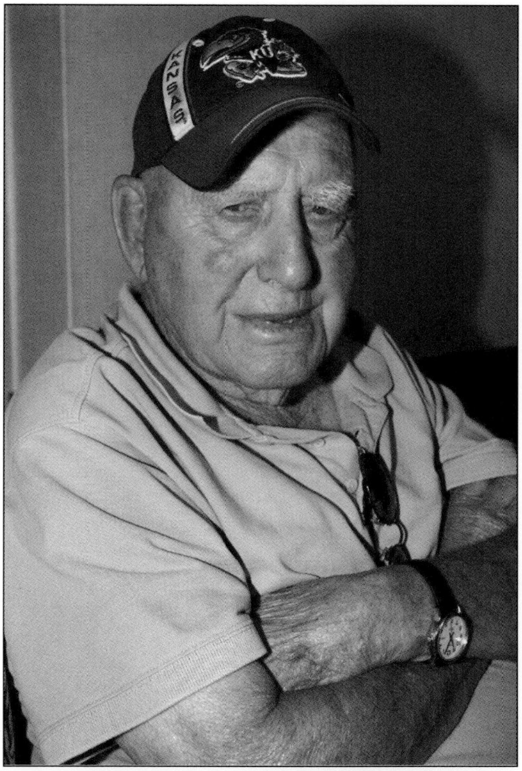

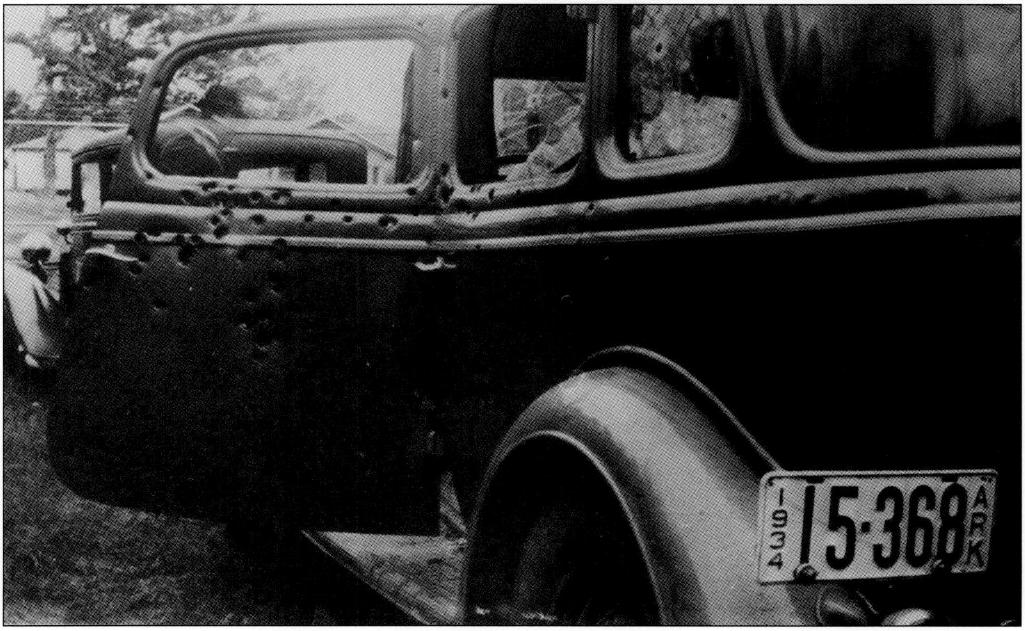

Bullet-Riddled Car. The Barrow Gang had arrived in Dexter with one car. Due to Buck's condition (he had been severely injured in the Platte City, Missouri, shoot-out), gang members decided they needed a second car and stole Ed Stoner's 1932 Ford Model A in Perry. The fugitives were always on the move, trying to keep one step ahead of the "laws," as they called them. This police photograph shows Buck Barrow's car after the Dexfield shoot-out. (Courtesy of Dexter Museum.)

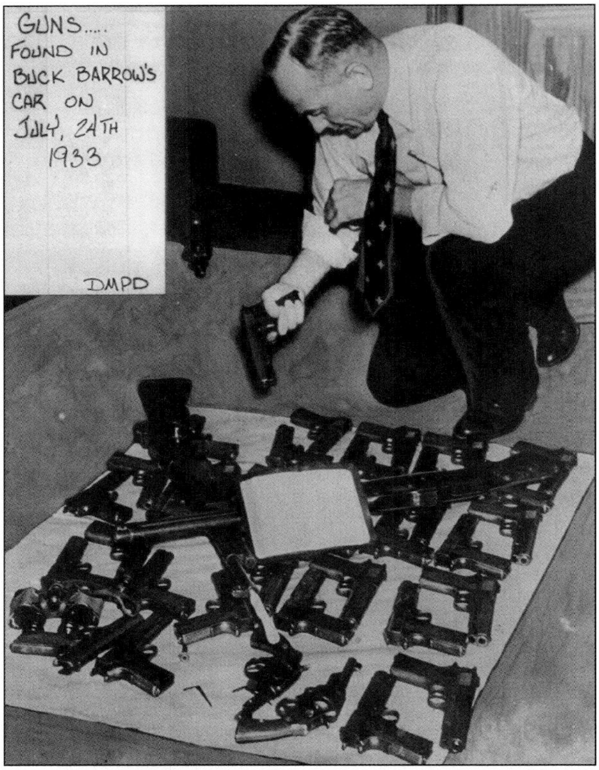

PLENTY OF FIREPOWER. This Des Moines Police Department photograph shows the array of weapons recovered from Buck Barrow's car after the Dexter posse raided the Barrow Gang's camp near Dexfield Park. The Barrow Gang had established a reputation as thieves and murderers, having killed several police officers. The July 1933 shoot-out was not the gang's first trip to Iowa. Several past bank robberies across the state were attributed to gang members. (Courtesy of Dexter Museum.)

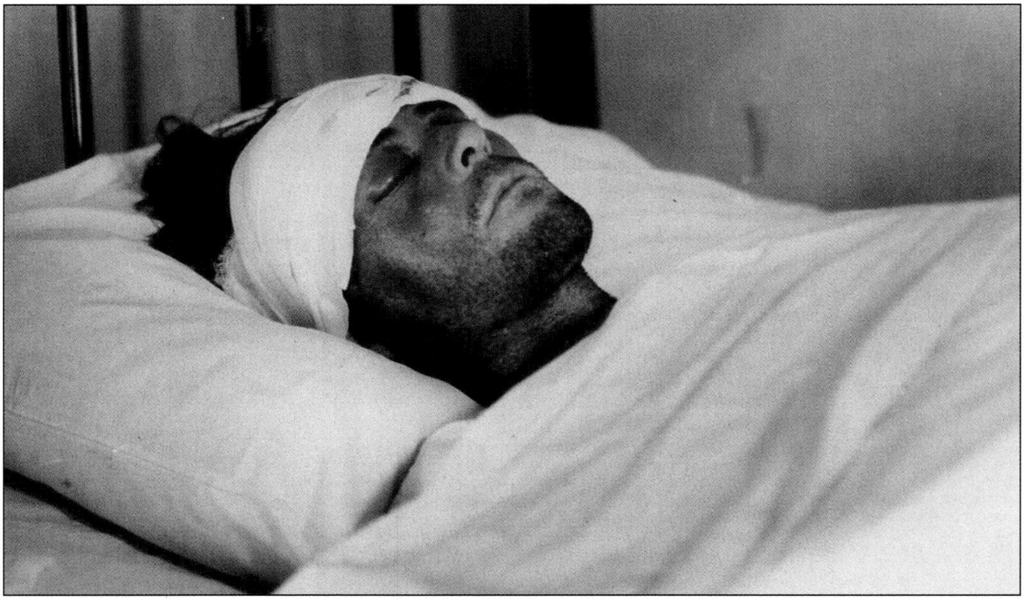

BUCK BARROW DIES. Buck Barrow, 30, was severely wounded at the Dexfield Park shoot-out and was taken to the Dexter Hospital, where he was treated by Dr. Keith M. Chapler and Dr. C. Robert Osborn. Barrow was sent to King's Daughters Hospital in Perry, where he died on July 29, 1933. While Bonnie and Clyde got away, Dexfield Park marked the beginning of the end. In less than a year, on May 23, 1934, they were ambushed and shot to death by police officers in Bienville Parish, Louisiana. (Courtesy of Dexter Museum.)

BIBLIOGRAPHY

Hastie, Eugene. *Hastie's History of Dallas County, Iowa*. Fort Dodge, IA: Walterick Printing Co., 1938.

Jenkins, Pamela J., and Martha A. Tanner. *Perry*. Charleston, SC: Arcadia Publishing, 2008.

Leslie, Sue, Linda Ayres, and Kathi Henely. *Building a Parish: A History of St. Patrick's Parish*. Perry, IA: Chief Publishing, 2012.

Perry Historic Preservation Commission. *Perry's Memory Lane*. Perry, IA: Self-published, 2016.

Pradarelli, Melinda. *Brenton: The People, History, and Legacy of Iowa's Brenton Bank*. Self-published, 2004.

Waukee Area Historical Society. *Waukee*. Charleston, SC: Arcadia Publishing, 2015.

Wood, Prof. R.F. *Past and Present of Dallas County, Iowa*. Chicago: The S.J. Clarke Publishing Company, 1907.